THAT GOOD NIGHT

THAT
GOOD NIGHT

LIFE *and* MEDICINE

in the

ELEVENTH HOUR

Sunita Puri

CONSTABLE

CONSTABLE

First published in the US in 2019 by Viking, an imprint of Penguin Random House LLC

This edition published in Great Britain in 2019 by Constable

Portions of this book appeared in slightly different form in *JAMA: The Journal of the American Medical
Association* as "Extraordinary" and *The New York Times* as "Unequal Lives, Unequal Deaths."

Excerpt from "Diving into the Wreck." Copyright © 2016 by the Adrienne Rich Literary Trust.
Copyright © 1973 by W. W. Norton & Company, Inc., from *Collected Poems: 1950–2012* by Adrienne
Rich. Used by permission of W. W. Norton & Company, Inc. Excerpt from "Poem with Two Endings"
from *Each Happiness Ringed by Lions: Selected Poems* (Bloodaxe Books, 2005) www.bloodaxebooks.com

A CIP catalogue record for this book
is available from the British Library.

ISBN: 978-1-47213-132-4 (hardback)
ISBN: 978-1-47213-133-1 (trade paperback)

Designed by Amanda Dewey
Printed and bound in Great Britain by
CPI Group (UK) Ltd, Croydon CR0 4YY

Papers used by Constable are from well-managed forests and other responsible sources.

Constable
An imprint of
Little, Brown Book Group
Carmelite House
50 Victoria Embankment
London EC4Y 0DZ

An Hachette UK Company
www.hachette.co.uk

www.littlebrown.co.uk

For my mother and my father, who gave me this life—
For my brother, who reminds me to enjoy it—
And for Sathya, who lights the way—
With love and gratitude

Therefore, because death stirs people to seek answers to important spiritual questions, it becomes the greatest servant of humanity, rather than its most feared enemy.

Lord Krishna to Arjuna, Bhagavad Gita

I came to explore the wreck.
The words are purposes.
The words are maps.
I came to see the damage that was done
And the treasures that prevail.
I stroke the beam of my lamp
Slowly along the flank
Of something more permanent
Than fish or weed.

Adrienne Rich, "Diving into the Wreck"

CONTENTS

Author's Note

I was five years old when I first heard that life is temporary.

During the years that my mother worked long shifts as an anesthesiology resident, my father became my guide and my best friend. He cooked me runny eggs in the morning, dried and brushed my unruly dark hair, taught me how to pray, and took me out to eat at fast-food restaurants that my mother would never approve of. One autumn evening after devouring hush puppies together, we sat on the couch next to the window in our small apartment, looking out at the evening sky as my father often did, my fingers still sticky from ketchup and cornmeal. An engineer by training, my father patiently and thoroughly answered my questions about why the sunset burned a thousand bright colors, and why I could see the waning sun and the bright moon in the same sky. When I told him that I wished the sky would always look as pretty as it did then, he told me that all of life is like the evening sky: beautiful, but temporary. Beautiful in part because it is temporary.

"Everything in life—you, me, the sky—will change and then disappear," he told me, pointing first at the navy blue, and then at the fading pink and orange. He told me that the plant in our living room would at some point wither and die, that someday he would have gray hair and struggle to walk with a cane, that everything and everyone in life changes and passes like the fading colors we watched. The voice he spoke with, quiet and solemn, wasn't his animated reading voice, his harsh scolding voice, or his melodious singing voice. I must have looked frightened; he told me not to be afraid. "This," he said, "is the natural order of things, something none of us can escape." The sooner you learn this lesson, he told me, the more you will value each moment in life, knowing that it is a temporary gift.

This was the first of many conversations he and my mother would have with my brother and me about death and impermanence, and what it means to live well with the knowledge of our transience. But back then, my father and I sat together quietly as I thought about his words, watching as the sun vanished and the stars appeared.

. . . .

More than two decades later, during medical school and residency, I found myself unprepared to face the mortality and suffering of my patients. Though my father's words echoed in the back of my consciousness, reminding me that death is both natural and certain, as a medical student I focused solely on preserving life. I began to believe that a longer life was a better life. A doctor's job was to manipulate, control, and postpone death, not to accept it as inevitable. We learned to rage against the dying of the light.

I savored the victories, the times when I could treat a terrible pneumonia or diagnose a new and treatable cancer. But sometimes I wondered if my efforts simply prolonged death instead of returning my patients to the quality of life they assumed our treatments could restore. Though I could mobilize an array of remarkable modern technologies to keep a patient alive, I hadn't the slightest clue how to acknowledge or discuss what all ancient civilizations could articulate and even embrace: the certain end we would all face.

I hadn't expected that my years of medical training would culminate in the choice to pursue palliative medicine—a relatively new specialty focused on treating the pain and suffering of patients living with a serious illness that often cannot be cured. Although people for centuries have suffered and died from terminal illness, the American Board of Medical Specialties didn't recognize hospice and palliative medicine as a distinct medical subspecialty until 2006. I also hadn't expected that, in choosing a field that embraces and addresses the human suffering and mortality that Western medicine overlooks and at times denies, I would come to a different and new understanding of medicine's role in our lives.

My work in the borderland between life and death has shown me how we—doctors, patients, families—talk around, rather than about, suffering, dignity, living, and dying. We rely on euphemism, silence, and jargon when we most acutely need to be clear and articulate. Medicine must find new language to discuss and destigmatize this experience that all of humanity shares; our silence and avoidance have resulted in much unnecessary anguish. The principles of palliative medicine have the capacity to transform medical practice by offering patients and doctors alike useful and probing language that could change the way we communicate about illness and end of life, both within our homes and in hospitals. This book is my humble attempt to inspire tough but necessary conversations in hopes of easing the suffering associated with the silence around mortality.

On a more personal note, tending to my patients has also shifted the meaning of my own life, forcing me to reevaluate what matters most to me, and to reconsider what it means to live and love well. My hope is that the stories of my patients, colleagues, and family may free us all to acknowledge that a deeper understanding and embrace of our own mortality may actually revitalize how we live, and what we consider to be most meaningful in each of our brief lives.

For we will each age and die, as my father told me years ago. We will lose the people we love. No matter our ethnicity, place of residence, income, religion, or skin color, our human lives are united by brevity and finitude, and the certainty of loss. Just as we strive for dignity and purpose throughout our lives, well before the light fades, we can bring this same dignity and purpose to our deaths, as we each journey into our own good night.

Part 1

· ·

BETWEEN TWO
DARK SKIES

One

SHIFT

Donna was in her mid-sixties, with wide brown eyes and the smoky voice of a jazz singer. Her skin, sprinkled with freckles and sunspots, stretched tightly against her delicate cheekbones and jaw. It was an unusually balmy afternoon in San Francisco, and somehow the day's heat and humidity had made its way into her room on the fourteenth floor of the usually chilly university hospital. Donna grasped a handheld electronic fan, closing her eyes as it cooled her face and tousled strands of the thin gray-brown hair that brushed her shoulders. When I met her, I was a fourth-year medical student weeks away from graduation, yet increasingly uncertain that medicine was the right career for me.

Five years earlier, Donna's kidneys began to fail from a combination of high blood pressure and diabetes. She was weak and nauseated, and missed so many days at work that she nearly lost her job as a secretary in a contractor's office. In order to feel better and to survive, Donna had to begin dialysis, a three-hour-long treatment three times a week that would clear her blood of the waste products and toxins that her failing kidneys could no longer remove. A vascular surgeon operated on Donna's arm to create a fistula, a connection between an artery and vein that enabled the dialysis machine to remove, clean, and return all of Donna's blood to her body. For the first few years, dialysis not only staved off death but actually improved her energy and outlook. She went back to work part time. Her nausea vanished and she managed to gain back the ten pounds she'd lost when kidney failure claimed her appetite.

But a few years later, her nausea and fatigue returned; dialysis began to cause the symptoms it had once fixed. Donna cycled in and out of the hospital with severe infections of the skin around her fistula and blood clots that plugged her fistula, rendering dialysis impossible. During a recent hospitalization, a team of physicians had placed a temporary dialysis catheter in one of the large veins in her neck while another team worked on repairing her fistula, which had clotted again. Yet she returned to the hospital several weeks later with a severe pneumonia, likely caused by powerful bacteria she'd been exposed to during her last hospital stay. When she finally left the hospital, she needed three weeks' worth of physical therapy in a nursing home before she was strong enough to care for herself at home. Though she was able to return home, she struggled to dress herself, cook, or drive to her dialysis sessions every Monday, Wednesday, and Friday.

She had come to the hospital today because a blood clot once again clogged her fistula. Her doctors wanted to place another temporary dialysis catheter and consult a vascular surgeon to create a new dialysis fistula altogether. But Donna said no.

I don't want dialysis anymore, Donna told her doctors. *I've lived a good life.*

If Donna doesn't want dialysis, her doctors wondered, then what *does* she want and how should we treat her? These were questions I had rarely encountered or considered in my years as a medical student. Like the doctors who taught and supervised me, I was hardwired to preserve and prolong life. On the few occasions I'd seen patients opt out of lifesaving treatments, I'd watched my supervising doctors struggle to articulate another plan—and the consequences and limits of any plan at all. Donna's team knew they needed help having that sort of delicate conversation with her, so they called the palliative care team to speak with Donna and help clarify what she wanted if she didn't want dialysis.

As it happened, I met Donna because I had chosen to spend two weeks of elective time on the palliative care service at the University of California, San Francisco, where I was finishing my last months of medical school before beginning three years of residency training in internal medicine. I'd completed all of the required rotations to graduate, having spent one to two months each learning from teams of internal medicine physicians, gynecologists, family physicians, surgeons, pediatricians, psychiatrists, and neurologists. Now, in these last months of medical school, I'd been able to choose which medical specialties I wanted to learn, and which doctors I wanted to learn from.

I searched the list of electives for inspiration. Medical school had been far more technical than humanistic, its emphasis heavy on the science of medicine, light on the art of doctoring. In the first few years of medical school, I understood why this might be the case: I couldn't diagnose and treat patients without an expert understanding of the body's physiology, the ways disease could alter it, and the proper ways to treat the dizzying myriad illnesses humans suffered. Yet during my rotations, when I actually saw patients under the guidance of a resident and attending physician, I'd been struck by how little time I spent with patients—no more than a few minutes on rounds, and occasionally a few more minutes later in the day, when absolutely necessary. Entire days whizzed by as we ordered and waited for the results of lab tests and CT scans, typed detailed notes about patients into their electronic health records, met with social workers to figure out how to get patients home as quickly as possible, and talked with cardiologists and gastroenterologists about their recommendations for our patients. Caring for patients somehow meant spending very little time with them. One day, out of curiosity, I timed myself completing my assigned tasks. I spent twice as long in front of a computer as I did examining and talking to my patients.

As graduation and the start of residency loomed, thoughts of quitting medicine arose unbidden in my mind. When I looked through the list of electives I could take, I was really searching desperately for reasons to finish my training. I'd go on to spend a month working with a psychiatrist who specialized in treating patients struggling with substance abuse. I'd spend another month working with a child abuse response team at the county hospital. A classmate recommended that I take a two-week-long rotation with the palliative care team, and I found myself signing up for an elective with them, too.

Donna was the first patient I'd see with Dr. McCormick, the physician on the palliative care team during my rotation. A handsome man with gentle brown eyes and a warm smile, Dr. McCormick wore a blue plaid shirt and khakis and worked closely with a social worker and a chaplain named Ellen. We sat together around a rectangular table and talked about each of the twelve patients our team was seeing, including Donna, our newest referral. "Sounds like the medical team wants to do what they can to help Donna continue dialysis, but she's not digging that plan," Dr. McCormick said, summarizing the dilemma that Donna's doctors needed us to address. "So let's go find out what she's got on her mind!" He was casual and personable, professional but not distant. As we walked together down a set of hallways to Donna's room, it struck me that Dr. McCormick had never met Donna before. I wondered how he, a stranger at the eleventh hour of Donna's life, would manage to earn her trust and ask her intimate questions that it seemed nobody had asked her before, including the many doctors who had been taking care of her since her kidneys began to fail.

Sunlight poured through the window across from Donna's hospital bed. I noticed her squinting and lowered the shade slightly. Instead of hovering over her or leaning against the wall as she spoke, Dr. McCormick, Ellen, and I sat in gray folding chairs facing Donna. On the table next to her hospital bed, there was a brown tray with plastic rectangles of smashed peas, fluorescent orange carrots, and a small chicken breast. Someone had checked the boxes "low sodium" and "renal diet" and "diabetic" on a pink slip of paper taped to the side of the tray. "It's *dialysis* food," Donna said, wrinkling her nose as she noticed me looking at her lunch. "Makes me more nauseated than my kidneys do." A copy of *Chicken Soup for the Soul*, many of its yellowed pages dog-eared, rested next to her untouched tray.

Dr. McCormick spoke to Donna in a soft tone that exuded compassion and presence. "We are from the palliative care team, and we're just here to get to know you and to support you as you think through some of the decisions your medical team is asking you to make," Dr. McCormick said.

"I need . . . all the support . . . I can get," Donna replied, her voice fading into a whisper as she made her way through her sentences.

Donna's fatigue penetrated her every word and attempted action. Lifting a forkful of green beans to her mouth had become an accomplishment, she told us. She scratched her arms during our conversation, and dry skin flaked onto the blue hospital blanket. I had seen patients who looked as chronically fatigued and debilitated by disease as she did, but none who refused the therapies we offered, even when I wondered if they were strong enough to benefit from them.

Dread had consumed Donna on the ambulance ride from her dialysis center to the hospital. She told us she had felt her heart thumping against her chest as though it were warning her of impending danger. She knew her doctors would offer her another procedure or surgery to fix her fistula and allow her to continue dialysis. But a question surfaced in her mind, one she'd considered from time to time over the past several months: Would a shorter life without dialysis be better than a longer life with dialysis?

"I'm not suicidal," she whispered. "I'm tired."

She told us about the many ways that dialysis had enabled her to enjoy the past five years. She would miss her adopted daughter and the view of the Bay Bridge from her front porch. She would miss making her mother's recipes for barbecued ribs and lemon tart. But she wouldn't miss the crushing fatigue of kidney failure that had slowly deprived her of one independence after another: The ability to use the toilet in her Spanish-tiled bathroom. The pleasure of taking a shower alone, scrubbing herself with lavender body wash, standing rather than sitting in a plastic shower chair. The full sensory immersion in her garden, hands deep in the fragrant earth as she tended her marigolds and daisies, leaving behind imprints of her knees in the soft dirt.

"I am sorry this has been so tough for you," Dr. McCormick said to Donna, handing her a box of tissues. "I hear you saying that dialysis has really helped you to live well and to enjoy your life, but I also hear that over the past year it's really been making you tired and sometimes it's even made you sick."

"Yes, it has," Donna said, pausing to catch her breath. Even crying wore her out.

"Have your other doctors talked with you about what stopping dialysis would mean?"

I held my breath, unsure exactly what Dr. McCormick was asking. Did he want Donna to say out loud that she knew she would die without dialysis?

"Honestly . . . they didn't really . . . say too much," she said, wrapping thin shreds of tissue paper around her right index finger. "What would . . . happen to me?"

"Well, the first thing you need to know is that it is okay for you to want to stop dialysis if it is not helping you to live well," Dr. McCormick began. "But it is also very important for you to understand what would happen without dialysis. The toxins that dialysis usually removes from your blood would build up."

"And then . . . I would . . . die?" Donna whispered.

"Yes, you would die from your kidneys failing," Dr. McCormick replied. I had never seen a doctor tell a patient so directly that they would soon die. I'd seen well-intentioned doctors try to soften the blow of hard facts by cluttering their sentences with rambling apologies or canned reassurances, talking around the truth. Their worry that a patient might be unable to handle plainly stated facts, that they must require unnecessary words and sentiments as a sort of shock absorber, struck me as a form of paternalism. Dr. McCormick's sentences, concise and compassionate, almost felt transgressive. I had never seen a doctor disclose a wrenching truth with acceptance rather than avoidance. His voice was steady and clear, free of euphemisms like "passing on" or "being at peace." I waited for Donna to stop the conversation, to say that discussing death so openly overwhelmed her. But all she did was nod. It was as though Dr. McCormick had validated what she already knew, as if she found this statement of truth comforting. "But our focus would be making sure that you are comfortable and free of any suffering during that time." He looked Donna in the eyes, placing his hand respectfully on her shoulder and nodding his head deeply to emphasize the last part of his sentence.

"How would . . . I suffer?" Donna asked, suddenly looking at me. Even though after years of studying I could tell Donna everything about how her kidneys work and what happens to her body when they fail, I hadn't the slightest idea how she would *experience* dying from kidney failure, or what medications could ease her suffering. My silence stunned me. I struggled to understand how I could be on the cusp of becoming a physician and lack the words to answer her question, to guide her through the one certain transition every patient of mine, every human being including myself, would experience.

"When you stop dialysis, one of the most common things that happens is that the fluid that dialysis usually takes out of the body can build up in the lungs, and you can have some difficulty breathing," Dr. McCormick began, and Donna nodded. "So I would give you medicines to help prevent any gasping or difficulty breathing you might have."

"Good," Donna whispered, adding, "I don't . . . want . . . to suffocate."

"There are two medicines I will make sure we give you so that you don't experience that awful feeling," Dr. McCormick said. "The other thing that can happen is that the toxins that build up when you stop dialysis can make you confused and eventually sleepy. Usually this isn't painful, but it can worry those around you."

"I don't . . . want pain," Donna responded, and Dr. McCormick quickly reassured her that kidney failure generally doesn't cause pain, and death would arrive only after loss of consciousness. Kidney failure, he told her gently, could be a very merciful way to die.

I had never seen this type of doctoring before.

As the conversation unfolded, I felt a knot in my stomach harden, realizing the enormous implications of Donna's statements. Intellectually, I knew that patients could choose not to start a treatment or discontinue a treatment that wasn't helping them, but I had never witnessed a patient say that their quality of life was actually worsened by a treatment intended to help them live.

"I'm ready," Donna whispered. "I know . . . God is . . . waiting for me," she whispered. Chaplain Ellen took Donna's hand and asked her if she found solace in religion or spirituality. Donna nodded, whispering that she was a Christian, asking Ellen to pray with her. As Ellen read from the book of Psalms, Donna's shallow breathing slowed, her face relaxing. "When the righteous cry for help," Ellen read, "the Lord hears and delivers them out of all their troubles. The Lord is near to the brokenhearted and saves the crushed in spirit."

"Thank you, sister," Donna whispered.

The dying I had encountered prior to meeting Donna had been either sudden and unexpected (the result of a terrible car accident) or a failure of the most aggressive possible medical treatment (the man with advanced cancer who died after twenty-five minutes' worth of CPR). In retrospect, I realize that these were examples of *death*. *Dying* was a process I hadn't been able to recognize during my years of medical school. I felt tears burn at the corners of my eyes and blinked them away, willing myself to stay composed. But I wasn't sad for Donna. I admired her.

Here, at the very end of medical school, mere weeks before I became a "real" doctor, I finally saw what it meant to care for a dying patient.

A portrait of a person, in forty-five minutes. What emerged as I listened to Dr. McCormick's conversation with Donna was different from taking a social history, a brisk collection of essential facts about a patient's life that could impact their health: Who was part of their family? Where did they live? What did they do for work? Did they drink or smoke? Did they follow a specific religion? I had always taken pride in memorizing facts about my patients that helped me to understand who they were: their children's names, their birthplaces, and their jobs. But those were still just facts, ones I collected earnestly because this felt like the closest I'd ever come to knowing my patients as people, seeing them as human beings, despite the ways in which medical training placed an increasing distance between us. This conversation with Donna was different. It was about understanding what truly mattered to her, and how she could make choices about her medical care that would privilege rather than sacrifice her priorities.

Up until this point, I'd come to believe that treating disease was the best way to alleviate suffering. The person and her disease collapsed together, the boundaries between the two ever more indistinct as medical school continued. But by unintentionally treating patients like a panoply of diagnoses, biological mysteries to be solved, I was losing sight of what had drawn me to medicine in the first place: the unique opportunity to become both a scientist and a humanist, translating book knowledge into relief of human suffering. The cumulative challenge of memorizing endless maladies and their treatments, rushing around the hospital to see patients and order lab tests and call consultants, the pressure to perform well, and the long hours in the hospital wore on me, even as the meaning I found in the work waned. During my palliative care elective, though, that meaning began to return. How ironic, I thought, that I began to find my purpose in a field that embraced what medicine sought to erase.

Over the next two weeks, I felt alternately uncomfortable and inspired, grateful to practice the type of medicine that felt genuinely humanistic, but also overwhelmed by the vast gap between palliative care and the medicine I'd been learning.

In those two weeks, Dr. McCormick taught me how to properly evaluate and treat pain and nausea, basic symptoms I realized I didn't feel prepared to treat even though I was on the verge of completing medical school. When we could ease a patient's cancer pain or shortness of breath from heart failure, some regained the ability to dress themselves or hold a comfortable conversation. Others slowly became strong enough to get more chemotherapy or enroll in a clinical trial. Dr. McCormick taught me the difference between hospice and palliative care: hospice isn't a place, but rather a type of palliative care that teams of nurses, doctors, social workers, and chaplains provided to patients, often in their own homes, when they had less than six months to live. I took notes as I watched him lead family meetings, asking patients about how the realities of their diseases reshaped their hopes and goals.

I hadn't considered that patients could have goals other than fixing a medical problem and returning home. I listened as a patient dying of pancreatic cancer told Dr. McCormick that she wanted to feel well enough to attend her daughter's college graduation in two months. An elderly gentleman found the courage to tell us that appointments with his oncologist took up too many hours of his waning life; he'd rather be at home with the family he loved than driving back and forth to the oncology clinic, spending hours in a cushioned chair as chemotherapy dripped into his veins. Though many of the patients I cared for were dying, we spoke mostly of their lives, of what it meant to live well in the time they had remaining.

Several days before the end of my rotation, I met Julia, a woman in her fifties with end-stage breast cancer who couldn't lie on her back because the cancer had eaten through half of her spine. Even when Dr. McCormick and I adjusted her pain medications so that she could finally sleep, the night-shift nurses left notes in her chart observing her to be "awake and alert" and "complaining of insomnia" at three a.m. I asked her what was troubling her, and she told me, "I am just not ready to leave my daughter and my grand-daughter. There's too much I have to tell them." I listened, nodding, but unsure what to say. I realized once I'd left her room that the version of myself before medical school might have been more capable of empathizing with her as a woman on the cusp of great loss, rather than looking upon her as a patient dying of breast cancer. The irony of this unconscious trade-off—my ability to relate to her human emotions in exchange for the profes-sional distance of medical expertise—left me ashamed. As I took the elevator back down to the room where our team discussed patients, I won-dered what other parts of myself I'd lost or forced into dormancy over these past few years.

Hours later, when our team sat together and talked about each of our patients, I described my conversation with Julia and turned to Dr. McCor-mick, suggesting that maybe we could increase the dose of her sleep aid. Ellen wondered aloud if there was something else we could do for her aside from prescribing a medication to help her sleep. "Have you ever heard of legacy work?" Ellen asked me, explaining that people often want to leave messages or remembrances or expressions of their love for those they will leave behind. Sometimes, people write letters that loved ones open on a specific event such as graduation or a wedding day. Others make videos re-counting their love for a spouse, or use paint and posterboard to leave a grandchild turkeys or hearts made of their handprints. I had never heard of legacy work before, but it struck me as a vital tool to attend to patients' emotional landscape, to help them mine their lives for meaning.

I returned to see Julia several hours later with Ellen, a tape recorder in her hand, and a notebook and pen in mine. "Which do you want to use to tell your family what you need to say?" I asked, as we both explained that we had the tools to record her voice or to serve as her scribe.

She did both. Her voice, alternately strong and broken, for her grand-daughter. Her words in my handwriting on lined journal paper for her daughter. She read my letter twice before she signed it in shaky cursive, folding and pressing it against her heart. "Thank you," she said, "for helping me leave a piece of myself for my girls." That afternoon, I'd done nothing that specifically required medical training, but Julia slept well that night, waking up only once.

. . . .

Both Donna and Julia died. Although she had hoped to die at home with the support of hospice, Donna became confused and then slipped into unconsciousness three days after we met her. Dr. McCormick said she might not survive the ambulance ride home, so we cared for her instead in her hospital room. We covered her with extra blankets when she shivered, and wrote orders to stop nurses from waking her to take her blood pressure and temperature every six hours. Her comfort became our most important vital sign. We stopped by her room several times a day, carefully adjusting doses of her medications to ease her shortness of breath, confusion, and pain. Her family tied balloons to her bedpost and surrounded her with photographs of people who loved her. They encircled her and sang, the melodies of hymns fractured by their tears. She died in the middle of the night shortly after her family left, alone in a quiet but peaceful room.

Julia took her letter and tape and went home with hospice care. Several weeks after my rotation ended, I ran into Ellen, who told me that Julia's family had written a thank-you note to our team. "I think that letter and that recording gave her some real peace and helped her feel that she could finally let go," Ellen told me.

What I learned from Dr. McCormick and Ellen was so distinct from what I'd learned and experienced in medical school that I wondered if it was "real" medicine. The medicine I'd learned was fast paced and lifesaving, an enterprise that relied on plastic catheters and ultrasounds, operating rooms and endoscopy suites, a rainbow of pills for diabetes and high blood pressure, saline and antibiotics that coursed through the body from bags attached to an IV pole. The effort to extend life left no space for accepting death.

Still, I left the rotation drawn to palliative care and haunted by the patients for whom my new knowledge came too late. This shift in focus, the inspiration I sought, had everything to do with what I hadn't learned in medical school, with what wasn't modeled for me rather than what was.

What was it about this negative space, about learning to articulate the unsaid, that called to me?

When I look back on those two weeks, I realize that I did not do for my patients what I had been trained for years to do: I did not diagnose or fix their ailments. They didn't live for more than days or weeks after I met them. But it is not their deaths that I remember. It is the peace they found in the honesty we offered, in the opportunity for them to articulate their suffering and what they wished for in the time they had left. My acquisition of a particular language, and my shifting relationship to empathy and truth, nagged at me even when I tried to convince myself that I couldn't possibly do what Dr. McCormick did every single day. During those weeks, I'd felt both human and humane, like a person and a doctor rather than one or the other. I couldn't dispute that I'd left my rotation feeling the closest I had felt to the doctor I always wanted to be.

Two

WORDS

I'm not sure whether I became a doctor because I loved medicine or because I wanted to be just like my mother.

She was born in Mumbai to Hindu refugees from West Punjab, where her parents had operated a cotton factory in the industrial city of Gujranwala. Upon India's independence from British rule in 1947, religious politics had cleaved Punjab in two: West Punjab, home to a Muslim majority and to my grandparents, became part of Pakistan. East Punjab, home to mostly Sikhs and Hindus, became part of India. Sectarian violence among Hindus, Muslims, and Sikhs, communities that had coexisted for centuries, claimed the lives of between one million and two million people. Silent trains filled with murdered refugees pulled into railway stations on both sides of the new border. Temples and mosques became sites of genocide. My grandfather recalled entire villages set ablaze, orange flames quivering as they consumed the homes of his friends and the park where they'd walked together most mornings. Dismembered corpses bloodied fields full of sugarcane and wheat.

Around fifteen million people lost their homes, including my grandparents, who barely survived their migration to independent India. After a Muslim neighbor warned my grandfather of an approaching mob, he and my grandmother left their home empty-handed, desperate to reach the border with their young daughter, my mother's oldest sister. Years later, my grandfather would learn that a mob torched their entire neighborhood just fifteen minutes after they fled. My grandparents went from one refugee camp to another, moving through Punjab and Delhi, eventually staying for five years in Deolali, once a transit camp for British troops in the western state of Maharashtra. Desperate for money and work in a new land, my grandfather decided to change his surname to that of a powerful, well-connected family in Mumbai, hoping that perhaps the illusion of a relationship with them would result in employment opportunities or even a refugee flat. Neither hope materialized, though my grandparents somehow made their way to Mumbai and raised five children in a two-room flat on my grandfather's erratic and meager earnings as a taxi driver. My grandmother found solace in prayer, firmly believing that God would help her and her young family endure and possibly even transcend the hunger and deprivation that marked their first years in a foreign city, still reeling from the aftershocks of upheaval.

My mother was born in the corner of a room where she and her four siblings and parents slept next to one another on scratchy mattresses. Because she was born at home, my grandparents never knew her birthday with certainty. It was one of the many unknowns in my mother's early life, far less consequential than the daily uncertainty of my grandfather earning money, of a warm evening meal, of enough clean water to bathe. But one certainty that emerged early in my mother's life was her desire to become a doctor.

She found her calling at age seven, when she met the family physician who visited their flat with a shiny black bag whenever someone fell ill. He had soft hands and a quiet manner. His bag had a copper clasp that snapped open and shut with a professional *click*. She imagined it was a magic bag, full of pills and potions that scared away the illnesses that made people sick. She sat next to him as he sewed up her brother's chin after he tumbled down a flight of stairs, and watched as he offered cool towels and a bottle of bright blue pills to her mother when her face burned with fever and her throat swelled. Just being around him made my mother feel better. She peered into his magic bag and thought that it was bottomless. Maybe when he put his hand in, she wondered, he actually reached into secret worlds. Once she reached into his bag to see what she might find, but quickly withdrew her hand when he turned around. She wanted to comfort people the way he did, to shoo away fevers and to sew up people's accidents. She wanted a magic bag of her own.

Her dream buoyed her through discouraging stretches of bleak monotony. There was the incessant honking of cars and metallic scuttle of rickshaw motors, the relentless sonic chaos of Mumbai that greeted my mother when she awoke and persisted after she fell asleep. There were her father's outbursts—screaming matches with her mother followed by cool silences—when the humiliation of having gone from a thriving business owner to a struggling taxi driver consumed him. There were the fumes from her mother's stove, vapors that stung her nose and made her dizzy. The fumes meant her father had earned enough money for her mother to make *daal* and rice for dinner, eventually filling the small flat with the comforting scent of garlic, ginger, and onions. No fumes meant the sharp twisting of her stomach turning on itself as she read her schoolbooks at night, remembering the magic bag when sleep seemed the preferable alternative to studying. She thought of the magic bag on Sundays as she picked lice from her siblings' hair, crushing their small black bodies between her index finger and thumb, rinsing her hands in a bowl of blood-tinged water.

Prayer brought my mother peace. She placed vines of jasmine atop a silver figurine of Lord Ganesha and a framed picture of Goddess Durga perched on a small bench in her mother's kitchen. She and my grandmother sat together on the dusty floor of the *gurdwara*, a Sikh temple steps away from their flat that they entered with solemnity, their heads bowed and covered with thin cotton *dupattas*. She considered the practice of medicine holy, and begged God for the chance to become a doctor, keeping the image of the magic bag in her mind as she whispered prayers in Sanskrit and Punjabi.

When my mother earned a spot at a medical school in Mumbai, my grandmother cried tears of pride and shame. She and my grandfather could not afford the mandatory admission fee. Later that day, quietly determined, my mother pleaded for help from a wealthy neighbor, who listened to my mother's predicament and gave her the money she needed. Every time my mother had to pay school fees that she lacked, she begged the dean of the medical school for a scholarship. A combination of her insistence, determination, and excellent grades swayed him each time. Throughout medical school, my mother continued to live with her parents, taking two trains and a bus to and from school each morning, returning as she always had to the smell of her mother's stove and the scratchy mattresses on the cold floor.

. . . .

During my childhood, my mother and medicine were inextricably intertwined, sometimes indistinguishable, each shaping and shaped by the other. It was almost as though medicine was the fifth inhabitant of our home, living quietly alongside my parents, my younger brother, Siddarth, and me. Medicine lived in our hallway closet, where my mother stored the green operating room scrubs that I occasionally wore as pajamas. Medicine carpeted my mother's car, long strands of her black hair stuck to the wispy blue operating room caps and shoe coverings always underfoot in the passenger seat. Medicine even made its way into my father's wardrobe. In a number of family photos taken in the 1980s, my father is wearing a shirt my mother gave him, one that advertised a medication she'd started to use in the operating room: "I'm in Control: Tracrium."

The hospital was my second home, and my mother's colleagues became my aunties and uncles. On school holidays, she would bring my brother and me to the hospital with her, leaving us in the surgical lounge under the not-so-watchful eyes of surgeons who snacked on doughnuts and chips between their cases in the operating room. They gave my brother and me operating room hats and gowns so that we could pretend to be just like them. I examined my face in the mirror in hospital bathrooms, hoping that I would one day have my mother's long black hair, her hazel eyes and long eyelashes, her smile so wide and warm that it could both comfort and disarm anyone. I helped her to pack suitcases full of sterile gloves and needles and operating room equipment to donate to Indian hospitals where she volunteered as an anesthesiologist every year, treating patients who lived in the poverty she had escaped. Medicine hovered over my shoulder when my mother and I sat together studying biology and physiology when I was in middle school, reviewing what I still consider to be the awe-inspiring mechanisms of the heart pumping, the kidneys filtering, the liver cleaning, the brain commanding.

In high school, when I told her what I was learning in biology, she told me I finally knew enough for her to share with me the details of her everyday work. She traced her finger along the side of my neck, showing me how she found a patient's jugular vein, and telling me why she had to place IVs there to give powerful blood pressure medications to patients undergoing surgery. She traced a similar path along the artery lining my wrist, and showed me where and how she put in a thin, flexible catheter that would sense and report changes in blood pressure. She taught me to trace a path down the front of my neck, showing me the anatomic landmarks she used to insert a breathing tube into a patient's throat, which would connect him to the ventilator, a machine that would assume the work of his lungs during surgery. She pulled out her stethoscope from her purse and showed me how to listen to my own heart, and then hers, the heart that had nourished me in her womb.

Her heart made the two distinct sounds that my high school physiology textbook described: *Lub-dub*, the steady, reliable sequence of the closure of one set of heart valves and then the second, ensuring that blood flowed in one direction, from atrium to ventricle to the rest of the body. Years later, in medical school, I would remember the sound of her heart as I learned how to read an EKG, its elegant tracings corresponding to the electrical impulse that blazed a path across the heart's tissue eighty times a minute. During periods of sadness and stress, I would place my hand on my heart, marveling at the fist-shaped muscle that pumped inches below, reminding me that I was just as strong and capable of resilience as the woman whose own heart gave life to mine.

Yet along with my mother's intense presence was her absence. Even though medicine fostered our bond, the demands of her career also tested it, keeping her at the hospital for stretches of time that felt endless. I was always the last child picked up from an after-school day care program if she was in a complex or emergency case. The hospital operator recognized my voice because I would call to talk to my mother every night she was on overnight call, which for a time was every third night. When I came home from school and found her asleep after working a thirty-hour shift, I would jump on the bed to wake her up, wrapping my arms around her and hoping she would take me to the beach or the park. I would breathe in the scent of her damp hair, freshly washed before she napped, and try to burrow my head in the narrow space between her jawline and collarbone. She would push me away, barely awake, and groggily ask me to let her rest.

I couldn't be without her, but I came to realize that she couldn't be without medicine. I followed my mother into medicine because that's where she was.

....

Six months into my internship, the grueling first year of internal medicine residency training, I met John Tan.

Because Mr. Tan couldn't speak, he wrote me notes instead. He lay in a bed in the intensive care unit of the university hospital, steps away from the ward where I'd met Donna and Julia. He was a thin man in his early sixties with a fringe of gray and black hair that lined the lower edges of his skull. About a year before I met him, he'd survived an aggressive cancer that grew from the lining of his nose and pharynx. But the chemotherapy and radiation that treated his cancer left him vulnerable to infection. A fungal infection invaded the base of his skull and eventually made its home in the lining of an artery feeding his brain. Periodically, pieces of the fungus would break away from the wall of the artery and, carried upward by tides of blood into his brain, lodge in tiny blood vessels that fed his delicate brain tissue. The resulting unpredictable strokes he had suffered robbed him of his ability to walk independently, swallow food, and speak.

"There's no surgery to remove the infection," our hospital's neurosurgeon told me when I asked if there was a way to remove or reduce it. "It's just a matter of time before he has another stroke. All we can do is continue the antifungal medications and hope that that will slow down its growth and buy him time. But in the long run he isn't going to do well."

Though it posed a constant threat to his life, John's fungal infection wasn't the reason he had been admitted to the hospital this time. He'd developed a severe pneumonia and was in the hospital for powerful intravenous antibiotics. But as his pneumonia began to resolve, he suffered a life-threatening bleed from an ulcer in his stomach. I ordered multiple blood transfusions for him and he underwent CT scans and endoscopies to identify and stop the bleed's source. Shortly after he stabilized, his heart started racing, portending another infection, this time in his bladder.

Mr. Tan was one of ten patients I'd been assigned. The time I spent with him, and every one of my patients, was brief and hurried. Efficiency was every intern's holy grail, and patients could slow us down by talking for a very long time. Despite convincing myself I wouldn't follow in the footsteps of the residents I'd learned from, I spent far more time on paperwork and note writing and studying than I did talking with and examining patients. My habits troubled me, but I'd remind myself that I'd need to survive residency in order to practice medicine the way I wanted to. After all, my residency classmates and I joked that we were experts in delayed gratification. But Mr. Tan's situation set off an internal alarm I couldn't ignore, the severity of his condition convincing me that taking care of him required me to stop glancing at the clock when I was in his room.

Every morning when I examined him, he greeted me with a crooked smile on his stroke-struck face, left cheek higher than the right, his bright eyes lined with deep crow's-feet. He extended his left hand, every blue vein visible and protruding, and motioned for me to sit down and join him. His perpetually chapped lips, always partially open, revealed thinning gums and teeth covered in thick saliva, which pooled on the side of his face and collected in the crevice of his collarbone as he napped. The sick-sweet stench of bloody stool, a result of the internal bleed he'd recently suffered, filled his room as I examined him, pressing my stethoscope along the points on his torso where I could best hear his heartbeat and breathing. Again with his left hand—the hand unaffected by his most recent stroke—he picked up the whiteboard and red dry-erase pen that lay at his bedside, next to a navy blue UC Davis mug and what appeared to be a letter written in Chinese characters, and began to write to me.

My mouth feels very dry. Can you give me some gel for it?

His main discomfort seemed so small in light of his pneumonia, bladder infection, stomach bleed, and the ever-present possibility of another stroke. I glanced at his medication list and noticed that the gel I'd ordered had somehow expired. I promised him I'd reorder it. He never had many questions for me. But as he developed one new malady after another and two and a half weeks in the hospital passed by, I realized how many questions I had for him, questions that I'd first heard Dr. McCormick ask: Did he understand how sick he was? How would he want me to take care of him if he got sicker? Had he and his family ever discussed what quality of life he valued, and what decisions he would want them to make on his behalf if another stroke destroyed his ability to communicate? Would he want CPR if his heart stopped? Though I had watched Dr. McCormick open these conversations with a graceful ease, I doubted my ability to do the same. Just as I began to tell Mr. Tan that I'd be back later in the afternoon to make sure his mouth felt better, he started to write me a note.

Do you ever go home?

I chuckled and promised him that I did.

You are here in morning, afternoon, night. When do you go home?

"Okay, now you sound like my mother!" I joked with him, and we both laughed. A patient had never conveyed concern about my own well-being, and I was touched. "I promise you I go home. And it's very kind of you to even ask me about that!" What I didn't tell him, what I was ashamed to admit, was that a part of me preferred being at the hospital rather than outside it. Within these walls, I had a clearly defined role, one that brought me a degree of purpose even when it frustrated and exhausted me. Outside in the world, I was uncertain of who I was: I'd invested so much time studying and preparing for work that I no longer knew what to do with myself when I had free time. I became synonymous with my work, even in the moments when I doubted that medicine was the right profession for me. Becoming a doctor had taken up so much of my life that I promised myself I would find a way to make it feel like the right fit. Outside of the hospital, I had been fighting with my boyfriend at the time, an engineer who had come to resent the emotionally depleted intern who took hours to respond to text messages and who sometimes fell asleep in the middle of a phone call after work. I was impatient in grocery store lines and curt to cashiers. My friends from college slowly stopped calling and emailing me because I mostly didn't write back; there was always something more pressing—a test, a research project—that seemed to get in the way. I wasn't good at my life. But I thought I could be good at medicine. I reminded myself to embrace the concept of delayed gratification. What I'd sacrificed now could be mine when I finished my training.

Thank you for helping me, he wrote, giving me a thumbs-up sign.

"You are very, very welcome, Mr. Tan. I promise you I'll take care of that dry mouth for you."

As I left his room, I knew I had to muster the courage to have an honest talk about his condition with him and his family. Nobody on the long roster of physicians who treated him—surgeons, neurologists, infectious disease specialists, and oncologists—raised a concern that he might die during this hospital stay. Or that he might survive but leave weaker and more debilitated than he'd been before. Of my ten patients, he was the one most vulnerable to catastrophe. And if he suffered a complication we couldn't control, we had no plan in place other than to sustain his dying body with every possible invasive machine and technology, regardless of their benefit to him at this late stage of illness. I found myself wondering if I was just treating one of his maladies to buy time for another one to manifest. Yet with many more experienced doctors involved in his care, I felt the least qualified to voice this observation.

Was Mr. Tan slowly dying? I wondered after observing the setbacks he had suffered in the weeks since I assumed his care. And if indeed his time was short, would he want to spend it in the hospital as we chased one problem after another without changing where things were heading? Instead of fearing his mortality, what if I respected him enough to name it, to invite the end of his life into the conversation I knew I'd have to have with him? Would he be alarmed or relieved to know what I was thinking?

I wanted more than anything to be a good doctor—to Mr. Tan, to every patient I'd see now and in the future. But what did it mean to be a good doctor to a patient in his predicament? Was a good doctor the one who promised to do everything in her power to save his life, or the one who was honest about medicine's limits? Was the good doctor the one who maintained a hopeful silence about Mr. Tan's uncertain future, or was she the one who broke it?

I moved through the rest of my day, seeing my other patients and discussing my care plan for each one with the two physicians supervising and teaching me: Andrew, a second-year resident, and Dr. Michaels, an attending physician who had finished his residency ten years earlier. As the late-afternoon sky darkened into night, I sat in the residents' room on the ninth floor of the hospital, writing the ten patient notes I had to complete before going home. The room was a workspace lined with computers and lockers for my fellow residents and me. Battered couches surrounded a table littered with half-eaten bags of chips, crumbs from a grease-stained pink box of muffins, and takeout menus from nearby Chinese and Indian fast-food restaurants. This was where we alternately shared the details of challenging cases and bemoaned the inconveniences of residency. During overnight calls, we huddled together in this room, sharing late-night ice cream bars from the cafeteria and draping warm blankets from the ICU over our shoulders as we typed our notes or researched the treatment of unusual diseases. Though the residents' room was often cluttered and smelled of a strange combination of coffee and sweat, it boasted a view that consistently brought me peace.

From this windowed room, I could catch the first glimpse of the evening fog's gray fingers stretching forth from the San Francisco Bay, grasping the city in its embrace. During overnight calls spent seeing and admitting new patients to the hospital, I wrote my patient notes in this same room, pausing to watch the sun spill slowly across the city like liquid gold against the rust and pink of the day's earliest sky.

Between my four years in medical school, two years doing research, and the start of my residency, I had been living in the Bay Area for nearly seven years. But I'd never found a view of San Francisco as incredible as the one from inside the walls of this hospital. From a conference room on the fourteenth floor, I took in the reliability of the sunrise and sunset over the city's bridges, hills, and vast patches of greenery, which contrasted sharply with the controlled but unpredictable atmosphere of the hospital. I meandered up to this room most mornings to take in the view before rounds. I pressed my palm against the cool window, its pane bejeweled with the day's earliest dew. I pressed my palm against this window now, as I took a break from note writing, wishing I could reach through to the wisps of scattered clouds, a mess of stars emerging around them. This window, the thin barrier between the order of nature and the chaos of the hospital.

....

I wasn't on call that day, which meant that I arrived at the hospital at 6:30 a.m. and would leave around 6:30 p.m., taking a university-operated shuttle bus back to my small apartment. Every four nights, when I *was* on call, I worked a thirty-hour shift to care for my list of current patients and admit new patients to the hospital. I lived in student housing near the Giants' baseball stadium and Caltrain depot in the Mission Bay neighborhood of San Francisco. During my ride home, I turned my full attention to the scenery of San Francisco as we passed the green edges of Golden Gate Park, streets in the Tenderloin lined with hotels and clusters of homeless people outside narrow cafés, and a lonely concrete stretch of Seventh Street, where speeding cars on Interstate 280 rumbled on the freeway overpass that hovered over a set of railroad tracks.

Everything about my apartment reflected my harried life. My refrigerator was largely empty save for a few cans of Diet Coke; in one cupboard, I'd gathered a few bruised bananas and apples and bags of baked chips I'd bring home from the hospital cafeteria. A cream-colored futon and an old television I'd bought from Craigslist faced each other in the small living area, where a few of my half-written essays and medical textbooks covered my old Ikea desk. I'd taped a few photographs of my parents and brother throughout the apartment; picture frames I'd bought on sale at Rite Aid sat, unopened, in a sad pile underneath my desk. I slept on a sinking mattress under a maroon and orange duvet, and the empty half of my bed was covered with novels, collections of essays, and poetry I read before sleeping and didn't bother to return to the bookcase: Rainer Maria Rilke's *Sonnets to Orpheus*, Arundhati Roy's *The God of Small Things*, Joan Didion's *Slouching Towards Bethlehem*. I'd discovered them in college, when I collected syllabi of English classes I longed to take but couldn't squeeze into a class schedule dominated by prerequisites for medical school. I bought used copies of *Black Boy* and *The Color Purple*, *My Own Country* and *Native Speaker*. I underlined passages of prose and lines of poetry that stirred emotions I couldn't name. Though I'd sold my biology and physics textbooks years ago, and long since recycled several notebooks' worth of chemistry lectures, I continued to sleep next to books assigned in classes I never took.

I always resolved to organize my apartment on my one day off each week, but when that day rolled around, I instead spent it sleeping in and walking along the Embarcadero to the Ferry Building. I'd meander from the bookstore to a vegan doughnut stand to a small café for lunch and walk for hours, letting the sunshine, which I sorely missed at the hospital, warm me. I'd occasionally go out to dinner at tasty, affordable places—a Vietnamese café in nearby Potrero Hill, a South Indian restaurant in the Mission—with a friend or two from my residency program. We talked about the lives of our friends who weren't in medicine, friends who were married, who lived in homes rather than student housing, and had enough vacation time and money to leave the country or enjoy a spontaneous weekend getaway.

When I began my residency, I was thirty years old. When I caught glimpses of myself in the mirrors of our hospital's bathroom, I saw a young woman with long black hair and a newly visible strand of gray, dark eyes encircled by faint new shadows, and a narrow face with eyebrows in need of threading. I had never been married, my few relationships crushed by my hours of studying and work and my naïve expectation that those I loved would implicitly understand the physical and emotional demands of my training. By the time my mother turned thirty, she had married a man she'd known for one week, moved with him to a new country where she didn't have a single blood relative, given birth to two children while juggling a grueling anesthesiology residency, and started to save her meager resident's salary for a home and for the future education of her children. At thirty, I still felt like a child, floundering to find my footing in the world, troubled by the endless transience of my training: I saw patients at three different hospitals, working with an ever-changing roster of fellow residents, students, and attending physicians, adapting my work to meet the expectations of each new supervisor. Change was the one constant in my life. I longed for stability.

My mother called me almost every day, though I wasn't always able to pick up. Tonight, she called just as I lay down in bed, and asked me how my day had been.

"It's been busy," I said, closing my eyes, relaxing as her voice, in lilting Hindi, washed over me. I told her about the patient whom I'd correctly diagnosed with new-onset heart failure caused by a prior course of chemotherapy, another patient whose back pain was due to newly discovered multiple myeloma. I told her about Mr. Tan, and wondered aloud whether he would ever be well enough to leave the hospital.

"He sounds very complicated," my mother agreed. "Nowadays, people are much sicker than before. But I didn't take care of people the way you do in internal medicine. My job is simple—intubate them and put a few IVs in and then just wait!"

She told me that she and my father were planning their yearly trip to India; they liked to travel in January or February, when the weather was tolerable. We talked about how much her home country has changed, how she could no longer imagine living in a city swollen with people, devoid of silence, its skies darkened by the haze of pollution. I could tell this caused her great pain, returning to a place she had lost. "I don't think so much about the past or what it used to be," she told me when I asked if returning to India caused her more sadness than joy. "It is all temporary anyway. We have it, and then it's gone." This is what she often said when she spoke of India, of how it had transformed into a place that she could neither recognize nor consider home. But her voice swelled with longing and regret that she couldn't disguise, and I could sense acutely everything my parents had given up for my brother and me to have the lives we did. When I thought about pursuing a career in literature or anthropology instead of medicine, she was supportive even though she and my father had always assumed I'd follow in her footsteps. But the mix of nostalgia and grief in my mother's voice haunted me, and I would ask myself if those careers would be worth her sacrifice. I could feel the weight of what she said and left unsaid pressing upon me in a place beyond language.

....

The next morning on rounds, when I spoke to Andrew and Dr. Michaels about Mr. Tan, I said aloud the words I'd practiced as I took the shuttle to work hours earlier. "I think maybe it's time to sit down and talk with his family about . . . where this is going," I said haltingly, struggling at first to state my recommendation clearly, then continuing boldly. "I am worried that he may get sicker quickly, and I haven't talked with him or his family about what we should do if that happens. Should we intubate him if he has another stroke and can't breathe on his own? Would he want CPR to keep him from dying? Does he even really know how bad his situation is? Those seem like things we should address sooner rather than later." I couldn't quite articulate my other motivation for the meeting: Everyone taking care of Mr. Tan knew how dire his situation was, how the next illness could take his life. Everyone knew this, except for him.

"Sure," Dr. Michaels said, "that's a good idea. Those are important things to clarify. For now, let's continue his current antibiotics and antifungals, and make sure his blood counts remain stable. Let us know how the meeting goes." I trembled anxiously. Wouldn't Andrew or Dr. Michaels join me? Had I been doing a technical procedure on Mr. Tan— placing an IV in a large vein in his neck, or drawing fluid out of his swollen belly—Andrew would have prepared me for and overseen the entire procedure, possibly with Dr. Michaels there to supervise both of us. Procedures were both necessary and risky, but so were family meetings, as I'd seen when working with Dr. McCormick. Words and silence, like needles and catheters, could harm or help, illuminate or injure. I thought back to my time with Dr. McCormick, when he and I would review the medical facts of a patient's situation and decide, together, what we wanted to communicate to the patient and how. We brainstormed the sorts of questions a patient or family might ask us, and considered how we might answer. We chose our words carefully, looking for that elusive balance of discussing the reality of a patient's situation without destroying the hope they might have for their future. I considered asking Andrew to help me plan for the meeting as Dr. McCormick had, to figure out what I wanted to communicate and how, but as an intern I often felt I had to assume an air of knowledge and competence even if I had neither. Nothing was more bothersome to supervising residents than interns who couldn't handle supposedly simple tasks like talking to a family, especially since family meetings tended to be draining and lengthy, requiring at least an hour out of an already compressed day. As I prepared for the meeting, I remembered that I had a pocket guide to family meetings that Dr. McCormick had recommended to me, complete with bullet points to help me prepare for and carry out the meeting in an organized, compassionate way. I grabbed the guide from my backpack and hunched over a desk in the residents' room to scribble notes that I hoped would approximate the planning I'd learned to do with Dr. McCormick.

I called Mr. Tan's wife, Laura, and daughter, Noelle, and asked them to come into the hospital for a family meeting. No, I told them, there was no emergency. Yes, he's doing about the same, I said. What I didn't know how to say was that his stable instability was the problem. I had to find a kind and precise way to tell them what the surgeon had told me, to figure out what to do not if, but when, the worst-case scenario manifested.

My family is all here, he wrote later that day, when they had all arrived and gathered in his room.

A petite woman wearing baggy black pants and an oversized cardigan, Laura stood no taller than the middle of my chest. Her short dark hair, parted down the middle, framed an open face with smiling eyes and simple glasses, and she wore a circular jade pendant at her throat. "I am his wife," she said in slightly halting English.

"Yes! I am so glad you could be here," I said, shaking her hand. Taller than me by several inches and gracefully poised with the long torso and neck of a ballerina, Noelle had long dark hair streaked with faded high-lights that she had tied back in a high ponytail. A loose dark sweater obscured her slim frame. She was in her early twenties, a junior at UC Davis. Her expression, initially grave, gave way to a warm smile when I told her that her father always kept an eye on his precious UC Davis mug. Still, her tightly folded arms betrayed the tension she was feeling, as if her arms could both steady and protect her from what this vague "check-in" might be about. Noelle spoke to me in English and to her mother in Cantonese. I knew from reading Mr. Tan's chart that Noelle accompanied him to his doctors' appointments, often interpreting for him and Laura. I would learn later that she chose her class schedule to accommodate her father's clinic appointments, making sure that she could travel back home to pick up her parents, listen to the doctors' rec-ommendations, and ensure that all the right medications were ordered, filled, and picked up at the right pharmacy.

"Don't worry," I told Noelle, motioning to the hospital's Cantonese in-terpreter in the room. "You can just listen today. No need at all to inter-pret."

"Thank you so much," she said quietly, her expression and folded arms unchanged.

I scanned the room quickly, trying to figure out where I should stand to lead the meeting. Next to Mr. Tan's bed? Sitting down with his family? My anxiety got the best of me, and I stood next to his bed, even though I asked his family to please take seats in the chairs I had brought into the cramped room from the nursing station. "So, um, thank you all for being here today and coming in to talk about how Mr. Tan is doing." The Can-tonese interpreter, who stood next to the family, translated and looked back at me. I glanced down at my outline, a list of points I wanted to cover in the meeting, many of which I had cribbed from Dr. McCormick's cheat sheet.

I felt totally alone in this room with my oldest tools—words. I took a deep breath.

1. Ask the patient/family what they know about his illness.

"So, could you tell me, what is your understanding of your medical problems?" I looked first at Noelle and Laura, then shifted my gaze back to Mr. Tan. He started writing down his answer in slow, wobbly characters: *My mouth is very dry.*

Huh? I thought to myself. "Oh, okay. Let's get you some gel for your mouth," I said, as I tried to think of another way to ask my question that would encourage him to answer it more fully. Laura smeared artificial saliva onto Mr. Tan's lips and I tried again: "What are the neurosurgeons and infectious disease doctors telling you about your fungal infection?"

As the interpreter repeated my question in Cantonese, I glanced at the next point.

2. Correct any misunderstandings they have about how sick the patient is.

On his whiteboard, Mr. Tan responded: *I don't know.*

How is that possible? He's been here for almost a month. How could he not understand what is going on with his fungal infection? I thought.

How do I begin to explain this?

"So I need to make sure you and your family understand a few things," I started, glancing at my notepad: *Fungal infection → another stroke at some point → no surgical option, only IV antifungal medication.*

3. Share information in clear, simple language.

"Unfortunately, we can only treat the fungal infection you have by giving you the medications we are already giving you through your IV," I began. "But those medications will not cure or take away the fungus. In the best-case scenario, the medications will only prevent it from growing more. In the worst-case scenario, the infection will continue to grow even though we are giving you the IV medications. The neurosurgeon who operated on you thinks that the fungus that is already in your blood vessel will probably break off at some point and cause another stroke. But we can't do a surgery to take out the fungus."

I stopped myself from continuing, allowing the interpreter to do her job, wondering how she translated these concepts effectively. I saw Laura's expression contort with concern, Noelle's eyes glaze over. I felt responsible for but unable to handle the growing emotion in the room.

Mr. Tan remained expressionless. He stared at his notepad and wrote out another question.

Can I have laser therapy to kill the fungus? Can you filter the fungus out of my blood?

I could see his engineer's mind at work, reaching to the farthest corners of possibility for a solution. I shook my head and forced myself to say what I was dreading. I hated the thought of crushing Mr. Tan, of dashing his hopes, but I hated even more the thought of withholding from him what I was just about to say: "It's just a matter of time before you have another stroke. And it could severely impact your life even more than the other strokes have."

4. Offer empathy. "I wish" statements can be helpful.

"I wish there was something like a laser therapy that we could do," I said. The interpreter spoke. And a heavy silence followed.

5. Allow for silence and expression of emotion.

When I couldn't stand the silence any longer, I went off-script. "What are your thoughts on this, Mr. Tan? What do you think you want to do?" As soon as the words stumbled from my mouth, I wanted to push them back in and swallow them.

About what? he wrote, expressionless.

About the fact that you're suffering from the complications of the treatment for your cancer, and every time we think we have treated one complication, another one shows up. About the fact that you have been in the hospital for three weeks and you probably will be in and out of the hospital until you die, probably here. About the fact that you could have a huge stroke anytime and we can't prevent it or fix it. About the

fact that I'm afraid that your heart might stop if you get really sick, and I'll break
your ribs and hurt you if I have to do CPR.

My words raced in my mind but stuck in my mouth. It was clear from
the palpable tension in the room that neither Mr. Tan's family nor I had ever
had this type of conversation. And yet now that this subject had been
broached, no matter how awkwardly, we needed to grapple with his mortality, which was now as obvious and tangible as the stench of his mouth
burned by radiation, his recently used urinal hooked to the side of his bed.
I couldn't help but wonder whether, instead of providing honesty and guidance, I had caused only fear, alarm, and confusion. "I guess . . . I mean, do
you want us to do *everything* we can for you if that big stroke happens? Even
if it ultimately wouldn't help?" I wanted him to tell me that he wanted to die
peacefully. I didn't know how to tell him that we were already doing everything we possibly could to prevent another stroke. And I couldn't bring
myself to admit that there was little more we could do if he suffered a
stroke. I couldn't find the words.

Mr. Tan looked at his notepad and wrote again.

Don't read this aloud. How long before I kick the bucket?

I pursed my lips tightly. I was a fledgling intern, a neophyte doctor. How
could I possibly tell him how long he had to live? And yet, how could I have
attempted this conversation without anticipating that he'd ask me just that?
Wouldn't I want to know if I were him?

I studied him. His temporal artery pulsed visibly at the corner of his
forehead. Bruises from IVs darkened his arms. At any time, any one of his
complications could suddenly take his life: a huge stroke, another sudden
bleed from his belly, a terrible infection with an antibiotic-resistant bug. But
what if none of that happened? If he did manage to leave the hospital?

"Probably months," I wrote on his notepad. I worried that Noelle and
Laura would ask what we were writing, that they would demand that I read
our conversation aloud. "I can't say exactly how many, but that is my best
guess." I paused and wrote more. "I am also worried that you might have a
very bad stroke that would keep you from ever leaving the hospital." He
looked at me and erased my words.

Sorry doc but you are wrong. I plan to walk out of here with a cup of coffee in my hand. He paused, and wrote more.

And I will see my daughter graduate from UC Davis in two years.

As if to demonstrate that he meant business, Mr. Tan put down his notebook and pushed himself up in bed. He carefully placed his right side on his pillow and rose to a fully upright position. Small beads of sweat dotted his forehead. His nurse rushed in. "No, Mr. Tan, you can't stand up alone!" she said, seeing that there might be no stopping him.

But Mr. Tan didn't listen. He grabbed the handrail of the narrow hospital bed with his good hand and steadied himself. He stood up right in front of me, wobbling at first, then growing sturdier, then still.

His nurse stood next to me and I sensed her fear and uncertainty. Somehow, I understood Mr. Tan's rising from the bed to be just a gesture of emphasis rather than defiance, his way of underlining and boldfacing what he had written with his shaky hand. He stood inches away from the nurse and me, his gray hospital gown hanging off his ghostly frame. He looked around the room for what seemed like minutes, quietly determined, saying nothing, before slumping down onto his bed.

"I understand," I said, in awe of what I had just witnessed, unsure what else I could possibly say. As he lowered his body onto the bed, I wondered how I could get out of his room as quickly as possible. "I know we've talked about a lot of really hard things today and I hope I didn't upset you or cause any confusion." The interpreter spoke to Laura, and turned to me with a question. "She wants to know if it is okay not to talk about this again."

Her words stung, but I forced myself to smile and respond, "Of course. I know this was a little awkward. I didn't mean to upset you. I just wanted to, you know, try to make sure you all know everything that is going on with his health." Laura, Noelle, and I shook hands, and I promised Mr. Tan I'd be back in the morning to check on him.

Thank you for your time, he wrote on the whiteboard, followed by a thumbs-up sign.

I retreated to my call room—the room reserved for the on-call resident to sleep in while at the hospital overnight—for some quiet. I replayed the meeting in my head, squirming at my questions and the family's confusion and bewilderment. My intention to provide clarity and guidance had only led the Tans to request no further such meetings. What would I do for him now if the worst happened? The default protocol would be to offer every extreme life-sustaining intervention possible. I imagined him undergoing CPR, or attached to a ventilator, and felt nauseated. If his heart or breathing stopped, our machinery might restore his heartbeat, but almost certainly wouldn't bridge his body, already ravaged by fungal infections and pneumonias and bleeding, back to the health he'd probably expect. Our technologies might prevent him from dying, but they would almost certainly fail to restore his quality of life. More intervention would almost certainly mean doing more harm. And I had taken an oath to do no harm.

Overwhelmed by the ramifications of my well-meaning but poorly delivered words, I found myself wanting to call my mother, to find out how she had grappled with her own mistakes, how she had managed to find peace when she retreated to her own on-call room, the place she went to to pause and make sense of what she encountered every day.

. . . .

I was seven years old and in second grade. My brother, Siddarth, was four years old and in preschool. It was a three-day weekend, sometime in January or February, and, as usual on long weekends, my mother had woken us up at six a.m. and taken us with her to work. Neither she nor my father could take a day off from their jobs to watch us at home, let alone take us on vacation to Catalina or Palm Springs or Morro Bay, the places my classmates went with their families, all places we would never visit.

We stuck to a routine those mornings. First, we would stop at the cafeteria and get snacks. I always chose a Grandma's fudge brownie with nuts, eager to rip off the red and brown plastic packaging and quickly devour it. My brother, who even at the age of four was the healthier eater, favored Cheerios and milk. The hospital had recently installed a frozen yogurt and ice cream machine, but my mother firmly marched us both past it. She noticed what my brother and I liked from the cafeteria, and she often brought home Grandma's brownies, boxes of cereal, and leftovers from anesthesiology lunchtime potlucks that she and her colleagues organized.

After the cafeteria, we followed our mother down the fluorescent-lit hallways of the hospital, past nurses' stations with stacks of stamped papers, past sets of elevators ferrying patients in wheeled beds and long poles with hanging bags of fluid, past the surgeons' lounge, where there was always a box of pastries surrounded by abandoned Styrofoam cups.

"Rita, you're here with your munchkins!" a tall nurse called out from behind us. I never remembered her name, but I can never forget how she enveloped my brother and me in loving hugs, leaving on us both the scent of flowers. "Be good today, kids," she said, "and I'll give you more stickers!" The stickers she gave us never made sense to me. Small, round, and multicolored, they had one word on them: STAT. I had seen her place yellow stickers on one set of papers, red on another, and green on yet another. Nonetheless, a sticker was a sticker, and she gave my brother and me plentiful multicolored STATs, which we then used to decorate everything from the birthday cards we made for our parents to our cat's flea collar. My mother smiled her usual large, glowing smile, waved to her colleague, and continued to walk quickly down the shiny, squeaky hospital floors toward her call room.

My brother ran into the room and turned on the TV immediately, then arranged his small body on the bed. As he ate his Cheerios, I watched my mother remove a small figurine of Lord Ganesha, the elephantine Hindu deity revered as the remover of obstacles, from her purse and place it on the desk next to the bed. Setting an apple from the cafeteria next to the tiny statue, she closed her eyes and clasped her hands together in prayer, just as she did every morning after rising and every evening before sleeping. I heard her whispering the *Gayatri* mantra, a powerful prayer for God's protection and guidance, the first prayer she taught me as a three-year-old child. I would learn years later that, in her practice of medicine, science and spirituality sat side by side; she prayed every morning for God to help her do the right things for her patients, to help difficult procedures go smoothly. As an anesthesiologist, there were ways she came quite close to playing

God. She administered medications to put patients into a deep sleep, manipulate their breathing, heart rate, and blood pressure throughout a surgery, and awaken them afterward, asking them to breathe, to tell her where they had pain so she could treat that as well. My father would tell me years later that my mother would take on medically complex, fragile patients whom other anesthesiologists didn't feel comfortable taking to the operating room. She did so only after praying first and asking God to guide her decision making on behalf of these patients. "He has always given me an answer," she would tell me. "I can only do so much as a doctor, but ultimately a patient's fate is in His hands." She prayed before every case for God to guide her every action so that she would keep each patient safe. After whispering the mantra three times, she pressed the figurine against her forehead and then against her heart.

"No prank calls," she said right before leaving, referring to the time when I'd dialed random extensions out of boredom. "And don't call the operator to page me. I'll be back as soon as I can. Stay here and watch *Scooby-Doo*," she said as she pulled back her thick black hair and stuffed it in one graceful swoop underneath her operating room cap.

I climbed onto the hard call room bed atop an itchy frayed tan blanket that smelled like antiseptic, looking up at the blurry TV mounted on the sickly green wall. The alarm clock next to the bed blinked continuously in bright red numbers: 6:57 a.m. No photographs or decorations brightened the room; just a bed, a television, and a nightstand with a big brown and blue textbook titled in large gold letters: ANESTHESIA. We had been in the hospital with our mother so often that her call room had the familiarity of a relative's home.

My brother would become my best friend. As we grew up and graduated from afternoons in day care or my mother's call room, we would become latchkey kids, taking care of each other in the hours we waited for our parents to return home from work. I'd warm bowls of frozen peas or make us macaroni and cheese from a blue box, and he'd force me to take a break from studying to watch *Alvin and the Chipmunks* with him. His sense of humor balanced out my intensity. Though we'd argue bitterly over the freedoms he was given instead of me—a car in high school, permission to stay out late without a curfew—I could be honest and vulnerable with him in a way I couldn't with anyone else.

My mother returned to check on us between cases, telling us about the patients she saw. She spoke excitedly, jumping from one incomplete strand of thought to another, talking about medicine as if my brother and I, mere grade-school children, were her colleagues. When I was in my own training years later, I'd realize that these stories weren't just about medicine: they were about her trying to make sense of what she witnessed, grasping for words to articulate the moral and spiritual questions her work raised. She told us about a nineteen-year-old patient who died because cocaine constricted his arteries and his heart stopped. She had only been responsible for putting a tube down his throat and connecting him to a ventilator, but still found herself wondering why cocaine stopped *his* heart when using it hadn't stopped the hearts of people older than him. She told us about the man with lung cancer who was diagnosed only because he was hit by a truck and taken to the hospital, where a routine chest X-ray revealed a bulky growth with jagged edges in his left lung. His lung cancer had been accidentally discovered early enough that the surgeons could cure his cancer just by removing the tumor. If he hadn't been hit by that truck, my mother told us, the tumor would have silently spread to other organs, becoming incurable and taking his life. She told us about the woman in her twenties who delivered her first baby, a healthy boy, only to die an hour after his birth from a massive blood clot that traveled to her lungs, stopping her heart before she had a chance to name her son.

My brother and I chewed the grilled cheese sandwiches she brought us from the cafeteria, looking at her as though she were a hero. I asked her why she couldn't save the young mother.

"Doctors aren't God," she told me. "We can only do our best to help people, but everything that happens is because of God's plan." I wanted to ask why a young mother's death would be part of any plan, but my mother's pager went off and she told us she'd have to leave. Years later, in my own training, I'd wonder if this was how my mother sought to find meaning in the tragedy she regularly encountered, if her faith was her parachute, her shock absorber.

. . . .

I could guess what my mother would advise me about Mr. Tan's situation: "Don't get too attached. You can only give him the antibiotics and tell him there isn't much more to do, and he should pray. And you should pray for him." She would advise both compassion and distance, doing what was medically feasible and leaving the rest to God.

But doing that didn't come naturally to me. I'd always admired my parents' strong spiritual beliefs, the way they offered every major life decision and attributed every success to God. I tried to do the same, but my efforts didn't always feel genuine. My parents had clung to God to find a way to endure the circumstances of their respective childhoods. I went through the motions they considered sacred, mainly because I wanted to please them, but I didn't experience divinity the way they did. We sat together singing devotional songs every Sunday and Thursday evening in the company of other Indian immigrants in our neighborhood. Because my parents believed that service to others was a form of worship, on Sunday mornings my brother and I would help them to make and distribute peanut butter and jelly sandwiches to homeless people in downtown Los Angeles and Long Beach. I did these things impatiently, waiting for my time to be my own again. While my parents emerged from prayer restored, I remained bored and irritated. Yet some part of me was envious of their spirituality, their ardent faith that since God oversaw their lives, there was no such thing as a good or bad event. That everything that happened was an intended part of a greater plan than they could understand, one they tried to accept with complete surrender.

But I didn't see how I could apply this to medicine, where I'd come to see prayer as a last resort. Would I pray to influence the outcome of Mr. Tan's situation, or would I pray to help him find the strength to endure no matter what the outcome? Would I pray for guidance to care for Mr. Tan the right way? To bargain with God over Mr. Tan's mortality? I couldn't ignore the nagging feeling that I was running out of ways to fix Mr. Tan's many problems. Maybe now *was* the time to pray.

Three consecutive shrill beeps punctuated the silence. I had to go to the emergency room to see several new patients. Hours later, on my way back to my call room, I stopped by to see Mr. Tan. He felt absent. He was there but not there, eyes overcast, a heaviness to his wave hello.

"You seem down," I said, and he shrugged but picked up his marker and whiteboard.

I am scared. I don't want to lose my family.

I nodded, pulling up a chair next to his bed. He erased his board, which could fit only a couple of sentences at most, and wrote more: *Noelle, she went to Davis after junior college.* I nodded, and he erased and wrote more: *Laura and I owned a restaurant. We cooked everything.*

Pointing at his feeding tube, he wrote: *So this is hell.*

I nodded and winced internally, imagining the horror with which a former chef accommodated a feeding tube.

I do all this for them.

I started to feel the slightest bit uncomfortable, unsure what I would say once he stopped writing and erasing. He did stop, and he looked at me.

"This must be so difficult for you to go through, Mr. Tan. Do you ever think about what you would want if we couldn't get you better?"

There. I tried. I said it. Imperfectly, and not as clearly as I had hoped. But I had tried.

I will suffer if you give up on me, he wrote and erased. *As long as I am with them, I will be OK.*

I peered intensely at his whiteboard, at each word as he wrote it, at each word that took its place. I had been thinking about how to talk to him about dying, but he was telling me instead about his life, about why he continued to live it despite his suffering, because to him the ultimate suffering would be losing his family. In the six months of my residency, I learned just how much pressure to apply when plunging a needle from the skin of the neck into a large vein just below the surface, leading to the heart. I learned how to place my finger inside a patient's rectum until I felt the smooth surface of a healthy prostate or the knotted irregularities of a diseased one. I viewed a patient's abdomen using an ultrasound, seeing the intestines floating in his natural juices and identifying where unnatural juices produced by a cancer had collected. But nothing felt more invasive, more intimate, than this exchange of words between Mr. Tan and me. With his words, Mr. Tan illuminated that cavernous resting place of his hopes, fears, and anxieties.

"What is a good day for you, Mr. Tan?" I asked.

A day with them, he wrote back.

"What gets in the way during a good day? What can make it turn bad?" I asked, feeling around in my mouth for the right string of words.

Dry mouth. Or too weak to get up.

"So I think we need to make sure that no matter what is going on with you, that you are getting the gel for your mouth as often as you need it," I said. "I also think that on good days we need to make sure physical therapy is working with you."

He gave me a thumbs-up sign. "It's really important to me that we get you feeling the best we can." Another thumbs-up.

"I didn't mean to scare you or your family earlier. I'm really sorry about that." I felt my face burn with shame.

He smiled his biggest, most lopsided grin I had yet seen, and shook his head.

It's OK. It is important to discuss.

As he wrote and erased, it occurred to me that to anyone passing by Mr. Tan's room, it might have sounded like I was talking to myself. In our exchange of words, mine spoken and his written, I felt myself relying on language in a new way, in a situation where the medicine I was learning to practice collided with the innermost worlds of the patients I cared for—the places I could not find with needles or ultrasounds or stethoscopes.

. . . .

As the remaining days of my rotation passed, Mr. Tan slowly improved. His infection resolved and his bleeding stopped. He got well enough to leave the ICU, and regained enough strength to begin physical therapy. He made it to a nursing home. I remember high-fiving Noelle the day before he left. She was thrilled that the caseworker had gotten him into a specific nursing home just south of San Francisco, a place where he could see the ocean from the foyer. I was grateful for being wrong, though I knew that he remained as prone as ever to a sudden catastrophe. He would later thank me for having the courage to bring up a delicate subject with him and his family, for motivating him to think about how to plan for a worst-case scenario.

During my intern year, I fretted about whether I was smart enough to make adept diagnoses based on a patient's description of their symptoms and a careful physical examination. I worried about misdiagnosing, about not knowing how to recognize and treat every illness I'd encounter. But focusing only on diagnosing and treating my patients' problems continued to feel like an incomplete fulfillment of my duty. I began to sense my own natural inclination toward understanding what I'd think of as the "bigger picture" for patients, especially those like Mr. Tan, who needed not only medications and CT scans but thoughtful conversations about how his diagnoses might suddenly change his life. I wanted to use my training to prolong life without sacrificing the *quality* of life a patient valued. Helping someone to live well, I realized, was just as important as helping them to live.

I couldn't have known then that in two years I would sit next to Mr. Tan in a large gymnasium at UC Davis, bringing along my camera and capturing moments from Noelle's graduation that I'd later print and give to her: Noelle in her graduation cap and gown. Noelle playfully placing her graduation cap on her father's head. Mr. Tan and his wife looking on as an officiant called out Noelle's name and she walked toward the large podium. Mr. Tan's determination to be at graduation had propelled him through many additional hospital stays for everything from a malfunctioning feeding tube to an infectious diarrhea. What role had something within or beyond him played in his defiance of the physical constraints imposed by his flesh? After the ceremony, as I watched him embrace his daughter under the relentless Central Valley sun, I thought of my mother's words, of the idea that doctors knew only so much about the fate of a human body, that God knew more about the destiny of a human spirit.

Before Mr. Tan left the hospital that December, he wrote me another note, one that I kept in the pocket of my white coat and then in my wallet, and then in the shoebox full of letters and cards and messages on scraps that have meant something to me over the years. In shaky handwriting, he'd written a clear message, one that taught me about grit and resolve, love and loyalty.

I told you I would get out of here!

Three

DECISIONS

When I was a toddler and my mother was in her residency training, the sky was dark when she left our apartment early in the morning and dark when she returned late in the evening, hours after my father had fed and bathed me. She spent the hours between two dark skies under intense fluorescent lights in the operating room and the intensive care unit.

Using medications and machines, she took patients to the brink of death so that, with the aid of surgery, they could live a longer and better life. If surgery began to overwhelm a patient's heart or lungs, my mother would inform the surgeon immediately, identify the source of the problem, and help decide whether continuing was safe. She saw people through open-heart surgeries, hip replacements, liver transplants, appendectomies, and removal of cancer blocking the intestines. Patients this sick were inherently unpredictable; my mother would leave their sides only in the late evening, when she was certain that she had done everything she could to ensure that she would see them alive hours later, on the next dark morning.

Though it became her life's work, anesthesiology hadn't initially been her calling. She had assumed that she, like most Indian immigrant physicians at the time, would begin a residency in family medicine after completing her internship. Family physicians were in demand in the United States then, and it was relatively easy for a foreign-trained physician to earn a spot in a family medicine residency program. But her plans changed entirely after a colleague named Dr. Patel told her to consider a less conventional choice. "I remember him and that conversation very clearly," she told me when I was in high school and asked her what drew her to anesthesiology. Toward the end of a quick lunch in the hospital cafeteria, Dr. Patel suggested that she look into a residency in anesthesiology. The field of anesthesia was rapidly growing, and well-trained anesthesiologists were badly needed all over the country. It would pay more, with the added benefits of better hours and less paperwork. Family medicine was a tried and true path, Dr. Patel acknowledged when my mother expressed concern over how few interns chose anesthesiology. But he himself wished he'd taken a risk, been open to a new and growing field.

Aside from expressing her one concern, my mother didn't question Dr. Patel, nor did she wonder whether she might enjoy being an anesthesiologist. "I didn't think so much about it," she told me when I asked how she made such a big decision based solely on a passing suggestion of an acquaintance. "He told me it was a new and exciting field, that it would be good money. And I just did it. That's what your father and I had to do. We had to make decisions, not think too much about them." And just like that, my mother applied for a residency in anesthesiology. When she received her acceptance letter from the University of Louisville, she and my father had to look up Louisville on a map of the United States. They shrugged, deciding that living there must be part of God's plan for them.

"Now looking back on it, I guess you can say I took a big risk," my mother eventually conceded when I insisted that her decision making was rather impulsive compared with the more reasoned, deliberate approach I'd seen her use. "But I can't explain it. Something told me it was the right decision to make, so I didn't think too much and I just did it."

In September of my second year of residency, I, too, had to consider what type of doctor I would be. Did I want to practice general internal medicine or apply for further training—called a fellowship—in a more specialized field of medicine? Many of my co-residents were applying for fellowships in fields like cardiology or gastroenterology. These added years of training would let them specialize in treating diseases of one bodily system, be it the heart and circulatory system or the gastrointestinal tract or the lungs. I'd seriously considered fellowship training in pulmonary and critical care medicine, a branch of internal medicine focused on the care of patients in the ICU and patients with lung disease; I'd leave fellowship training able to intubate patients and ease them off breathing machines, monitor their heart function with invasive devices, and give them powerful pain medications and sedatives to make their time in the ICU bearable. I'd be able to do many of the procedures my mother did, though I'd take care of patients in the ICU rather than the operating room.

Right around that time, I began a four-week rotation in the intensive care unit, and my mother's residency routine became my own. My jarring alarm clock reliably screeched at 5:15 a.m. I quickly brushed my teeth, twisted my hair into a high bun, and pulled on my thin, sky-blue scrubs before racing to the shuttle stop, my breath a series of white puffs against the dark courtyard and predawn sky. The same dark sky and empty courtyard greeted me when I returned late each evening, eager to wash off the day with a hot shower. In between my shuttle rides, I'd spend my days under the intense fluorescent lights of the ICU, where desperately ill patients lay in individual rooms behind sliding glass doors and gray-purple curtains. Throughout my four weeks there, I'd learn and practice the same procedures my mother had done multiple times a day for almost thirty years.

By that point in residency, I'd treated pneumonias and bladder infections in elderly patients, learned to distinguish between shortness of breath caused by emphysema and that caused by a heart attack, recognized and responded immediately to emergencies without panicking as I imagined I would. But the most gratifying moments were the ones I'd spent with patients like Mr. Tan, and Donna, the ones whose situations weren't easily fixed, whose chronic diseases distorted their daily lives and shrank the perimeters of their worlds. My role in their care seemed far more expansive than making and treating a diagnosis. I was interested in questions with no easy answers. I was drawn to medicine's gray areas. When I closed my eyes and imagined the type of medicine that would bring me happiness and fulfillment, what I returned to again and again was the practice of palliative medicine. I didn't quite understand why I'd find fulfillment caring for patients I knew I would lose soon after I met them. Neither did my parents.

"What is that?" my mother asked when I told her I might apply for training in palliative medicine. I'd come home for a weekend toward the end of my intern year, and my parents and I sat at our kitchen table, drinking tea and nibbling on almond cookies. When I explained that the field focused on easing the suffering of patients with serious, usually incurable illness, my mother scoffed. "Don't all doctors help patients suffer less? Isn't that what we are all supposed to do?"

My parents weren't alone in their confusion. Most people, including medical professionals, don't know much about palliative care or hospice or the difference between the two. Many assume that hospice is a place that cares for patients in the last days to hours of life; in reality, hospice teams most often care for patients in their own homes, easing their physical and emotional suffering in the last six months of their lives, usually when treatments such as chemotherapy or dialysis have been discontinued. As the medical world began to see that more Americans enjoyed improved symptom control and quality of life on hospice care, many wondered if patients with a serious illness would benefit from a similar service well before the last six months of their lives. And this became the focus of palliative medicine: attending to a patient's quality of life shortly after the diagnosis of a serious illness rather than in the last months of life. This meant that patients could simultaneously get palliative care and treatment of an underlying disease—be it cancer or heart disease or kidney failure. Although hospitals began offering palliative care services during the 1980s, it was recognized as a medical subspecialty by the American Board of Medical Specialties only in 2006, five years before my conversation with my parents. I'd be a young doctor in a young specialty that was still articulating its identity, which I found exciting even as my parents urged me to apply for a field that was more respected and established. I chuckled internally as I listened to the repetitive hesitation of two souls who had taken far greater risks and endured far more daunting unknowns than this one.

"That's not what I've always seen," I said, reminding my mother of the many times she'd wondered aloud why my attendings insisted on providing aggressive treatments for patients who were close to death.

"Why not do something more useful, like cardiology or intensive care?

You can use those skills all around the world, but you can't do that with this . . . what is it called again? This field you are interested in?" she said.

"Pall-ee-uh-tive care, Mama," I said, annoyed.

"That's a strange word. You really want to care only for dying patients? Is that really why you became a doctor?" My father nodded as she spoke. "At that point, isn't it between the patient and God?" he asked. "What are you supposed to do for them if you can't fix their problem?"

I exhaled hotly and pushed my cup of tea away, shaking my head and crossing my arms across my chest. My sudden anger surprised me. The tea spilled onto the table, and my dad admonished me. "Hey, you watch it!" he said sternly.

"I don't think you understand. I was on the verge of totally quitting medicine and then I did the palliative elective. That's pretty much what kept me from throwing in the towel." I clenched my jaw.

Our old tensions boiled. There had been other fields that caught my eye—anthropology, literature, social work—but I knew it had always been expected that I would become a doctor. I'd gone to medical school on what I thought were my own terms, though the boundary between my sense of obligation to fulfill my parents' expectations and my own vision for my life had always been blurry.

"But this field is so depressing," my mother continued. "Don't you think it will just bring you down? At least in other fields you can actually help people."

"That's what you don't get! It actually isn't depressing. It's pretty amazing to get someone's pain under control or to help explain to them the reality of what's going on with them. You're an anesthesiologist—you know all about helping get people comfortable," I said, my voice pressured, eyes narrowed. My mother avoided my gaze.

"Look, you asked us for our opinion. If you don't want to listen, then don't ask," my father said, waving his hand and getting up to wash his empty teacup.

I slammed my hand on the table. "I actually didn't ask! I was telling you!

I'm the one who's had to do all of this work, so why can't you just support this decision?"

My father returned to the table and hovered above me. He spoke quietly but firmly. "You wouldn't have been able to do this work if we hadn't worked so hard ourselves. Show some respect. Come on, Rita, let's go for a walk." My mother got up and left with him.

I'd always chased my parents' approval, and their skepticism about my potential subspecialty unsettled me. They made important decisions with the intense practicality and foresight they needed to survive the poverty of their childhoods and weather the rocky, unanticipated transitions of immigrant life. And their decisions were almost always good ones, a curious mix of risk taking and adherence to convention. I trusted their judgment more than my own. Their agreement with the major life choices I made—about my education or career or finances—gave me confidence in my own judgment. When they disagreed, I doubted myself intensely.

I sat alone at the kitchen table for an hour, fixated on the questions my parents had asked me, the last few sips of tea cooling in my cup, a brown skin of milk skimming the top. Would palliative care really be the best use of my education? Why wasn't I more interested in fields that worked to improve patients' survival? Wasn't that what I had signed up for when I chose to go to medical school? Would I be able to handle the emotional intensity of palliative care? I tried to imagine myself working mainly in the ICU or as a cardiologist or primary care doctor—reputable specialties with transportable skill sets. I could see myself enjoying any of those jobs. I wouldn't have to explain or defend my work, I'd be able to join my mother as a medical volunteer in India, I'd be able to help patients in familiar, well-understood ways. Maybe I could just integrate my interest in palliative medicine into the practice of a different subspecialty, just as some primary care physicians specialized in caring for patients with HIV. I threw myself into my ICU rotation, hoping that maybe I would enjoy it enough to part ways with palliative care.

The procedures and technology of the ICU thrilled me. It was immensely satisfying to do something very concrete to a patient with my hands and immediately relieve a bothersome symptom or administer a necessary medication. Each of us secretly hoped that our patients would require as many procedures as possible so that we could master each one. I loved learning to manage a ventilator just as my mother did every day; when we spoke in the evenings, I'd tell her what I learned about using certain settings on the ventilator to treat a patient with pneumonia, and other settings to support a patient with a flare of asthma. I told her how nervous I'd been to place a large catheter in a patient with kidney failure, and how relieved I'd felt when I finished the procedure successfully, enabling the patient to start dialysis.

When patients' lungs filled with fluid—due most often to heart failure or to advanced cancer—I learned to cut the skin on patients' backs and use a catheter to drain the fluid, quickly easing their shortness of breath. I pierced the skin of other patients' necks and threaded catheters through the veiny highway leading directly to the heart so that I could give them medications too powerful to be given through a regular IV. I threaded larger catheters called pulmonary artery catheters from their necks into their hearts, through the right atrium and the right ventricle all the way into the entrance of the pulmonary artery.

Sometimes the heart reacted to the foreign catheter by fluttering in a dangerous pattern called ectopy. "Did you watch for ectopy when you advanced the catheter?" my mother asked me the first time I placed a pulmonary artery catheter.

"Yes, I saw it. I was so scared for a second," I replied, remembering my anxiety as I watched the patient's heartbeat become erratic as the catheter advanced and irritated the heart.

"I used to put them in every patient before they went to the operating room," my mother replied, adding, "Now you know how long each one of those procedures takes. That's why I left home so early for so many years."

I suddenly saw myself at four, clinging to my mother's leg, begging her not to go to work. My father would pull me off her and hold me as I cried, watching her disappear quickly through our front door without looking back. I saw myself at seven in a trailer behind our elementary school stuck for hours in the after-school care program for children with working parents. It was Friday, and I overheard the two women in charge whisper to themselves that my mother was late, *yet again*. It had been an hour since the last child was picked up. I pretended not to hear them, instead focusing my attention on the herculean task of trying to play Hungry Hungry Hippos alone. My face burned with embarrassment, then with anger. *Where was my mother?* She eventually showed up, running from her car to the trailer, unaware that she'd forgotten to remove the blue operating room cap that still covered her hair. "You're not in the hospital anymore," I told her angrily as I pointed to her head and pushed her away when she tried to hug me.

She was late because she had been doing the things I was learning now. I could understand her absence. In the quieter moments of my ICU rotation, I marveled that she'd made time for anything other than work and her own survival during her residency.

I quietly celebrated the success stories of some people I treated in the ICU. These were people who needed only a few days' worth of machines and medications until their severe infections abated or the unexpected complications of surgery resolved. They persevered through painful but necessary procedures, and endured the disruptive noises and tense atmosphere of the ICU that left them disoriented and sleep deprived. The payoff for their discomfort was surviving and going home. It was incredibly satisfying to care for patients who survived, and upsetting to lose those whose illnesses outsmarted our best lifesaving efforts and technologies. But it was outright troubling to care for the patients who neither survived nor died. These were people who might remain in the ICU for weeks or months, their hearts and lungs and kidneys stuck in a cycle of incremental improvements and sudden setbacks. I treated these patients with the same care as every other patient, but doing so set off a slow burn of unease: No matter what I did, they remained gravely ill. Sometimes, the more I did to them, the sicker they became.

Dennis was a retired businessman in his sixties whose lungs began to fail shortly after undergoing surgery for a broken hip. His lung failure caused his heart to fail, and we tried every possible medication to manipulate his heart's physiology, prodding it unsuccessfully toward healing. Fluid from his failing heart began to fill his lungs, which required more and more support from the ventilator until there was no more support to give. As his heart and lungs deteriorated, his kidneys shut down, so we started dialysis. Because we could. Because that's *what you do* when your patient's kidneys start to fail. *But is it what you do when kidneys start to fail because other organs are failing and aren't getting better?* I asked myself, though I never voiced my concern on rounds with my team. The pace of the days left me breathless and unable to focus on anything other than performing procedures, ordering medications, and manipulating machines to keep each patient alive. Yet as I outlined my treatment plan for Dennis in the daily notes I wrote in his chart, I wondered whether anything I'd done for Dennis had actually helped him to get better. I had intubated him, attached him to a ventilator, placed a pulmonary artery catheter into his heart to monitor its function, requested the expert opinions of cardiologists and nephrologists and infectious disease physicians about his care. I had done everything that my mother would have done for Dennis. But I wondered if the life I sustained for him was one he would find acceptable. He could not speak or eat. He couldn't recognize or interact with his wife and son because of the chemical haze of pain medications and sedatives he needed to tolerate being pinned in place by the tubing and needles that connected him to monitors and machines. As his days in the ICU turned into weeks, I began to suspect his losses weren't temporary ones. I continued to hope that he would recover, though I couldn't exactly envision what recovery might look like for him.

One afternoon, I sat with Dennis's wife, a thin woman who wore matching turquoise and silver earrings and bracelets. I told her that even with the maximum possible support from the ventilator, Dennis's blood oxygen saturation hovered around 85 percent, far from the normal range of 92 to 100 percent. I told her I worried about the extent to which his low blood oxygen levels had damaged his brain and his heart. I explained that I would order another CT scan of his lungs to assess for any new injury they might have suffered. If fluid had once again accumulated in his lungs, I could insert a needle to remove it and help improve his oxygen levels.

Dennis's medication pump began to beep, signaling that one of his medications needed to be refilled. I fumbled with the buttons on the pump, trying to silence it. "Do you think he's suffering?" his wife asked me as she stroked his hair, matted and greasy after three weeks in the ICU. His face, now rough with salt-and-pepper stubble, was doughy and ruddy, his once sharply defined features now swollen with the fluid his heart and kidneys could no longer manage, even with the help of our machines. Yet even though he scarcely resembled himself, he didn't appear to be suffering: he was sedated, seemingly unaware of being attached to devices that enabled us to support his ailing heart, breathe on behalf of his lungs, and clean his blood since his kidneys could not. "I don't think he is in any pain because we are giving him medications to keep him comfortable," I said gingerly, "but I think that going through all of these treatments and not being able to live his normal life has got to be very hard on him." She nodded, her eyes darting between his face and the ventilator and the gray monitor that hovered above him, capturing the rainbow of his physiology: The green line of his heart rate and rhythm. The red line of his blood pressure. The white line of the percentage of oxygen in his blood. The yellow line indicating the pressure in his pulmonary artery. I watched Dennis's monitor more closely than I had ever watched him.

It occurred to me later that evening that when I gave Dennis's wife updates about his condition, I spent more time explaining how I would address his health problems than I did explaining their significance. I was quick to offer next steps and treatment strategies without explaining that each setback—a bladder infection, or worsening heart failure, or a pneumonia caused by being on the ventilator for too long—made hope for recovery an even more distant twinkle on a dark horizon. I felt ashamed as I remembered describing to her the next steps in Dennis's care that I'd discussed with my attending on morning rounds; by only discussing next steps, I might have also offered false assurance that his persistently low oxygen saturation might be fixable.

If I could redo this conversation, I would have asked Dennis's wife what prompted her to ask that question, whether she observed Dennis to be suffering. I'd ask her how Dennis himself might define suffering in this situation. I wondered about the suffering he might have experienced because of our well-intentioned efforts to treat him. What must it have been like for him to be unable to live without the support of machines, and unable to die because of the support of machines? Perhaps what I could offer him most urgently was pausing to think clearly about what would truly help rather than harm him. I did not want to expedite his death, but I also did not want to commit him to that hazy purgatory of being alive but not necessarily enjoying the quality of life he might value. I had seen that before in my teenage years, when I met Rajiv.

Los Angeles, 1994

Just past the entrance of a place I'll call Bright Clouds Nursing Home, a red-haired nurse in lavender scrubs waved hello to my father and me and motioned us to go on ahead past the front desk. I held my breath as I stepped through the foyer, bracing myself for the usual putrid mix of urine, bleach, and a faintly floral air freshener. Around the cluster of tables in the dining room sat the same people in the same places: A frail, ghostly man swaddled in a fluffy blue blanket, his head slumped forward and mouth agape. Next to him, a woman whose hairline began midway down her skull and who made continual smacking motions with her lips and occasionally screamed. A man, who I guessed was around my father's age, walked around these two to get a fruit cup, though he seemed to waddle with an unusually wide space between his feet and carried a bag next to his leg, filled with what I would later realize was his urine.

This was a place with a large, empty guest parking lot.

The December cafeteria menu hung on the wall above the ghostly man and the screaming woman, the daily staples of pancakes, sandwiches, and pastries written in red and green ink. Off to the side, a Christmas tree sagged under the weight of too many silver ornaments and twinkling lights. Brightly wrapped boxes were arranged at its base, and I wondered whether those were real gifts or decorations. Overhead, music from the 1940s and 1950s played.

This was my third visit to Bright Clouds. My parents were horrified by the very concept of a care facility for the elderly, who they believed should be cared for by family, not strangers. They were especially horrified that some Bright Clouds residents had no family, or had family who never visited them. Throughout middle school and the beginning of high school, I reluctantly tagged along with my parents as they brought Christmas gifts and Easter baskets to residents without families. Though they didn't practice Christianity, my parents nonetheless considered Christmas and Easter to be holy days that should be spent with family. Visiting Bright Clouds was one of many quiet community service projects that my parents voluntarily adopted. They reminded my brother and me constantly that service to others—particularly society's most vulnerable—was an act of worship. Though I was a sullen adolescent, I agreed with my father, but wished for a community service project anywhere other than Bright Clouds. I groaned when he would place a bag of gifts, wrapping paper left over from last Christmas, and tape in front of me. "Take care of this," he would tell me. "Then we will go to Bright Clouds."

The combination of the residents' debility and the isolation at Bright Clouds overwhelmed me. I smiled and shook their hands as my father instructed, trying to suppress a mix of tears, nervous laughter, and a strong impulse to run away. Once, I excused myself to go to the bathroom while my father distributed gifts to a demented lady who babbled softly, a gentleman whose legs had been amputated, and a very old lady with severe scoliosis who had told him that she wished she could see the sky again. I would occasionally cry on our rides home. My father offered no solace. "Growing old and getting sick is all part of life," he would tell me. "You should learn this now. We will all grow old, and one day we will all die, too." I would ask my father why he told me this every time we drove home from Bright Clouds, why we couldn't instead just stop at McDonald's for an apple pie and soft serve and put the afternoon behind us. Why did we have to talk about such sad things? Why did we have to go back to this sad place on happy holidays each year?

"This is part of life," he would repeat. "And some of these people are in very sad situations on days when you and I and so many others are enjoying ourselves. So why not spend some time bringing them some happiness when they are clearly suffering?"

My father knew a few things about suffering. The youngest of seven children, he grew up in Darya Ganj, a district in Delhi that my father remembered fondly for the few things he enjoyed as a child: sticky orange *jalebi* and milky chai, a rare outing to Golcha Cinema, and narrow, interconnected alleys where he would hide from his mother and play cricket with friends from school. From the rooftops of apartment complexes, he would fly kites he'd made himself from paper and string, lying down to sleep on these same rooftops when summer arrived. Gazing at his neighborhood from this vantage point, he observed that suffering was inescapable because he saw it everywhere: the lepers who had so little that they begged the poorest families for scraps from dinner, an apartment complex filled with women who had been raped in the violence of Partition, only to be abandoned or rejected by their families. And he saw the suffering of his own mother, whose rheumatoid arthritis was so severe that my father came straight home from elementary school to help prepare the family dinner. He'd mix together flour and water into a doughy paste and make oddly shaped *chapattis* with his tiny hands. Since my grandfather could never seem to keep a job, my father devised his own ways to help my grandmother buy food for dinner. He began to play marbles with local children and would bring home the prize money he won in street tournaments. Occasionally, he'd even trek to wealthier areas and clandestinely attend weddings. When guests threw money at the bride and groom after the ceremony ended, my father would grab as many rupees as he could and race home.

Witnessing her suffering was unbearable for my father. He prayed to God to give him his mother's arthritis; it would be easier to have the arthritis himself than to bear witness as she endured it. "But this is my share of suffering," my grandmother would tell him when he shared his prayer with her. "This is my luck, not yours. You cannot suffer for me."

"So you couldn't fix Dadiji's suffering," I would say, though in retrospect I'm not sure if I was making an observation or asking a question.

"No," my father acknowledged. "But I had to learn that a part of lessening her suffering was just seeing that she was suffering, and doing what I could to help her." My father didn't speak of suffering as something to lament or avoid. He spoke about it as part of being human, as something we all had the power to endure, even transcend. Suffering didn't preclude survival.

As we left Bright Clouds that afternoon, my father noticed an elderly Indian gentleman in the foyer. We had never seen him, or any other Indians, in the years we'd visited Bright Clouds.

And yet here was Bajwa Ji, standing in high-waisted pants with a tightly bound belt, white shirt, and thick glasses that reminded me of my father's. He clasped his hands behind his back as he walked, just like my father did. He had the tired, overwhelmed eyes of someone perpetually displaced. My father immediately began speaking to him in Hindi, startling Bajwa Ji.

Namaste, Ji. Kii haal hai?

We quickly learned that he was from Delhi, and that his forty-eight-year-old son, Rajiv, had been in a car accident in Los Angeles about five months before, leaving him in a permanent vegetative state. Rajiv's wife and children left him after the accident, and the only place he could be properly cared for was at a nursing home like Bright Clouds. Bajwa Ji and his wife, Amita, both in their early seventies, moved from Delhi to a small apartment near the nursing home and spent every day and many nights at his bedside, hoping that God would reward their vigil with the miracle of Rajiv talking, thinking, walking, eating, and returning to his former self. Both Bajwa Ji and my father wondered how they hadn't crossed paths before at Bright Clouds. I cringed, realizing that our visits to Bright Clouds would now become more frequent.

Rajiv's room was on the right side of a long gray hallway. He was the only Indian patient the nursing home had ever had, according to the red-haired nurse, who told us that the orderlies and nursing assistants had comforted him in Spanish, assuming that he was Latino. Rajiv lay in his bed, eyes wide, brow wrinkled, wearing an expression of permanent surprise. I wondered if this was how terror twisted his face when he first saw the oncoming car, when he tried unsuccessfully to swerve out of its way, when he heard the crunch of metal on metal, suddenly airborne and then amid concrete and shattered glass. He always wore a white gown, white sheets covering him, as though he awaited cremation at a Hindu funeral.

I was expressionless during these visits, watching as nurses gave him a sponge bath, carefully lifting and moving his stiffened limbs, offering soothing words when he flinched in pain. They refilled his feeding tube formula, took his blood pressure and temperature every few hours, emptied the plastic bag that collected his urine, changed the diapers that collected his waste. His mother sat next to him, helping the nurses when she could, smearing holy ash on his forehead and whispering prayers. She wore brightly patterned saris, collages of burgundy, marigold, and emerald, bringing warmth to Rajiv's sterile room.

He's a living dead man, I remember thinking in my sullen teenage way.

Bajwa Ji began to call our home frequently, quietly saying, in Hindi, *"Beta, me Bajwa huu."* Child, I am Bajwa.

He never had to tell me that he was looking for my father. My father never had to tell me to interrupt whatever he was doing to speak to Bajwa Ji. I hovered outside my father's office, observing the long stretches of silence as he listened to Bajwa Ji, telling him that he shouldn't cry, that God certainly heard his prayers, that God could do anything, including healing Rajiv. I wondered if my father believed what he said, and how exactly he thought Rajiv would "get better." It was miraculous that he had survived, he would tell Bajwa Ji. Perhaps he needed to remember that, by remembering God, another miracle could take place. "Sometimes, God tests us," my father told me. "Believing in the impossible is a part of having faith." But, I later wondered, isn't accepting the unbearable also part of having faith?

Was Rajiv's predicament a miracle or a prison sentence? I wondered as I overheard my father's conversations with Bajwa Ji over the next three years, as I neared the end of high school and my visits to Bright Clouds grew increasingly rare. Would it have been better had he died in the car accident?

....

I wondered the same thing about Dennis: Had he died from his respiratory failure, would we have spared him and his family the agonizing suffering that accompanied his prolonged purgatory? Had we done him greater harm in saving his life than letting him die peacefully? But how could we possibly have known that our valiant attempts at saving his life would result only in the slow collapse of one organ system after another? It was our mission as doctors to use our skills and technologies to try to save Dennis, but what was our duty now, when both our efforts and his own body failed him? I left the ICU most days exhausted, not just from the intensity of the hours I'd worked, but also because these questions swirled around in my head about Dennis and about half the patients in that sixteen-bed unit. My father's conversations with me about suffering came back to me often during that time. Human suffering wasn't a topic we discussed in medical school, which I found shocking once I began residency and encountered every possible permutation of patients' physical and emotional suffering. I memorized how to diagnose and treat a panoply of illnesses without considering how a person might suffer regardless of whether we could cure their ailment or not. On a quiet overnight call in the ICU, I searched for articles in medical journals about human suffering in medicine and found a piece written by Eric Cassell in 1982 titled "The Nature of Suffering and the Goals of Medicine."

"I will begin by focusing on a modern paradox," Cassell wrote. "Even in the best settings and with the best physicians, it is not uncommon for suffering to occur not only during the course of a disease but also as a result of its treatment." His words rang true as I thought of the patients our team cared for. Many had been sick for years with some combination of diabetes, emphysema, heart failure, or cirrhosis, and had now landed in the ICU because of a serious final blow that we couldn't necessarily fix: a new and aggressive cancer, a large stroke, another failing organ. In the room next to Dennis, there was an extremely thin gentleman in his fifties with colon cancer that had migrated to his lungs, the tumor ferociously destroying delicate lung tissue and rendering him completely dependent on a ventilator to breathe; he soon died from pneumonia often caused by being on a ventilator for weeks. Across from him was a woman whose ongoing heart failure had worsened over the past two years, and in the past three months she'd been in the hospital more often than she'd been at home. Her heart grew weaker no matter how many aggressive medications I gave her, and finally one night her heart stopped entirely. After twenty minutes of CPR, we restored her heartbeat, but the damage to her brain left her unable to communicate or move. Her family agonized over whether to keep her alive with the support of machines or let her go.

Even before coming to the hospital, the combination of Dennis's COPD and arthritis made it nearly impossible for him to exercise or, on bad days, dress himself or get out of bed without help. The day that I prepared to place a dialysis catheter in him, I didn't feel an ounce of excitement even though a co-resident told me she envied the number of procedures I had gotten to perform. I felt sheepish as I gathered the supplies I needed, wondering how I expected dialysis to help him when, even before he came to the ICU, he sometimes struggled to get out of bed on his own.

I would have to insert the dialysis catheter into a large vein in Dennis's upper thigh, adjacent to his groin. Pulling back his gown, I pushed an ultrasound probe against the skin overlying the vein. I found it, marked its location with a black X on his skin, and began to shave the gray and brown hair on his upper thigh. As I moved the razor over his skin, I noticed how thin and bruised his leg had become, how his once faintly contoured thigh muscle had given way to a wasted linearity. I looked at his neck, where I'd placed a large catheter about ten days earlier. I glanced at his wrist, where just the day before I'd had to place a new catheter to monitor his blood pressure; it had taken me three attempts to get it in the right place, and I'd left behind a large purple bruise that spanned his wrist and the base of his thumb. His nurse had recently placed eye drops in his drying eyes. A few drops had escaped and dribbled down to his pillow, leaving behind streaks that looked like tears. His vulnerability pierced me as I stood over him, readying another catheter for another vein.

A deep sense of unease rose within me, a feeling beyond language that moved through me quickly like a shiver. I covered Dennis's exposed leg with his hospital gown and stepped out of his room. I paged another resident and asked her if she'd like to place the catheter instead. *Totally! Glad to help out. Give me about ten minutes to get there*, she said enthusiastically. I was grateful that she didn't ask me why I offered the procedure to her; I don't know how I would have responded.

She would go on to place the dialysis catheter, and Dennis would be connected to a tall green and gray machine that would do the work his kidneys could not. His oxygen saturations would not improve. His blood pressure would drop dangerously low, and he would need even higher doses of medications to maintain a normal blood pressure. His heart rate would begin to slow, first just for a few seconds here and there, and later for minutes. His once pink face would turn ashen. The tips of his fingers would turn blue and then black, a consequence of being on medications to support his blood pressure for many weeks.

My attending and I would sit with Dennis's wife and son on a Saturday evening and his wife would again ask if Dennis was suffering. I would gently answer with two sentences that I had recited while in front of my mirror that morning: "Even though we have been doing everything medically possible to help Dennis's heart and lungs and kidneys recover, he has only gotten sicker. This is important for you to understand because I do think that we may be causing more harm and suffering when it seems that his body is dying." I spoke slowly and gently, though I couldn't manage to suppress the tremor in my voice.

"Dad wouldn't want to go on like this," his son said, sifting through a tangle of IV lines and wrist restraints to find his father's hand. Dennis's wife gazed at her hands, fingering her wedding ring. "This isn't him anymore," she said, looking first at me and then at my attending. "It's time," she said, nodding as she looked at him and cried. "Please, can you make him look more like himself?"

There was a time years ago when doctors wouldn't have considered stopping Dennis's life support. In the 1970s, a young woman named Karen Ann Quinlan fell into a coma after she took tranquilizers and alcohol and stopped breathing. She was placed on a ventilator and given a feeding tube. When her doctors determined that she was in a persistent vegetative state and would likely never be herself again, her parents requested that she be taken off the ventilator and allowed to die naturally; they did not want such extraordinary means to extend her life in a manner that caused her tremendous pain with little to no hope of neurologic recovery. But her doctors refused, believing that stopping the ventilator would constitute homicide. Eventually, the New Jersey Supreme Court ruled that Quinlan's right to privacy enabled her father, who was eventually appointed her legal guardian, to refuse continued support from the ventilator on her behalf. Since she continued to be fed through a feeding tube, Karen went on to live for nine years after the ventilator was discontinued, dying, as her mother put it, "in God's time."

The Quinlan case was the first of several important legal cases that recast life-sustaining technologies—ranging from a ventilator to dialysis to feeding tubes—as options, not requirements, for dying patients. Since patients ultimately held authority over their own bodies, they—and, eventually, their legally recognized medical decision makers—could request life-sustaining treatment to be withheld or withdrawn. Though morally complex for physicians, patients, and families alike, turning off a ventilator or removing a feeding tube didn't legally constitute euthanasia or suicide. Turning off Dennis's ventilator and dialysis machine, and stopping his blood pressure medications and his tube feeds, for example, would allow him to die naturally from the failure of his lungs, heart, and kidneys—a death that machines and medications had until now postponed. Still, I felt uneasy writing the orders to stop Dennis's ventilator and dialysis. Intellectually, I remembered that it was his dying organs that would take his life, not the order I wrote to stop the ventilator. Emotionally, though, there was a finality to this decision that unsettled me even though I knew it would bring Dennis a hard-won peace. *This isn't about me or what I should have done differently for him,* I reminded myself when I signed my handwritten orders to discontinue the ventilator and dialysis after giving him pain medication. But it felt personal. I'd failed both in treating him and in relieving his suffering.

After a Catholic priest visited to give Dennis the sacrament of the sick, I began to undo the work I had done. After giving him a dose of pain medication, I removed the catheter I'd threaded through an artery in his wrist, the larger catheter I'd threaded from his neck into his heart, and the dialysis catheter my colleague had placed in a vein near his groin. I gave him additional pain medication to ease any shortness of breath or discomfort he might experience. Under the guidance of a respiratory therapist, I gently removed the breathing tube from his mouth, watching him carefully for any signs of gasping. The nurse turned off his blood pressure medications, and I shut off the monitor, telling his wife and son that the most important vital sign at this point was his comfort.

Dennis didn't gasp. He didn't grimace, sweat, or moan. He looked like he was sleeping peacefully. About ten minutes later, his breathing began to change. He took deeper breaths followed by long pauses. When his breathing stopped entirely, his wife rested her face next to his and kissed his lips, then his cheeks and his forehead. Her voice choked with tears, she turned to me. "Thank you," she said, turning then to embrace her son. The conversation I'd had with her about the reality of Dennis's condition felt like my most helpful and merciful contribution to his care. I wished we had spoken sooner.

Los Angeles, December 1997

Over Christmas break during my senior year of high school, I went with my father to Bright Clouds to see Rajiv for the last time. Rajiv hadn't been at Bright Clouds for nearly six weeks because he'd been in and out of the hospital. The first time, he'd accidentally regurgitated some of his tube feeding formula into his lungs and suffered a severe pneumonia; the infection had stressed his kidneys and he briefly required dialysis. Just two days after returning to Bright Clouds, his feeding tube became infected and he was taken back to the hospital, where he was temporarily fed through a tube snaked down his nose to his stomach until a surgeon placed a new feeding tube in his belly. In the year since I'd last seen Rajiv, his eyes looked more vacant, his skin had yellowed, and his once plush arms had thinned. Bajwa Ji sat in a plastic chair next to Rajiv, massaging his arms with baby oil while Amita sat with her eyes closed and her hands folded in prayer. Whenever I spoke with Rajiv's parents, I felt guilty about resisting our visit. "God bless you always, child," Bajwa Ji and his wife would say to me each time I saw them. "You are going to college, your father tells me," Bajwa Ji said. "You will have our blessings for your studies and for your life, always." He had become more frail, and walked with a cane. He now had to take medications for blood pressure, something he'd never needed before. "Please think of Rajiv, and please come visit us," Bajwa Ji said as my father and I turned to leave.

My father and I drove home silently. "Do you think it would have been better if he had died in the car accident?" The words escaped me before I realized how cold they must have sounded.

"Do you mean would it have been *easier* if he had died in the accident?" my father responded.

I could tell by his tone of voice that my father was about to go all philosophical on me. If my mother had a doctorly tone of voice, my father definitely had his analogous Mr. Socrates tone of voice.

"No, I mean would it have been better. For him and his poor parents. They don't do anything but take care of him and he's never gonna get better. And it's clearly affected their own health," I said, suddenly angry on behalf of Rajiv's parents but also angry at them. "I mean, they left their whole life to watch their son lie in a bed like this. But if he had just died, then they would have obviously been sad for a while but this is just torture for all of them!"

"I would do the same if it were you," he responded. "I would be there every day."

"Yeah, but I would never want to end up like that!" I said, waiting for him to respond by saying that I could learn something about faith from Rajiv's parents, that sometimes things that seemed impossible were within reach if one prayed earnestly. "I would never want you to suffer that way either," I told my father.

"What do you think life is? All about avoiding suffering?" he asked, laughing.

"I don't think anyone should have to live the way Rajiv is living. It's not really living. Isn't that suffering? Being trapped like that?" I said.

"Sunita, we can't pick and choose the ways we might suffer in this lifetime," he replied. "Rajiv is probably suffering. You can see that his parents clearly are. But that is why they need our support. It is difficult to suffer through this alone."

"I wish you would just tell them that Rajiv is never going to get better and they should just let him go. Put an end to all their suffering!" I snapped.

"What you still have to learn," he said in his best Mr. Socrates voice, "is how to deal with life's suffering, because you can't avoid it. Nobody can. But if you pay attention and help ease the suffering of others, that is God's work."

....

In residency, I began to understand the truth of my father's words in a way I hadn't before. As a teenager, I'd often been annoyed by my father's seeming indulgence of Bajwa Ji's wildly improbable hope for Rajiv's recovery. But looking back on it, I am moved by his willingness to bear the unbearable with a family he didn't know. He acknowledged their suffering. And he would continue to do so until Bajwa Ji and his wife, desperately homesick for India, somehow arranged for Rajiv to be flown back to Delhi, where he would be cared for at his childhood home with the help of nurses his parents hired. Bajwa Ji and my father continued their conversations until Bajwa Ji died in his sleep about two years after returning to Delhi. Rajiv would outlive both of his parents, until he, too, died in his sleep in his childhood home.

As a young doctor, I was learning how to prevent or fix the body's dysfunction, but that was different from the act of acknowledging and being with the suffering of another. Doing what my father did required a certain type of slowing down, which felt like a luxury during my residency, particularly in the ICU. I jumped from patient to patient and procedure to procedure, learning as much medicine as I could in a compressed period of time. Yet successfully treating a physical malady didn't necessarily mean I'd eliminated a patient's suffering. And treating suffering didn't always mean curing a disease. What my father had been trying to teach me was that simply being willing to see and be with suffering was a part of treating it. I think he wanted me to know this regardless of whether I became a doctor or not.

What is the purpose of medicine? I wrote on a Post-it note that I stuck to my refrigerator the night that Dennis died. Throughout my time in the ICU, I had tried so hard to enjoy and find meaning in the fast-paced, procedure-heavy, lifesaving work that echoed my mother's career. But the quieter and slower moments still called to me. The ones when I could pinpoint exactly if or how a highly technical procedure would help a patient. The ones when I had the mental space to consider and answer questions about suffering. The ones that took me back to the weeks I'd spent with Dr. McCormick, when words were my tools and conversations were my intervention. If I'd had the right conversations with Dennis's family earlier in his ICU stay, maybe his wife wouldn't have had to keep asking about his suffering before our team finally acknowledged that we were probably prolonging it.

Maybe every individual would define the purpose of medicine differently, I thought. *But*, I suddenly understood with clarity, *my purpose in medicine is in palliative care*. I wished that a more conventional specialty called to me, one in which I could envision myself fulfilled doing what other doctors seemed to enjoy. But no number of procedures or weeks spent in the ICU or the cardiology unit would change what I knew to be true.

I'd followed my mother in a different way than I had expected to—into the certainty of medicine, yes. Yet I found myself compelled to step away from her path, into the uncertainty of palliative medicine. I decided to forgo convention for exploration, leaping into an unknown just as she had. On the last night of my ICU rotation, I sat alone in my apartment, too exhausted to join friends for drinks, sipping a glass of wine alone. I thought of how my mother had chosen anesthesiology, turning over her words in my mind as my body relaxed.

I can't explain it. Something told me it was the right decision to make, so I didn't think too much and I just did it.

Four

EXTRAORDINARY

San Francisco, Spring 2012

Six months after finishing my rotation in the ICU, I was nearing the end of my second year of residency. I had applied for and been accepted into a palliative care fellowship program at Stanford, which would begin just over a year later—after I finished my third and final year of residency. I'd been both relieved to have made a decision about my future specialty, and overjoyed that I'd be able to stay in the Bay Area. The acceptance letter from Stanford arrived over email one morning during my rotation at the veterans hospital in San Francisco, where I was overseeing two interns and a medical student. Our team was on call that morning, evaluating sick patients in the emergency room and admitting them to the hospital under our care. We had already admitted nine new patients by late morning, when I finally had a moment to read rather than skim my electronic acceptance letter. Just as soon as I'd read the letter through once and started to read it a second time to be completely sure that I wasn't dreaming, my pager beeped, and off I went to the emergency room.

Mr. Smith was the tenth and last patient our team admitted to the hospital on that busy morning in mid-April. As was customary, the emergency room physician told me the details of a patient's case so that I could make initial recommendations for his care and decide which unit in the hospital (the intensive care unit, the cardiac monitoring unit, or simply the main medical unit) Mr. Smith needed based on the severity of the illness. Deceptively simple sounding, this task drew upon several critical skills: identifying how dangerous the patient's ailment currently was or could become; thinking about the most life-threatening and most likely diagnosis; integrating these possibilities with the physical examination of the patient; and coming up with a treatment plan.

The emergency room physician spoke quickly. "He's got esophageal cancer that has spread throughout his liver and his lungs, and on top of that, now he has a huge blood clot in his lungs. The notes from his oncologist say he's got a do-not-resuscitate order, but he's disoriented and I can't really get him to talk to me about his wishes. His labs are a mess, and his oxygen saturation is really low. He's not looking good."

"This does sound bad," I responded. "Are you treating the clot with heparin?" I asked, referring to a powerful blood thinner given through an IV to treat blood clots.

"One of his notes says he had some kind of hemorrhage about a month ago, somewhere in his abdomen. No bleeding since, but if we start heparin, he might bleed again. Since *you* are admitting him, though, that decision is yours."

Nice sidestep, I thought grimly, even though I recognized why he did so.

"And he's totally out of it?" I asked.

"He's so disoriented that he's trying to eat his oxygen monitor."

I headed to the emergency department to evaluate Mr. Smith, walking slowly to give myself time to think. He had incurable cancer of his esophagus that had spread to his liver and lungs. The blood clot in his lungs deprived him of essential oxygen and dangerously strained his heart. The clot was almost certainly caused by his cancer. The dilemma he presented was both typical and acute: heparin wouldn't dissolve the blood clot he currently had, but it could prevent another blood clot from forming and worsening the strain on his heart and lungs, killing him. But with heparin, given his recent abdominal bleeding, he was at high risk for a fatal bleed.

People with cancer often die of blood clots, I told myself. *Is he dying?* My own question scared me. Even though I had nearly completed two years of residency training, had a license to practice medicine in California, and had been accepted into a fellowship in palliative medicine, I doubted my ability to determine whether a patient's malady was a natural part of the dying process or just another problem to be fixed. Dennis came to mind: A ventilator and dialysis assumed the work of his failing lungs and kidneys. He needed powerful medications to help him maintain a normal blood pressure. His muscles withered away from lack of use, and his gut couldn't absorb the artificial nutrition we gave him through a tube in his nose. We'd all acknowledged he wasn't getting better. But was Dennis *dying*? This wasn't a question we had asked ourselves until his wife pushed us to consider his suffering.

Why am I so afraid to acknowledge that Mr. Smith might be dying? I wondered, puzzled. I'd been far more comfortable wondering about Mr. Tan's mortality, even though what I'd heard of Mr. Smith suggested he was closer to the end of his life. Yet when I imagined forgoing treating Mr. Smith's clot, I felt ashamed. The impulse to keep a patient alive was deeply ingrained, I realized. We as physicians in training were impelled to prolong life, enable survival. We hadn't become doctors to recognize and accept dying.

The culture of American medicine focused mainly on saving or extending lives. New medications studied in medical journals were evaluated for their "survival benefit," the additional months or years they could add to a patient's life. Most departments hosted weekly or monthly "Morbidity and Mortality" conferences to discuss among colleagues why certain patients died, and whether they could have survived if only their care had been handled differently. Medical professionals and the public alike were socialized to believe that saving lives was medicine's mission, as a seemingly endless string of medical television dramas and movies suggested. And if patient deaths represented medicine's failures, I thought, then it shouldn't surprise me that we struggled immensely to identify, name, and discuss anything other than survival.

What did surprise me was that my impulse toward intervention seemed to have strengthened after my ICU rotation, particularly when I was in charge of a team including two interns and a medical student. As a senior resident, my job was to see all of the patients admitted to our team, but also to teach the interns and medical students how to develop a plan of care for each patient's condition. I was still in my training, but also now teaching and leading. And though I couldn't explain why, I felt pressure to model the type of doctoring I'd often questioned as an intern. If a patient was in the hospital, there must be some intervention I could offer, some problem I could fix. I recognized that I could do harm trying something, anything, to fix what was wrong. But it was one thing to know this and another to act on this impulse, especially when I was charged with treating patients and teaching younger colleagues.

I can't let him die, I thought to myself. He's got cancer and a related blood clot. I've treated so many blood clots. It would be easy to treat this one.

Hold on, said another voice, something deeper, calm and firm.

Go see him first.

. . . .

Mr. Smith's room was dark except for the green glow of his heart monitor and the flash of a red alarm, drawing my attention to worrisome vital signs: an abnormally rapid heart rate in the 120s, low blood pressure in the 90s, and a dangerously low blood oxygen saturation in the mid-80s. Collectively, these numbers indicated that his lungs and heart were failing as a result of his blood clot. I pressed a button to silence the alarm and heard a broken voice. "Darlene, Darlene, Darlene," he murmured.

"Mr. Smith?" I said, hesitantly.

"Daaarrrleeeeeene," he responded, his voice stronger.

I began to examine him. Tangles of matted brown hair framed his fragile face. Deep wrinkles gathered at the corners of his eyes. His ribs protruded like speedbumps along the narrow path of his torso, leading to a concave belly. EKG leads, oxygen tubing, and three intravenous lines tethered him to his bed. His skin was covered with bruises from multiple attempts at blood draws. A white device was taped around the first finger of his left hand, monitoring the amount of oxygen in his blood. He gnawed on it and stared past me. On his right arm, I saw serpentine veins, the pull of flesh against bone, a faded green tattoo of the sort I had seen on many military veterans. It read, "Where there is light there must be darkness."

I listened to his heart, a flutter in the great hollow of his chest. His breath was shallow and quick, a distant whisper. He coughed when he tried to swallow, his saliva unable to slither around the tumor in his esophagus. His body told me a story that he couldn't tell me. His chart filled in a crucial detail.

"Patient would not want extraordinary measures," his most recent oncology note said. "No known family or friends. Cannot name a decision maker. Code status: DNR/DNI." This meant that if his heart stopped and he died, he would not want us to resuscitate him by performing CPR or delivering an electric shock to his heart. He would not want to be intubated and placed on a ventilator if he couldn't breathe. He instead wanted us to allow him a natural death.

I looked at his CT scan. It was difficult to tell where he ended and where his cancer began. Tumors glowed throughout his body like a macabre Christmas tree.

Giving anticoagulants for blood clots isn't an extraordinary measure, my textbook voice said. *It is possibly one of the most ordinary things I do in internal medicine.* But, my deeper voice inquired, is treating *his* blood clot extraordinary? That is a different question. He could bleed and suffer more than he is currently. He also might not bleed. Would that result in a better life, or a more drawn-out death? None of the 2,500 notes in his electronic chart provided any answers. The only documentation that really told me anything about his perspective on life was his tattoo: *Where there is light there must be darkness.*

I called his oncologist, his internist, and his nursing home, looking desperately for guidance, and possibly also for someone to validate my impulse to treat the blood clot. Nobody could give me the information I needed: Who was this man? What did he know about his cancer? What quality of life did he value? Is there anyone else I should try to reach? The answers I got were almost always speculative. Only one staff member at his nursing home could tell me something with certainty: "All I know is that he always asks for root beer, but he can't swallow it because he coughs. It makes him happy, though."

And so I remained exactly where I started, looking at the sweetly disoriented man before me, wondering whether to place him on an oxygen mask that would fit tightly across his face, treat him with heparin and risk causing him to bleed, or get him back to the nursing home with hospice services the next morning to keep him free of pain and shortness of breath during his final days. Perhaps what I could offer him most urgently was pausing to think clearly about the best way to care for him. I didn't want to cause him suffering, but I also felt an obligation to treat the problem that brought him to the hospital.

....

On afternoon rounds, I sat down with my attending physician, Dr. Doyle, our intern, Ryan, and our medical student, Erin, to discuss the patients whom we had just admitted to the hospital, so that each patient had a clearly defined plan before I settled in, alone, to care for them overnight. We discussed Mr. Smith first.

Ryan and Erin had both evaluated him in the emergency department after I did. Ryan's role as an intern was to come up with a plan to treat Mr. Smith, and my role was to listen to and critique his plan, particularly if I disagreed with it. Ryan wanted to give him heparin for his blood clot and intravenous fluids to bring down his blood calcium level, which was elevated because of his cancer and which could have contributed to his confusion. Ryan hoped that, if Mr. Smith became less confused, he might be able to tell us exactly what he wanted for himself. If we tried his plan, we would draw Mr. Smith's blood multiple times per day (to make sure that his blood was sufficiently but not excessively thin), run several liters' worth of IV fluids rapidly through his arm (to bring down his blood calcium level), and strap a plastic mask around the bridge of his nose and his mouth, connecting him to a machine that helped him to breathe but without a tube in his throat. Ryan wondered whether physical restraints would be a good idea, since during his hours in the emergency department Mr. Smith had removed his breathing mask several times. Also, Erin piped up, perhaps there was a way to tape the mask to Mr. Smith's skin, since even the smallest adult-sized mask available couldn't conform to his angular, narrow face.

Their plan was stunningly comprehensive. If Mr. Smith died in spite of these valiant efforts, at least I would know that we had left no stone unturned, that we had tried everything possible to keep him alive. Yet I felt a stab in my gut as I imagined Mr. Smith tied to his bed, his oxygen mask pressing into the delicate skin of his nose and cheeks, plastic bags filled with cold saline running through the veins we would pierce throughout the night to draw blood. None of this would take away his advanced cancer, I reminded myself. But what if it bought him a few more days at his nursing home, less confused and breathing easily?

"Thanks for this thoughtful plan," I began. "It sounds like you want to give fluids for the calcium level and heparin for the blood clot so that you can hopefully hear from him directly what he wants in this situation."

"Yes," Ryan said, nodding. "I mean, we considered that he could bleed because of the heparin, but if that happens we could always send him to the ICU and stabilize him with blood transfusions and maybe an endoscopy."

"Sure, we *could* . . . ," I began slowly, then paused. Sure, we could always send him to the ICU in case he bled, but shouldn't we seek to avoid that scenario in someone this fragile? Why was I even entertaining the option of giving him heparin when he had bled so recently? Yes, Mr. Smith had been brought to the hospital because he couldn't breathe, and, as a doctor, I was supposed to fix the problem. *But you can't make decisions about his treatment to make yourself feel like a "good doctor."* The same voice that encouraged me to see Mr. Smith before deciding what to do for him reminded me that what I *could* *theoretically* do for him wasn't necessarily what I *should* do for him.

"Do you think that he is this confused because he is dying?" I asked Ryan and Erin, trying my best to channel the calm with which Dr. McCormick had asked me that question about a patient we'd seen together more than two years ago.

Erin looked at me, surprised. *Is this a trick question?* Ryan glanced at the pages he had printed from Mr. Smith's medical records, the results of his blood tests, his CT scans, his oncology clinic notes, and said, "I still think there's a way for us to get him more oriented so that we can hear from him what he wants us to do."

"Yes, but what if the reason he is so disoriented is because his body is shutting down from his cancer?" I was talking to myself as much as I was talking to Ryan and Erin. How much were we willing to do to Mr. Smith to see if we could "get him more oriented"? If his blood oxygen dropped to more dangerous levels and rendered him too sedated to breathe on his own, would we override his do-not-intubate order, place him on a ventilator, and send him to the intensive care unit? *Even if Mr. Smith "got more oriented,"* I thought to myself, *what options can we offer him?* Treating his clot but risking a large bleed? Was it fair to "hear from him what he wants us to do" if all we could ultimately do is keep him free of pain, anxiety, and difficulty breathing as he goes through the dying process?

"Don't we still have to treat the blood clot, though?" Ryan asked. "Yes, he's going to die from his cancer because we can't treat the cancer, but shouldn't we still try to fix what we can?" *Yes, but what if trying to fix him kills him?* I thought. My whole team stared at me. Ryan and Erin observed my decision-making process, Dr. Doyle studied my teaching skills and medical knowledge, and our pharmacist waited to tell me what dose of heparin to give Mr. Smith if that was how I chose to treat him. I felt as though they could sense my unacceptable uncertainty, that its scent overpowered the stench of hand sanitizer and stale potato chips that filled the hospital.

"This is a very tough situation," Dr. Doyle said, breaking the brief silence. "He's already on some fluids and sounds like he is somewhat stable right now on the mask, so you have some time to think about what is really the best plan for him." I wished that Dr. Doyle would just tell me what to do. But he often didn't. "You're going to be an attending in just over a year," he'd told me when we initially met each other and discussed his expectations of me during the month we'd work together. "You have to learn to make decisions as though I'm not here. And you have to trust that if you are making dangerous or poorly thought out decisions, I am going to tell you." He had a shock of white hair and a kind, slim face. Believing him meant believing in my own judgment, which was sometimes a challenge.

As we went over the plans for the other nine patients we'd admitted, my mind kept drifting back to Mr. Smith. Several other patients were far sicker than he was, one suffering from severe liver failure and another from a heart attack, one from end-stage dementia and an infected bedsore, another from a kidney infection and severe diabetes. But although several were so tenuous that they might soon require ICU-level care, I felt confident rather than conflicted about my plan for each of them. Their treatments came with risks, as all medical treatment plans do, but the risks paled in comparison with the very clear benefits.

After rounds, I stared at the computer screen intently, as though the intensity of my stare could produce the clarity of the right answer. It was second nature for me to treat a blood clot, and my fingers started to fill out the order set. I made it halfway through, then pressed Delete. I started it again, then paused. Looked at the screen. Pursed my lips. I still felt the weight of Ryan's and Erin's confused stares. Was I a fraudulent physician because I wanted to forgo treating a blood clot? Because I thought treating a blood clot wasn't necessarily treating Mr. Smith?

With trepidation, I called Dr. Doyle and told him that even though it would be very easy to try giving Mr. Smith heparin for his blood clot and liters of saline to treat his high calcium, ultimately both were clear signs of his body dying from cancer. To halt that natural process, especially with heparin, would risk severe bleeding that would only worsen his suffering. "Even if he did wake up," I said, "we would not be able to offer him options aside from hospice, so perhaps it's best to keep him comfortable and not do anything risky. I just think he's dying." Silence followed. I wondered if Dr. Doyle was about to tell me that he had serious concerns about my decision making, that he wondered if I was really ready to move on to my third and final year of residency.

"Well, that's the difference in thinking between an intern and a resident," he replied. "You and I both know where Ryan and Erin are coming from. Maybe in another patient, or the Mr. Smith from a year ago, we'd treat the clot. But we can both see that Mr. Smith's confusion is the beginning of dying from his terrible cancer. I agree with you—let's just treat any pain or shortness of breath he has tonight and try to get him home in the morning."

I unclenched my fists, relieved that he agreed with me, but also acutely aware of the gravity of my plan for Mr. Smith. "I was worried you would think I'm a bad doctor," I confessed. I immediately regretted being so forthcoming about my insecurity. "Not at all," Dr. Doyle said. "I think it's far more difficult to recognize when we need to step back and allow nature to take its course than it is to just start treating any and every problem." I let his words sink in, and thanked him.

After our call, I wrote something like this in Mr. Smith's chart: "The risks of anticoagulation outweigh the benefits in Mr. Smith, as he has sustained a recent GI bleed and has a limited life expectancy due to his metastatic esophageal cancer. I will order medications to treat his shortness of breath and confusion, and will arrange his discharge back to his home nursing facility with hospice services in the morning." Instead of reducing his situation to a series of medical abbreviations and half sentences as I did in most patient notes, I wrote about him in paragraphs, as though complete sentences in his chart could somehow add a measure of dignity to a man dying alone. Instead of ordering medications to treat his blood clot, I ordered medications to treat his shortness of breath. I asked to space out the checks of his vital signs to minimize disturbance of his sleep. I requested no further lab draws. I signed these orders and called Ryan to let him know of the change in plan. "Okay," he said quietly. "I guess we'll see how he's doing in the morning."

I continued to stare at the computer screen after hanging up the phone.

. . . .

I spent the next few hours checking on each of my patients, reexamining them if needed, adjusting medication doses, speaking with their family members. It was two a.m. when I retreated to my overnight call room.

I had not been paged for thirty minutes, the longest stretch of respite that day. I lay down on the saggy call room bed and closed my eyes. I could still see the image of the computer screen in my head, the orders I had signed seemingly pinned to the lining of my eyelids. I thought of how difficult it had been to tell Ryan that I'd decided not to give Mr. Smith heparin, even though Dr. Doyle had agreed with my decision. Disagreements between colleagues about serious decisions for patients could sting, as I had learned from my mother.

I was nine years old when she first began to tell me about the decisions she struggled to make at work, especially if her opinions were at odds with those of her colleagues in surgery. She would sit on our gray-and-black-striped couch and I would sit on the carpet, closing my eyes as she brushed the unruly frizz that was my hair at the time, smoothing it with coconut oil, weaving it into a braid. My head was tilted back from the cumulative force of brushstrokes, my eyes fixed on the white puffs that lined our ceiling, reminding me of vanilla cake crumbs. While she brushed, she told me her schedule that day: "Today I have two cases with one surgeon, then I have to help out in the clinic in the afternoon." Her usual honeyed voice, a mixture of English and Hindi, was replaced by a detached evenness, a tone that I didn't yet know I would adopt years later: the doctorly tone. As I heard her talk about work, I wondered why her voice changed.

She set the brush down and picked up the blue bottle of coconut oil from Asia Sweets and Spices, the only Indian grocery store within driving distance of our home. It was the only place at the time that carried staples we needed: coconut oil, saffron, giant cardamom that my mother kept in the freezer, bootleg videotapes of old Hindi movies and the newly released *Ramayana*, calling cards to India, Ayurvedic toothpaste, velvety red *bindis* that my mother wore to prayers and parties, and, behind a glass counter, a multicolored assortment of the Indian sweets my parents loved.

Her hands, small and soft, massaged the drops of oil first into my scalp and quickly down to the last stretch of my hair, pausing at the end to massage her own hands with the traces of oil that remained.

"This surgeon always wants to do very aggressive operations I don't think we should be doing. One of the cases is a guy who is ninety. He has so many problems already with his heart and lungs, and now he broke his hip and the surgeon wants to fix it."

I was still looking at our ceiling, wondering whether the big earthquake I kept hearing about at school would cause the flecks of white to flutter down in the closest thing to snowfall I'd probably ever see in Los Angeles. "I don't think it's right," my mother continued. "His heart and lungs are badly failing and you want to do a surgery?" I felt her hands moving rhythmically between the three sections of my hair, weaving them together, stopping, reinforcing what she had already braided, and continuing. "I really don't think we should be doing this but it is hard to argue with the surgeon."

She tied a purple scrunchie to the base of my braid and stood up. "Time to go," she said.

It would be years before I understood the complexity of the relationship between anesthesiologists and surgeons, but even as a child I could sense the normalcy of professional disagreements—with their occasionally serious consequences—during my mother's workdays. I wonder now why she began telling me these stories when she did, when I sat at her feet and she could only see my back, not my face. Maybe it wasn't me she was speaking to. Maybe it was just herself. Maybe there was something about the simplicity of braiding your child's hair, of trying to tame it, that enabled her to say out loud how tough it was to bring order to the chaos in which she worked.

I now wished there was something I could do to slow the tumble of repetitive thoughts in my head. Was Mr. Smith actually dying? Could I know that for sure unless I tried treating what might be treatable? Yet why did the mere thought of trying that feel nauseating? Did I do a good enough job of translating my gut reaction, the combination of sickening nausea and sinking of my stomach that arose when I thought of thinning his blood and placing him on a breathing machine, into a rigorous and intellectual care plan? Was I being doctorly rather than emotional?

I was midway through a yawn when my pager let out a series of beeps from Mr. Smith's nurse. "His breathing has changed," she said worriedly when I called her back. "Please come evaluate him."

Dying has a certain cadence and tempo, which is a recognizable prelude to an infinite stillness. When I first entered his room, Mr. Smith looked like he was sleeping. His chest rose and fell intermittently, then more slowly. His eyes remained closed when I shook his shoulder. His heart rate slowed. The tempo increased.

A hot wave of panic moved through me. Every contour of my stomach burned. I hadn't expected him to die tonight. Had my inaction expedited his death? Could heparin have helped him have a few more good days? I pulled up a chair to the side of his bed and sat down.

There was nobody to call on his behalf. There was nothing to do but be there. Goosebumps lined Mr. Smith's arms, and I covered him with warm blankets from the ICU one floor above him. I moistened his drying lips with artificial saliva. Remembering a note referencing his love of folk music, I used my phone to play bluegrass tunes, dispelling the heavy silence around us with banjo, guitar, and pensive lyrics.

I reread his tattoo. *Where there is light there must be darkness.* All the light and promise of modern medicine, inseparable from its dark potential for suffering.

At three a.m. I held the hand of a stranger. I watched his lungs expand and release air first in great heaves and then in diminished puffs, felt his pulse race and then suddenly slow, looked at his beard and tangled hair and wondered when he last took a shower, when anyone held his hand for this long, whether he would have wanted company or solitude. For a minute, our pulse rates were the same. When it became difficult for me to tell whose pulse I was feeling, I kept my hand on his wrist and placed my other hand against the juncture of my neck and head, noticing that my carotid pulse matched his radial pulse, that in this way, for this stretch of time, the pulse of an exhausted resident and her dying patient matched precisely. And then his breathing pattern became irregular. His heart slowed again.

The dark sky slowly gave way to the navy blue of early morning and the day's first blush. As the sky brightened, Mr. Smith's breathing slowed even more. At 6:37 a.m., he stopped breathing entirely. His body remained, but he had quietly and comfortably moved out, leaving behind his tattoo, his bruises, his clot, his cancer. I sat next to him for a few minutes before I rose and pressed my stethoscope against his still, silent chest.

Ryan and Erin approached me shortly after arriving at the hospital to ask how our patients did overnight. "So Mr. Smith died just about forty-five minutes ago," I said, almost as if I were confessing to a crime, forgoing our usual discussion of patients in alphabetical order. "What?" Erin exclaimed. "He went that fast? That clot must have been really big." Ryan took a deep breath and looked at me. "Wow," he said, shaking his head. "Don't you think that maybe the heparin would have helped? He could maybe have gotten back to the nursing home instead of dying here."

"To be honest, I think he would have died either way, but he could have suffered more with the heparin if he bled," I said, my temples throbbing with fatigue. "I went back and forth for a long time about whether or not to treat that clot. I actually agonized about it. I still am," I said. "But I was with him when he died. And he looked peaceful. It was like he just fell asleep."

Ryan nodded and turned to his computer quietly, looking through the charts of the patients who survived the night.

Rounds that morning were somber. "I'm surprised he went that quickly," Dr. Doyle said. I nodded in agreement, feeling the first sting of tears at the corners of my eyes, pretending to sneeze so that I could secretly wipe them.

Ryan and Erin looked at each other, and Ryan spoke. "I can't shake the feeling that maybe the heparin would have been helpful." I thought of my mother's disagreements with her colleagues over the years, of how arguments over life-and-death decisions betrayed deeper divides about the purpose of medicine, how a doctor's obligations to a patient straddled both existence and eternity.

"Even if that's what we had done, his time would have been very short," Dr. Doyle said, "and the most important thing was that he was comfortable." I wanted to feel more reassured by his words than I did. I half listened as Dr. Doyle redirected our conversation, reviewing the different ways to treat blood clots in the lungs depending on their size and severity. I couldn't concentrate, my mind wandering back over every decision I had made as I learned each detail of Mr. Smith's situation. Had I been right? I wondered. Had I been the doctor he needed me to be?

As I drove home that afternoon, I realized that what troubled me was just how deeply ingrained my expectation was that I should keep patients alive no matter what. I expected Mr. Smith to die soon, though I struggled to accept that he was already in the process. And I didn't want him to die on my watch. I initially found myself thinking more about fulfilling a certain professional obligation than recognizing the type of care Mr. Smith really needed from me. I thought of Ryan and Erin, who both seemed mildly traumatized to learn that Mr. Smith had died hours after he came to the hospital when *there was something we could have done for him.* Even though Dr. Doyle supported and even praised my decision making, their words made me second-guess myself nonetheless.

Becoming comfortable with the inevitability of patients' mortality seemed to rely on a certain unlearning of what I'd been taught in medical school about a doctor's obligations to her patients. My responsibility wasn't to keep Mr. Smith alive at all costs, though that's what my mind tried to convince me. Though my profession relied on science to halt the ways that nature affects and afflicts the human body, perhaps it was equally important to realize when trying to outsmart nature would inflict a different sort of suffering on my patients. It seemed to me that one of my most important responsibilities would be to know and remind myself of this difference.

Part 2

THE UNLEARNING

Five

THE UNLEARNING

On June 30, 2013, I completed my last day of internal medicine residency in San Francisco. Hours later, on July 1, I began my fellowship training in palliative medicine in Palo Alto. I'd spent most of June 30 driving back and forth between my old apartment in San Francisco and my new apartment in Burlingame, packing and dropping off boxes and bags I'd hastily filled with clothes and books. A quaint town midway between Palo Alto and San Francisco, Burlingame was home to a spacious tiled library, a main street lined with bakeries and restaurants, and an independent bookstore that stocked bestsellers and gossip magazines alike. I'd visited the town when I'd driven down to have dinner with an old friend who lived there with her husband. I liked the church steeple that came into view as I drove to my new home, an olive apartment complex set behind a garden filled with rosemary bushes and neatly arranged cacti. My street was home to trees adorned with leaves so green they seemed fluorescent; just a few months later, the same leaves would burn a deep burgundy. Across the way, a solitary willow bowed to the sky in reverence. Living here felt like respite. After making at least ten trips between the two cities in the span of a half day, I arrived at Stanford University Hospital bleary-eyed and lost, trying to make my way to the palliative care team office in the basement of the main hospital.

Certain things would remain the same in both residency and

fellowship. I would spend one-month blocks rotating between three different hospitals—the university hospital, the Palo Alto veterans hospital, and the county hospital. I still worked under the supervision of an attending physician, whose role it was to teach and mentor me, and who was ultimately responsible for the care of the patients I saw.

But in many ways, my role had changed overnight. Instead of admitting patients from the emergency room and addressing all of their medical problems throughout their hospital stay, I saw patients only when another doctor requested a consultation for a patient, usually to treat certain symptoms (such as cancer pain, nausea, shortness of breath) and to talk with patients and families about their treatment goals—what patients considered most important and dear to them when living with a serious illness. I'd gone from assuming that many of my patients would live for years after their hospital stays to knowing that some of my patients would die within the coming weeks or months after returning home.

After accidentally meandering into the cubicles of various social workers and the heart transplant team, I finally found the palliative care team's cubicles. A petite woman with warm brown eyes and shoulder-length brown hair greeted me with a wide smile. "Hi, Sunita! It's so nice to have you here! My name is Charlotte, and I'm the social worker on the team." I wondered how she already knew my name, and noticed that someone had written on the whiteboard in red marker, "Welcome Sunita Puri to Stanford Palliative Care!"

"It's great to meet you, Charlotte!" I said, already sensing that she and I would become good friends.

"Here, I printed you a list," she said, handing me a roster of fifteen patients. "We just got a couple new referrals from the oncology team, but we'll talk about them on rounds."

I scanned the list filled with patients' names, ages, and diagnoses. *There are some young patients here*, I thought. Age twenty-one, lymphoma. Age forty-five, metastatic gastric cancer. Age thirty-five, ICU day thirty, acute respiratory distress syndrome.

"Charlotte, are there patients on this list that I'm supposed to see before rounds?"

"No, it's your first day! So on our team we have two nurses and an attending physician and me. Everyone usually shows up for rounds at nine-thirty or so, and we will talk about each of the patients on our list. The attending this month is Dr. Harris, and she'll assign you a few patients to see. Oh, and you'll need that," she said, motioning to a pager on the corner of my cubicle. "The teams will page you when there's a new consult to see."

Charlotte showed me how to look up pager numbers on the hospital directory and told me what days of the week the cafeteria food was worth eating. She asked me where I was from and what brought me to Stanford, and showed me photos of her two children. "This rotation can be intense," she mentioned in a low voice, "so please make sure you have some way to let off steam. And always let me know if you need anything."

Dr. Harris arrived shortly, followed by the two nurses on the team. A short woman with bouncy black hair cut to her shoulders, Dr. Harris wore the sort of conservatively stylish outfit you might find at Ann Taylor. Businesslike and efficient as she introduced herself, Dr. Harris told me that her day was packed with meetings, but that she would assign me several patients to see and we would talk about them later in the afternoon. "We tend to get quite a few consults, usually around four or five new ones each day in addition to the other patients we are already seeing. You will definitely see a lot this month," she told me.

I listened as the team discussed each of the patients on our list. The twenty-one-year-old's lymphoma was getting worse, as was her bone pain and kidney failure. The forty-five-year-old wanted to go home with hospice care but his wife told him she refused to let him give up on his life. The thirty-five-year-old had a high fever overnight and the ICU team suspected he had a new pneumonia. Almost all of our patients required family meetings, and some also required better control of pain. Everyone was open to the suggestions of others; Dr. Harris suggested what medications and doses the nurses should use for patients in significant physical distress, and Charlotte offered ways to discuss hospice constructively with the forty-five-year-old patient's wife. The discussion was thorough but matter-of-fact, devoid of emotion. *Then again*, I thought, *for this sort of work to be sustainable, maybe it must also become routine.*

"By the way, the neurology team saw me in the hallway and said they needed help with a patient," one of the nurses said, turning to me. "She's eighty years old and had a large stroke. One daughter wants to be really aggressive about her care and put a feeding tube in her, but the other daughter says that her mother would never want a feeding tube." I jotted down the bones of the situation and agreed to see her right after rounds.

. . . .

Masaki had short black hair cropped close against her round face. She may have been eighty, but her skin was luminous and her hands were soft and delicate when I held them and introduced myself to her even though I knew she couldn't respond. Her daughter Emily sat in a brown chair. She had been typing away furiously on her computer but set it aside when I entered the room.

"Hi, I'm Dr. Puri. I'm a member of the palliative care team. It's really nice to meet you," I said as I extended my hand toward her, both excited and nervous.

Emily took off her glasses and squinted at me. She didn't shake my hand. "I'm sorry. You're from the *who?*"

"I'm from the palliative care team. I . . . um, I was here to see how I might be able to help with the, uh, with what your mother is going through," I said, unprepared for her surprise and uncertain how best to explain my role. "The neurology team had requested that I stop by to talk with you and your sister about how best to take care of your mother given her recent stroke."

"Our neurologist Dr. Scott never told me about this," Emily said sharply. "I still don't understand. What is pal . . . I'm sorry, what's the word you used to introduce yourself?"

"Palliative," I said. "I know that's kind of a weird word, but basically what it means is that I'm here to make sure that your mother is comfortable and not suffering from any of her symptoms. I'm also here to help you and your sister discuss the issue of the feeding tube for your mother." I wished I could stuff my words back in my mouth. I'd plunged right into a delicate discussion without really defining my role.

"Okay," Emily said. "But I don't know if we are ready for hospice or anything like that, if that's what you mean," she said.

"No, not at all. That's not what I am here to discuss," I said, flustered. "The neurology team had explained that your mother had a pretty severe stroke, and that you and your sister might have had different opinions about what your mom might want for herself in this situation," I said, trying again.

"Yes, that's true," Emily said. "I mean, this was all completely unexpected. Mom had filled out a living will or something where she said she wouldn't want anything aggressive when she's dying, but I don't think feeding her is aggressive. My sister disagrees. That's the basic problem."

"These types of situations are very tough, and my role is to help with the discussion about whether the feeding tube will help your mother in the . . . the right ways," I said, reminding myself not to appear as nervous and inept as I felt. "We call these discussions 'goals of care' discussions. It's another nebulous term but it means that when someone is really sick, we discuss their medical condition and what they are hoping for. From there, we consider whether doing certain procedures will actually help them to reach their goals."

"So there's a possibility that feeding my mother won't help her?" Emily said, her brow furrowed in confusion.

"No, that's not what I'm trying to say," I responded. "I'm sorry, I don't mean to confuse you more. I know you are in a really tough situation right now, and my only intention is to help you make decisions on your mother's behalf that she might make for herself."

"But that's what is so hard," Emily said, sighing. "My mother is a very private person and she never really shared any personal thoughts with us. We don't know what she would say about this situation, but I can tell you *I'd* never forgive myself if she starved to death." Her voice softened slightly. "What is the harm in just giving her the feeding tube?"

Masaki opened her eyes and stared at the ceiling. "Mommy, can you hear me?" Emily said, walking over to smooth her mother's hair. I looked on awkwardly, feeling as though I'd interrupted an intimate moment. "I think what's tough is that I don't know if this is her new normal or if she'll ever get any better," Emily said as she reached for lemon-scented lotion and began applying it to her mother's arms.

"That's a really difficult piece of this puzzle," I said, "and it is also part of the reason I think it will be useful to arrange a meeting with your sister, you, the neurology team, and our team to talk about that. I think what I was trying to say earlier is that if we think someone is going to recover, then doing certain things like placing a feeding tube can help. But if this is, as you said, your mother's new normal, we would really need to think carefully about the role of a feeding tube for her."

Emily took a deep breath. "Here's the thing. Maybe that makes sense in your head, but to me that sounds like you saying if Mom is only going to be lying in a bed, then there's no point giving her nutrition."

"I'm . . . I'm really sorry, that's not what I am trying to say," I stammered. "How about this: Is it possible for us to meet again tomorrow with your sister here? I'll be sure to get Dr. Scott from the neurology team to join us as well."

"Okay. I think around this time tomorrow should work." Emily refocused her attention on massaging her mother's arms and I snuck out of the room sheepishly. As I tried to find my way back to the palliative care office, I realized I'd been so caught off guard by Emily's initial questions and so focused on explaining how I could help that I'd forgotten to acknowledge the enormity of the question she faced: How do we make the right decisions for people we love?

When I described my meeting with Emily to Dr. Harris later that day, she told me that I would need to come up with a way of explaining my role. If patients, families, and other physicians don't understand what palliative medicine is, I can't effectively do my job. As I drove home that evening, I thought about how, in the last twenty-four hours, I'd gone from being a resident to a fellow, from living in San Francisco to living in Burlingame, from being a doctor who made every effort to keep patients alive to one who would likely lose each one she met. Yet the biggest shift was my new relationship to language, my attention newly focused on the words I used with patients and colleagues, and the words I heard them use.

. . . .

It wasn't an option for me to ease my way into my new role. I hit the ground running in fellowship, just as I had in residency, seeing patients who presumed I had an expertise that I was still cultivating. Controlling patients' bothersome symptoms was easier for me than navigating family meetings; after all, I knew the physiology behind cancer pain or chemotherapy-related nausea or the awful shortness of breath that accompanied heart failure. But learning to participate effectively in family meetings actually meant unlearning some of the communication habits I'd learned in residency. So when I could, I found myself taking on the role of an observer, taking in the communication missteps between doctors and patients that widened into consequential misunderstandings.

"I want you to set the timer on your watch when this meeting starts," Dr. Harris told me before we entered a meeting led by an oncologist in training. "Take note of how long the oncology fellow talks before allowing the family to speak." The oncologist, a brown-haired man with a kind face, spoke for twenty-five minutes about the gravity of the patient's diagnosis, the chemotherapies that theoretically could be used, and all the reasons why the patient was too sick to qualify for them. "So you're saying there are still options for my dad?" the patient's son asked the oncologist, legitimately confused because the doctor had spent more time describing treatment options for lung cancer instead of the reasons this particular patient couldn't receive them. In a meeting with the wife of our forty-five-year-old patient, I jotted down notes as Charlotte gently corrected her misunderstandings and fears about hospice care, but without insisting that the patient choose hospice. I cringed when I heard the neurologist taking care of Masaki tell Emily that there was "nothing more to be done" for her mother, that a feeding tube was the least of her problems. I sighed with relief when Dr. Harris spoke. "We may not be able to fix the stroke, but we can put together a plan to make sure that your mother is comfortable and not suffering from it. Your concern for her nutrition is very understandable, and we can talk about how to address that." As a resident, I'd made or witnessed the same well-intentioned mistakes I observed, though not always with a Charlotte or Dr. Harris around to steer a conversation back on course.

My intense engagement with language made every patient visit unpredictable in new ways. A patient with a failing liver asked me how much time I thought he had to live and begged me not to mince my words. Another patient, a woman with end-stage breast cancer, pleaded with me not to tell her adult daughters that she had chosen to stop chemotherapy. "I don't want them to think of me as a quitter," she said tearfully. "But I can't do this anymore." A confrontational patient asked Dr. Harris and me to leave, telling us that he knew we were only there to talk him out of treatments so the hospital could save money. The next patient we saw, a gentleman with kind eyes, took our hands and kissed them, thanking us for the medications we'd recommended to ease the shortness of breath caused by his failing heart.

Colleagues reacted to our team in equally variable ways. We were both the death squad and angels of mercy, sometimes regarded with suspicion and at other times with admiration. Some thought that our main function was to send people to hospice and start morphine drips. Others understood the difference between palliative care and hospice. "Wait, we aren't withdrawing care on this patient," a nurse told me, glancing at my badge before I went to introduce myself to a patient with advanced emphysema and a severe pneumonia. "Oh, I know," I said. "But the medicine team called me to help with a family meeting," I explained. "Yeah, but you're from *palliative*. So when you get involved, doesn't that mean that we kind of back off on taking care of the patient?"

I began to practice introducing my role, and memorized responses to the questions I fielded daily. "Hi, I'm Dr. Puri," I'd say in front of my bathroom mirror, looking at my reflection with a warm smile. "I'm from the palliative care team. What that means is that I'm a quality-of-life doctor. I'm here to help treat any pain or other discomfort you have, and to understand what you define as quality of life so that I can make sure we are doing what we can medically to make that a reality for you." I told fellow physicians and nurses that a palliative care consult simply meant a patient needed some expert help with their pain management or a conversation about their treatment goals. It didn't mean that a patient was imminently dying, or that they needed to stop their current treatments, or that they needed hospice care, or that their doctors and nurses had somehow failed and given up on them. It simply meant that their quality of life could in some way be improved.

The words and phrases I'd started to use routinely in fellowship still felt like a foreign language, one I stumbled over and used imperfectly. *If language reflects something about culture*, I thought one evening as I drove home, *then maybe my verbal fumbling made sense.* The language of medicine reflected its biggest priorities—identifying and solving problems, saving and extending lives. It was about CT scans and laboratory tests and survival benefit. Medical language atrophied when matters of suffering and mortality needed to be discussed, giving way to euphemism and avoidance. Lacking the language to discuss mortality is the ultimate way of erasing it. If we could somehow normalize instead of avoid the fact of death, perhaps phrases like "goals of care" and "advanced directive" would roll off our tongues as fluidly as words like "antibiotics," "chemotherapy," and "surgery." Or maybe in normalizing the language around mortality, the culture of medicine would evolve. After all, practicing medicine requires the drive to enable survival I'd learned to cultivate during residency, tempered by the acceptance of life's impermanence I was learning to articulate in fellowship. Physicians and patients needed fluency in both.

. . . .

In the third week of July I got a page from Jackson, an ICU fellow whom I quickly came to admire for his intelligence, sense of humor, and dedication to his patients. "We need your help with a family meeting for this lady, Alice," he began. He spent ten minutes exquisitely describing her illness and the ICU team's many attempts to treat it, his voice tinged with shame as he told me she wasn't getting better. I took notes as he spoke, and waited for him to tell me more about how I could help.

Jackson paused. "I know that's a lot of info."

I glanced over my scribbles and said, "This sounds complicated. Let me make sure I have all the facts. Alice is thirty-seven and had a bone marrow transplant three years ago for this rare lymphoma. She's been in the ICU for two weeks because of a fungal pneumonia that has gotten so bad that she needs the full support of the ventilator and continuous dialysis. But she's totally awake and can interact with you through writing. And you need some help discussing what should happen next with her and her family."

"Yeah, but not with her," Jackson said quickly. "Her family has been really clear that they don't want us talking to her about this and freaking her out. Alice is totally awake and writes out what she's thinking. She wrote that she would rather have us talk to her family instead of her right now."

Though we'd all been taught in medical school that an alert and coherent patient must always be involved in their own medical decisions, I'd found that rule to be imperfectly applicable. I could understand why Alice might want her family to be her ears and voice, and why her family would want to protect her from hearing the entirety of her condition. Other families had been similarly protective of their loved ones over the past two weeks: *Just talk to us about these things, not her. We don't want her to think we are giving up on her. We definitely don't want her to think she's dying. If she knows she's dying, she'll give up all hope and die sooner.*

"What have you discussed with family so far?" I asked.

"Well, we've told them that this pneumonia is extremely serious and it isn't getting better even on the strongest antibiotics. Because she's got such a bad infection, we can't treat the lymphoma," he replied. "But what we haven't told them is that she's probably going to die even despite everything we are doing." Charlotte noticed my expression on the call, which she'd later describe to me as a mix of confusion and horror. She cocked her head at me, and I scribbled a note to her: *What are they doing to this woman?* I wrote, shaking my head. But this is not what I said to Jackson. Just a few weeks into my new role, I could see how often I'd done what he and his team had done, how I'd muffled the truth by talking instead about procedures and remote possibilities of improvement. But I also understood what made the truth difficult to acknowledge.

"Thanks so much," Jackson said. "This has been a tough one for me. She's so young and she's totally awake and aware even though she's obviously never going to make it out of here. I think that's making it extra hard for my attending and me to have this discussion with the family." At least there was this: a recognition that they needed help.

"This is a really tough situation," I said, acknowledging his genuine dilemma. "I'll definitely join the meeting." It would take place in about an hour; Alice's boyfriend, mother, and aunts would be there.

. . . .

During my first month of fellowship, I'd started to visualize the treatment of serious illnesses as a journey the medical team took with patients, a hike taken together in a dense forest with only a sliver of moon visible overhead. The hike itself might be arduous and frightening, complete with trails that splintered into many paths, but both doctor and patient continued in search of their mutual destination. I thought of goals discussions as a necessary pause on the path, an invitation for both doctors and patients to take stock of the journey thus far, to discuss how best to reach the destination. Where on the map did patients think they were? Did the doctors agree? Was the destination still within reach, or had a boulder fallen on the known path to reach it? Was there a way around the boulder, or was it important to consider a different destination? Continuing on a tenuous journey blindly was a recipe for failure. But a goals discussion could be helpful only if the doctor could tell the patient, clearly and compassionately, if they were at a juncture where either of two trails would lead them to their destination, or whether they now found themselves unexpectedly at the edge of a cliff, their destination now out of reach. And if they needed to aim for a different destination, what sort of place would the patient want to see? What would they want along this new, different path?

"Family meetings are a procedure," a prominent palliative care physician named Susan Block had once said, "and they require no less skill than performing an operation." She gave me a new way of understanding how meticulously Dr. McCormick prepared for family meetings. I'd taken her words to heart and appreciated the way her explanation cast the intent and importance of a key intervention in our field as similar to any other time-intensive, critical, and useful procedure in medicine.

I prepared for my discussion with Alice and her family methodically, as a surgeon might prepare for surgery. I searched for any summaries of recent conversations with her about her treatment preferences in a scenario like the one she currently faced, or for documents like an advanced directive in which she might already have specified what types of medical interventions she would want if she couldn't be cured. If the territory I explored in a family meeting was based in the minds and hearts of my patients, then these notes and documents were my CT scans, giving me a glimpse inside their prior thoughts about worst-case scenarios. Even though Alice's disease was fast-moving and could come back with a vengeance, her lymphoma specialist hadn't discussed with her what would be important to her if that situation arose.

My conversations with the patient's care team were akin to the lab results I'd reviewed in other scenarios. I spoke not only with physician colleagues but also with social workers and chaplains who might have seen Alice. I tried to get a sense of how any prior discussions with Alice and her family had gone. Were there certain family dynamics I needed to be aware of in the meeting? Did Alice find solace in prayer or a particular faith?

And last, as I integrated the information I'd gathered about Alice, I wrote down a set of questions I hoped to pose during the course of the conversation. If surgeons memorized certain steps to guide them through an operation, my lists of questions were my own guide through the procedure I hoped to perform. For Alice, I wrote down the following: Was she bothered by any troublesome symptoms? What did she understand about her disease? If her time was shorter than we would like, where would she ideally want to spend it? In other words, what would she want her doctors to do for her if they couldn't cure her? But even after diligently reviewing a patient's chart, speaking with other members of their care team, and writing out a map of questions for myself, I approached family meetings with a healthy respect for what I couldn't possibly know or anticipate.

Ideally, palliative care specialists and other physicians helped patients think through these complex, deeply personal questions when they were still well enough to consider their options, talk with their families, and ensure that their wishes were known and written down. But Alice's situation was far more typical. We were on a trail with no map, our path blocked by a huge boulder.

Although I didn't find what I was looking for in Alice's chart, I did find great detail about how she'd gotten so sick. When Alice was in her early thirties—around my age at the time—she was diagnosed with lymphoma and, after nearly dying from the infections and organ damage the lymphoma caused, underwent a bone marrow transplant. It bought her three years of largely uninterrupted life. She went back to work. She adopted a puppy. But over the six months before her current hospital stay, she began to cycle in and out of the hospital with one illness after another: a severe pneumonia, kidney failure, an episode of confusion. Her lymphoma had returned, eventually devastating her immune system. An aggressive fungal infection soon made its home in her lungs. She became breathless and blue, and was placed on a ventilator.

The ICU team hoped that the ventilator would give her lungs time to rest and recover while powerful antifungal medications battled the infection. But the medications damaged her kidneys, and she needed dialysis. And then, when a second infection entered her bloodstream, her blood pressure dropped and she needed medications to keep her blood pressure high enough to continue dialysis and improve blood flow to her brain. Even though her anemia stabilized with daily transfusions, dialysis cleaned her blood continuously, and her blood pressure remained artificially acceptable with the help of medications, Alice couldn't inch her way off the breathing machine.

I looked at the computer screen intensely, jotting down the phrases I might use to distill the details of her medical situation in language that she and her family could understand.

Alice was sound asleep when I went by her room to introduce myself prior to the family meeting. I glanced at the clipboard next to her bed, filled with fragments of conversations in wobbly handwriting.

Did Giants win?

Pay electric bill

Pancakes

Where is he?

Around the words, I noticed doodles of flowers and butterflies sur-rounded by a border of concentric circles. There were stars circling a cres-cent moon. There was her own name, written in cursive and block letters. If she didn't have the breathing tube in her mouth or the IVs in her arms, she might have looked like any other woman in her late thirties taking a nap. I wondered whether it was miraculous or tragic that medicines and machines had gotten Alice well enough to be herself, but not well enough to leave the ICU.

I made my way to the ICU waiting room, where I sat at the edge of a half-moon formed by the ICU attending physician, Dr. Frankel, Jackson, and Charlotte. Alice's mother, aunts, and boyfriend, Chris, sat across from us. Dr. Harris couldn't join us, and had wished me luck. I listened as Dr. Frankel told Alice's family that Alice's pneumonia and lymphoma were both getting worse despite the support of antifungal medications, blood pressure medications, the ventilator, and dialysis.

"What probably makes Alice's situation especially tough for all of you is that she is really sick, but she can still interact with you, recognize you, write down what she's thinking for you. This makes it harder to understand that she's not likely to improve," Dr. Frankel told them gently. "We are very worried that Alice may not ever be able to breathe on her own without the ventilator."

Chris, a muscular man with thick black hair, looked at the ground, shak-ing his head. One of Alice's aunts, a tall brunette named Elaine, broke the brief silence by asking, "So what does that mean, then?"

"Well, part of the reason that we wanted Dr. Puri from palliative care to join us is so that we could all talk together about some of the hard decisions we might have to start thinking about," Dr. Frankel said, nodding at me and inviting me into the conversation. The reality of Alice's situation had been an understandable blow to her family. Perhaps my most important task was to get to know Alice's family and, through them, Alice. I started off gently.

"It's very nice to meet all of you, though I'm sorry that we are meeting in these circumstances. I think how I can be helpful here is to help you think about what Alice would want if, indeed, we aren't able to get her off the breathing machine," I began, nervously aware that many pairs of eyes watched me. "I know that right now you'd prefer that we talk with all of you, the people who love her, about these treatment decisions."

Chris began. "The first thing you need to know is that Alice is a fighter. She isn't going to give up easily. Not at all." He crossed his arms over his chest and sat up straight, continuing.

His voice was alternately fierce and tender as he recounted all the bad news Alice had received over the past few years, and the ways she had defied the odds delivered to her in similar meetings. "It's always a bad sign when a bunch of doctors want to meet," he said. "They'd have meetings like this one all the time when she was getting her transplant, but she made it through. She fought through that, she fought through the side effects of the medications she had to take, she fought through the last three times we've been to the hospital. So I knew coming in here what this was going to be about. But I'm telling you what Alice would say—she'd want everything done to get her better."

Now that I was more fully immersed in and attentive to the words that both patients and doctors used in these meetings, I'd discovered that the meaning of the word "better" could be fairly elastic. Dr. Frankel might describe Alice as "better" if she could live without the support of the ventilator. Chris might think Alice was better if her lab results improved. Alice might only consider herself better if she could return home.

So I asked: "How do you think Alice would define getting better? What would that look like for her?"

Chris raised his eyebrows. "Better is *better*. You know, meaning she gets off the machine and we can get her home."

I clasped my sweaty hands together, taking a deep breath and trying to calm myself. I tried again: "I guess what I'm trying to say is that we're not sure Alice is going to get off the breathing machine. I'm wondering what might be important to her if we can't get her better in the ways we hoped we could."

"I'm telling you, that's not going to happen. She's going to get better. She's pulled through worse before. She is a very strong woman."

Elaine rolled her eyes and shook her head. "Okay, Chris, you need to listen to what the doctors are trying to tell you. They are all trying to help prepare us for the fact that she might not ever come off machines and go home. And come on, I seriously doubt that Alice would want to be on machines for the rest of her life just because you think she is a fighter."

"You don't know her like I do," Chris snapped. "You haven't been there every single time she's gone to the hospital and come home so weak that I have to stay up all night watching her every move."

"I've known her for over thirty fucking years," Elaine said, exasperated. "Don't you dare tell me that you know my own niece better than I do." Alice's mother patted Elaine's leg. "That's enough, Elaine," she said softly, taking her hand.

Elaine spoke again, looking at me: "Are you saying she's going to die no matter what you do for her at this point? With or without the breathing machine, she's going to die?"

This was what Jackson struggled to articulate to me on the phone. Alice's young age and complete lucidity made the fact of her gradually dying body painful for her doctors to acknowledge, let alone communicate to her loved ones. We all secretly hoped that her age could help her to defy the odds. Still, even if she somehow made it off the ventilator, her lymphoma would almost certainly take her life shortly thereafter. We couldn't discuss Alice's goals without being honest about her decline, but could we be certain that our worst fears for Alice would actually become her reality? How certain did we need to be in order to discuss the worst-case scenario?

"We aren't sure what is going to happen, which is why we want to start thinking about what we should do if we come to see that she's not getting better despite everything we are doing. I know it is really difficult to think about that possibility." I was careful to speak slowly and softly, observing the body language of her family members.

"You seem like a very nice person, and I appreciate you trying to help us out. But if you're asking me to say we should stop the breathing machine at some point, the answer is no," Chris said. "Absolutely not. She's going to pull through."

"Oh, certainly not," I assured him, shaking my head vigorously. "We just want to be honest with you about the fact that right now our best treatments aren't working as well as we would like them to. And if they continue not to help Alice, she may get sicker very quickly. At that point, we may not be able to offer much more treatment than we are giving her already. It would be harder to have this type of discussion in the middle of an emergency, so we are just trying to give you all time to consider what we should do in a hard situation in case it arises."

"Thank you," Elaine said after a brief silence. "We really do appreciate it."

I glanced at Dr. Frankel, who spoke. "We should meet again three days from now to give you another update on how she is doing," he said. "I think that it's important for you to think about these questions as a family. You might even consider bringing up some of these topics with Alice."

Chris hunched over in his chair, looking down at his clasped hands, and then sat up and stretched. As I rose from my chair, he gestured at me and said, "I get this feeling that you're a nice person. I can see that you want to look out for us. Maybe you should talk to her," he said. "But promise you'll be gentle. Don't talk about death or anything like that. Just kinda get her thoughts on this situation. Maybe she'll open up to a new person."

His change of heart surprised me. I nodded. "I would be very happy to talk to her. And I promise I'll be very gentle." Although ideally Dr. Harris wanted us to meet patients as early as possible—when they first got sick rather than when they were close to death—I could see how at times being a new face might be helpful.

"Just please stop the conversation if you think it's getting to be too much for her. I can't have her demoralized. That might make her die sooner."

Hours later, I returned to Alice's room but found her asleep once again after getting a hefty dose of pain medication. Elaine sat next to her, flipping through *Vogue* magazine. "Doesn't she have a right to know everything you and the rest of the team just told us?" Elaine whispered before I left. "I understand why Chris has got his panties in a bunch about this, but I don't think lying to her is the answer. But then, how do you even tell someone the truth in this type of situation?" she wondered. I didn't know. Most of the patients I had seen in residency who were as sick as Alice were either too sedated or confused to participate in a discussion; my only option was to speak with their families. I had never had such a delicate conversation with a young patient who was connected to a ventilator but fully awake.

I left work most days asking myself questions with no easy answers. When I was in residency, I constantly made mental notes about the medical facts and conditions I needed to study: how to interpret blood gases more quickly and precisely, how to do a more precise physical exam of a patient in heart failure to decide whether or not their total body swelling was improving, the best way to remove fluid from a painful joint to make sure it was only gout, not an infection. These were generally matters I could look up in an endless number of educational resources online, on my phone, in study guides that lined our residents' workspace.

But there were no study guides or formulaic answers to the questions I asked myself after leaving work those days. What if Alice told me that she wanted to know every detail of her situation? How much should I actually share with her? How could I convey the truth of her situation in a way that didn't demolish whatever hope she might have for some semblance of recovery? If she asked me questions I didn't want to answer, would my silence, or well-intentioned euphemisms, cause her to have false hope for a miraculous recovery? In conversations with other patients over the past few weeks, I'd at least been able to discern their emotional state and reactions to our conversation by their tone of voice; when talking with Alice, I'd have to interpret her emotions through written words and facial expressions.

It would have been easy for me to comfort myself by saying that these questions were specific to Alice's situation, that her case and circumstances were exceptional. Yet although the medical details of various cases might differ, they shared certain tricky moral dilemmas. Should Alice be the one to make her wishes known? If the ICU team felt strongly that Alice was going to die no matter what they did for her, shouldn't they tell her that? But wasn't it possible, as Chris had said, that Alice might make it through this episode as she'd defied the odds before? Could we talk to her about the reality of her situation without destroying her hope? Or would a truly honest discussion about her illness force her to hope for something different?

. . . .

The next morning when I went by her room, Alice was awake. Her notebook was already filled with shaky scribbles, pieces of various conversations that fit together like a stream-of-consciousness poem: *no pain*; *can I have water*; *my boyfriend*; *the tube hurts*; *call her*.

"Hi, Alice," I said, pulling up a plastic chair to sit next to her, smiling nervously. She smiled back and waved slightly with her right hand. Her brown hair was pulled back into a low bun that rested on her right shoulder. Her delicate mouth, dried blood at its corners, wrapped perfectly around the breathing tube. "My name is Dr. Puri, and I am from the palliative care team," I continued slowly. She nodded. "Not everyone has heard of palliative care, so let me tell you what my role in your care is," I continued, watching Alice's face closely. "I want to help make sure your symptoms and discomfort are well addressed. I'd also like to make sure that you fully understand your medical condition. I'm here to talk through what you are hoping for in your situation and to be sure that you are as well supported as you can be."

Alice nodded, her expression neutral. I asked whether she'd had any pain, shortness of breath, or nausea. Alice shook her head no. She pointed to the breathing tube and grimaced. *It's scratchy*, she wrote. I asked her if she had tried a small dose of pain medication to treat her very understandable discomfort. She nodded again and wrote, *Makes me sleepy but it works*.

I asked her about her life before she got sick. She had been with Chris for many years. They lived a few blocks away from the apartment I had lived in during residency. She smiled as much as the tube in her mouth would allow as I asked her whether she had been to the neighborhood brunch joint (yes—and she loved the pancakes), how long she had lived in San Francisco (fifteen years), and what she did for work (she worked as a secretary but was thinking about going back to school to study psychology). She was raised Catholic though she didn't practice. She was hoping to go home soon; she missed her dog, her bed, the familiar smell of her kitchen. A minute of silence passed before she wrote: *Will I be able to go home?*

I wanted so badly to reassure Alice that we would get her home soon, healthy and recovered. But to do so would have been irresponsible. I had to measure my words carefully and with close attention to their effect, just like I titrated the doses of medication to get someone's blood pressure to the right number. But I could generally predict how a person's physiology would respond to a given blood pressure medication—which ones to avoid because the patient had kidney disease, which ones to give because the patient had heart disease. Choosing the right words, however, required some knowledge—or at least a somewhat informed impression—of a patient's *psychology*, a formidable task when I'd just recently met a patient. No matter how well I thought I knew a patient and family, and how accurately I might be able to anticipate their emotional response to a difficult situation, the mind and heart could be wild beasts, capable of interpreting the kindest gesture as the greatest threat. I had taught myself how to recognize emotional recoil, how to step back and allow the smoke to be seen as a signal, a notice, not always a sign of fire.

I explained that getting her home was the goal, but she couldn't leave the ICU if she needed help from the ventilator and dialysis machine. I asked her if she understood why she needed to be on the ventilator. *Because I can't breathe*, she wrote, and I tried my question again, asking for more specifics.

"That's right," I said. "What have the ICU doctors told you about the reasons you can't breathe?" It would be one thing if she were an otherwise healthy person who couldn't breathe because of a treatable pneumonia. It was another thing entirely that the infection in her lungs and the lymphoma in her blood grew stronger every day.

Lymphoma, she wrote.

I nodded and spoke slowly. "The lymphoma has made your lungs vulnerable to a very aggressive pneumonia. What we are trying to do is give you the right medications to help your body fight the pneumonia, and support your lungs with the breathing machine." She nodded.

I took a deep breath, readying myself for the harder part of the conversation, the part that I wish she didn't have to hear from a near-total stranger.

"Here's the thing about the tube, Alice," I started. "I think of it as a bridge from a bad situation to a better situation, a kind of temporary support for your lungs while they heal. We always want to take the tube out as soon as we can."

She nodded, her neutral expression unwavering.

"We are worried that we haven't been able to take the tube out for you yet," I said softly. "I imagine that worries you, too."

Alice nodded. *Yes*, she wrote. *I worry it won't come out.* We sat together silently as Alice played with her pen, drawing around the content of our conversation. More stars. A few trees. A cat.

I want to go home, she wrote, circling and underlining her sentence. *I want to sleep in my bed. I want my dog. I want this tube OUT.* She wasn't asking to be cured, or to be kept alive at all costs. She was asking for the most ordinary things. But our extraordinary technologies couldn't enable her to enjoy the most ordinary things. I felt cruel for asking her about wishes that I couldn't help fulfill.

I resisted my urge to respond right away with reassurances and platitudes. Alice closed her eyes and leaned back into her pillow. Her warm breath fogged the breathing tube and then vanished as the ventilator hummed and hissed, hummed and hissed.

"I wish that I could make all of those things happen for you right now," I said softly, meaning every word. Alice nodded, her eyes closed.

She pointed to her head and wrote that she had a headache and wanted to rest. Could I give her something for the pain?

Of course, I said quickly, secretly grateful that our conversation was drawing to a close. Had it continued, I feared she would have asked me questions I wasn't sure I could answer, questions about what would happen if she couldn't come off the ventilator, or whether she could go home with the ventilator. I asked her nurse to give her pain medicine, and told Alice I'd be back to see her in the morning. She nodded, her eyes still closed. I wondered what she was thinking and feeling. I wondered what I would think and feel if someone had this same conversation with me.

. . . .

Alice was one of the twelve new patients I met that week.

Joseph was a painfully thin man dying of lung cancer. He wanted to go home, a request his family wanted to support but couldn't. "I'm just really nervous that my sister and mom and I have no experience giving him the kind of care he needs," his teenage son told me outside his father's hospital room. "He's so fragile, like a glass I don't want to break." When Joseph asked me when he would get to go home, I couldn't bring myself to tell him what his son had told me. "Hopefully soon," I'd say.

There was Grace, a woman in her forties with breast cancer. Her twelve-year-old son snuggled next to her in her narrow hospital bed, begging her to stop screaming in pain. I'd stay in her room sometimes for an hour at a time, changing around her medications and doses until she could finally talk to him without wincing. There was Maria, whose constant nausea stemmed from an aggressive stomach cancer that had invaded her entire abdominal cavity and marched forth into her lungs. She took my hand every time I saw her and asked me to help her go to sleep. "*Por favor*," she pleaded, "*quiero dormir.*" Her voice was desperate and exhausted. She would rather die than live miserably until death came for her.

One night, I dreamed that Maria was pounding on my apartment door, begging for mercy. I awoke drenched in sweat, panting. I turned on the porch light and looked outside my window. Nobody was there.

. . . .

That weekend, my brother came to visit me. Since he'd been in medical school himself over the past three years, we saw each other only sporadically, mostly on the few holidays that both of us happened not to be at the hospital. But we texted often; he sent me funny videos of cats chasing laser pointers and pictures of obese gerbils getting stuck between the spokes of hamster wheels, things he knew would make me laugh. When he found out he'd have a whole weekend off toward the end of July, he decided to drive down from UC Davis for the weekend. We became our high school selves together, eating, laughing, and mercilessly teasing each other. He pestered me about the lack of decorations in my new apartment ("I'm only here for a year!" I protested) and wondered why I didn't just buy a bigger bookshelf instead of hoarding my books on the left side of my bed. "Why are you read-ing *these?*" he asked, holding up my copy of *He's Just Not That into You* and a glossy celebrity gossip magazine. "Because I basically need to turn off my brain," I said, blushing at his discovery. It somehow made sense for me to cap off my day by reading about anything and everything that bore no re-semblance to my work or patients. "How does Halle Berry still look so good?" he wondered as he leafed through the magazine.

We walked to a Japanese restaurant a block from my apartment and had steaming bowls of ramen. We meandered up and down the tiled stretch of downtown Burlingame and ducked into the bookstore, where we read other gossip magazines together. That evening, we picked up a takeout pizza and decided to watch a movie at my apartment. "We are so not cool," my brother said as he opened the steaming cardboard box. "It's Saturday night and in-stead of going to San Francisco we are sitting on our asses eating pizza and watching *The Joy Luck Club!*" We both laughed hard, and I nearly choked on my first bite.

We'd watched this movie many times since high school, and usually laughed at the overly dramatic stretches that seemed implausible. But as the early part of the movie unfolded, I began to cry when I'd otherwise have laughed. It was the first time I'd cried in months. I put my half-eaten pizza slice on my plate and trembled under the blanket I'd wrapped around myself.

My brother, meanwhile, was laughing and hadn't noticed my tears. "This is *soooooooo* unrealistic!" he said, turning to me and then putting his own pizza down. "What's wrong?" he asked, pausing the movie and turning to me.

I thought I didn't know, but I did. There was something about watching the main character in this movie go about her life shortly after losing her mother that pierced all the insulation I thought I'd put up between my patients and me. I thought I'd sublimated the twinges of sadness I felt by throwing myself into diminishing their discomfort, talking them through the unthinkable. I thought of Grace and the pain that persisted despite my desperate attempts to control it, the nausea that Maria couldn't escape. Alice's limbo. *This rotation can be intense, so be sure you have some way to let off steam.* My brother put his arm around me and leaned his head on my shoulder.

"Work is hard," I managed to say. I hadn't let myself feel anything about the patients I saw every day, or the intense and layered pain that consumed them. It was one thing to know intellectually that I'd be around death all the time. But it was another to be immersed in the enormity of the final experience all human beings would share. *What have I gotten myself into?* I thought in the brief pause between one wave of tears and another. *Am I in over my head?* Somehow, watching a movie about a daughter grieving the recent loss of her mother pushed me out of my head, away from the script I read from to comfort myself: *Life is temporary. Suffering is far worse than death. Death can be beautiful, just like birth.* I'd often criticized the common perception that doctors could be superhuman, capable of curing the impossible. But in these first weeks of fellowship, I realized I'd expected myself to be superhuman—to embody a certain peace with death so that my patients could more easily find their own peace. What my patients needed was not only my expertise and professionalism, but also my humanity. And perhaps that meant embracing life's impermanence but also allowing myself to be just as scared and overwhelmed by death as my patients were. Trying to be Ms. Socrates hadn't worked. I sobbed then for all of the people I couldn't sob in front of. I reminded myself that I wasn't a doctor right now. That, in order to go back to work and be a doctor, I had to let myself grieve, grapple with what it meant to lose a thirty-six-year-old to colon cancer, to care for a woman who would rather take her own life than live another day with nausea.

"Auntie *Lindo*!" my brother exclaimed, a goofy smile on his face, forcing some laughter out of me. We both thought Auntie Lindo was the most complicated character in the movie, one who both compelled and annoyed us. "You have a hard job," he acknowledged. "What you see every day is not normal." I smothered my face with a tissue. My brother reached over to pick a few strands of stray tissue out of my eyelashes.

"I have an idea. Let's watch *Mean Girls*!" he said, his eyes lighting up mischievously.

"Yes!" I exclaimed. "We haven't watched that in forever." I yawned; crying had relaxed me, left me lighter. My brother changed out one DVD for the other, and we both returned to our pizza in my small dark apartment.

....

Alice had gotten worse over the weekend. Her blood pressure dropped so low that continuing dialysis was becoming dangerous. She was just as dependent as she'd always been on the ventilator.

On Monday morning, eight people circled around Alice's bed—her family, Dr. Frankel, Jackson, and me. Dr. Frankel began the meeting with an update. "When we met a few days ago, we had talked about our goal of trying to see if Alice could get well enough to come off the ventilator and dialysis," she said gently. "Unfortunately, we have not been able to meet those goals. And we are dealing with new problems, like the fact that you can't move your legs," she continued, looking at Alice.

"Hey, we don't want to just hear all the bad news," Chris said, shaking his head. "We need positivity right now so that Alice can heal and get better. So what's the positive news?"

"I wish we had more positive news to share," Dr. Frankel said, "but I'm afraid that we are just seeing Alice get sicker."

"You have to listen to them," Elaine said to him. "They are trying to help."

"Babe, what do you think?" Chris said, turning to Alice.

Over the span of a few minutes, Alice slowly scribbled down her thoughts. She thought she was getting worse. She still couldn't eat or drink. She couldn't talk. The breathing tube made her want to throw up. How much longer would she need it?

"I want to tell you something that is going to be difficult to hear," Dr. Frankel began. "It's not looking like we will ever be able to get you off the breathing machine. I think you are too sick to live without the machine," she said, pausing. "But I also think that you might be too sick to live even with the machine." Alice closed her eyes. Chris drew in a sharp breath and looked at the ground.

"I am very worried about what is happening to you, Alice. And I am especially worried that you are getting so sick that your heart could stop," she continued. "And when that happens, I do not think you would make it through CPR, that procedure when we come in and press on your chest and sometimes shock you to jump-start your heart," she said, acting out chest compressions as she described them. "But sometimes people want us to try that for them. What do you want?"

I winced internally, hoping that Alice would say no, thinking of the times I had been the one to perform chest compressions on patients like Alice at the end of their lives. They should have been allowed to die peacefully, not with my hands pumping their chest a hundred times a minute as another doctor yelled for a crash cart while yet another doctor screamed out the results of lab tests that only confirmed they were dying. *Say no*, I thought to her, hoping that somehow she would hear and heed me.

Alice shook her head. "Are you saying you wouldn't want that?" Dr. Frankel clarified.

No, Alice wrote, *I don't want that.*

"I don't think she's thinking straight," Chris said, shaking his head. "I think this is all scaring her too much, the way you're all standing around her and talking to her. Baby, you want to live, right? You don't want to give up!"

Alice looked at Chris and shook her head slowly. *Like this?* she wrote, underlining her words forcefully. She lay still, and then angrily stabbed her bed with the pen. It was probably as close as she could get to screaming.

"We all want her to live," I said carefully, "but we also want her to have quality of life and as little discomfort as possible if we can't give her more time." Alice nodded as I spoke. *Quality*, she wrote, circling it.

"I've got to get some air," Chris said. He opened the sliding glass door and left quickly. Elaine followed him.

Alice looked at Dr. Frankel and then at me, pointing to what she had written.

. . . .

When I went to see Alice the following morning, she reached for her clipboard and pointed to a sentence she'd written for her nurse an hour ago. *I don't want this anymore.* She pointed at her tube when I looked at her after I read her scrawl. *No more tube.*

I hadn't expected her to have made a decision. "Tell me more," I asked, trying to understand it.

They can't fix me, she wrote. She shrugged, and began to cry. Her arms had become weaker, and she struggled to lift her hands to wipe her eyes. I grabbed tissues from her bedside and dabbed her cheeks and eyes gently. I tucked dampened strands of her hair behind her ears and held her hand, letting her squeeze mine as hard as she cried. I fought every impulse to tell her not to cry. I remained silent.

Her tears slowed, and she reached again for her pen. *I am not afraid*, she scribbled. She circled and underlined her words, and looked me straight in the eye. I nodded. The quiet that followed wasn't silence. I could hear the whir of her dialysis machine, the *ding* of the ventilator when she tried to cough, the beeping of an IV pump that had run out of medication.

"Have you shared your thoughts with your family?" I asked, and she nodded. *Tube out tomorrow*, she wrote, circling it. Her family knew this, too. She reached for my hand and squeezed it lightly. *Thank you*, she wrote, drawing a wobbly smiley face next to her words. She placed her pen down on her clipboard, where it rolled to a stop on the lower part of her torso, somewhere between an abdominal drain and her urinary catheter.

Tomorrow came, and I spoke with Jackson and Dr. Frankel to confirm the plan. They had already updated the other doctors involved in Alice's care, most of whom agreed that at this point all treatment options had really been exhausted. None of this made the situation easier.

"You know, I just keep thinking about whether we missed something earlier, or maybe if we'd started the antifungals sooner, she would have had a fighting chance." Dr. Frankel's voice trailed off, and Jackson nodded in agreement.

"I've been thinking a lot about this," I said slowly, "and I think that because you worked so hard for her, she's had this time when she's been awake enough to communicate with her family and hasn't been in much pain at all. She had this time with her family because of you." I could sense that Dr. Frankel and Jackson believed they failed Alice, when in fact they had succeeded in remarkable ways.

"And," I added, "she was awake enough to tell us herself that she didn't want to keep going. That decision didn't have to be made by her family. As awful as this whole situation is, at least she could be the one to tell us she's ready to go."

Jackson twirled his pen and nodded. "That's so true. I think the family would have felt really guilty for a long time if they had to make this call."

Dr. Frankel added, "You would think after all these years I've been doing this job that these situations might be a little easier for me. I should be able to know that it's okay and important to be able to let Alice go, but it's still so tough."

"And that means that you still care so much," I said. "It's a tall order for us to somehow get used to these situations and yet to still care about each one. But it would be weird if losing patients somehow became easy." I spoke the words I told myself the night before as I tried to reconcile the fact of Alice's dying with the emotions it stirred.

Dr. Frankel nodded deeply. "You're absolutely right," she said. "I love that I'm taking advice from a fellow, not an attending!" She laughed.

Sometimes, I was learning, I had to support my colleagues just as much as I support my patients.

Chris and Elaine sat next to Alice's bed, watching her. Her eyes were bright, and someone had applied blush to her cheeks. I noticed that she wore pink lipstick; its imprint brightened a stretch of her breathing tube.

"Good morning, Alice," I said, aiming for neutrality rather than sorrow. Chris fixed his eyes on her, and Elaine gave me a half smile and made room for me at the side of Alice's bed. Alice beckoned me closer to her and I knelt, wondering if she was going to give me a hug. Instead, she tried to reach up for my long hair, which I had left down around my shoulders today instead of pulling it back into my usual bun. As I bent closer to her, with some strained effort she lifted first her left hand and then her right, touching the ends of my hair and then running her hands through the strands. I watched her eyes move in all directions, taking in my hair as though it were a novelty, closing her fingers around soft sections, trying to memorize their texture.

Letting go of my hair, she pointed to the photographs that hung above us, a makeshift mobile of photographs that Alice had requested: Alice at a bar with Chris. Alice and her aunts at the Golden Gate Bridge. Alice alone, wearing a dark tank top and smiling widely, her hair identical to mine. She fixed her eyes on the dangling photographs as though she were newly born rather than dying slowly, watching the most ordinary moments rotate above her, out of reach, in a still room with no breeze.

Looking at me, she wrote, haltingly and with great effort, *I used to have hair like yours.*

I smiled, confessing that usually my hair was pretty curly but today I'd flat-ironed it straight. She gave me a thumbs-up and nodded. I wondered if we could do anything to keep her more comfortable. I'd noticed her mouth was dry and cracked—could we moisten and clean it for her? We could always reapply the lipstick afterward.

Alice nodded and smiled. She shook her head when I asked her about pain and difficulty breathing, anxiety and fear. She pointed to something she'd written earlier and underlined and circled.

I want to be like sleeping beauty, she wrote. *I am ready to fly!*

We all learn how to do things to patients, but not how to undo them. There is a grace to learning how to place a breathing tube into a patient's throat: the examination of the patient's mouth and neck before placing the tube to choose the correct tube size and to make sure that broken teeth, dentures, or drapes of connective tissue don't obscure the view of the windpipe. The nod to a nurse to push sedating medications into a patient's vein. The glide of the breathing tube through the mouth and in between the visualized vocal cords, those delicate sinewy landmarks that confirm the tube is going where it should. Just the right amount of pressure inching the tube forward. The confidence to ask for assistance when you're not sure if the tube is in the trachea and not the esophagus.

But undoing—removing the breathing tube when its purpose has been exhausted—often feels like an imperfect experience because it isn't as carefully taught. Usually, we extubate patients because they can breathe on their own. But when we extubate a dying patient, what follows may be the final impressions a family will have of their loved one. Intubations are closely supervised, but extubations aren't always.

"I'm begging you, I don't want her to feel a thing," Chris said to me outside her room after I first saw her that morning. "I can barely keep it together right now and if I see her in pain, I'll never be able to live with myself."

He began to weep, convulsing with sobs. A nearby nurse motioned toward the waiting room, which was empty and would be a much better place to talk. Elaine followed us.

"Can you tell us what exactly is going to happen?" Elaine asked. "Honestly, I think a couple other doctors have explained it but I just can't remember. It's . . . well, this is all pretty overwhelming."

I nodded, wondering whether I would be able to hear the details of the extubation if I were in their position, or whether I'd want to remain blissfully ignorant, staying at my loved one's side and pretending that I wasn't really losing her.

"I will definitely walk you through it," I said. "Our main goal at this point is to make sure that when we remove her breathing tube, Alice doesn't suffer any shortness of breath or pain of any kind." I paused. "The way that we do this is by giving her pain medication before we remove it."

"Will she still be conscious?" Elaine wondered.

"You're not putting her to sleep, right?" Chris said. "I want every precious moment I can have with her."

"I totally understand. We will give her pain medication only if she has any discomfort. We will try our best for her to be awake and available to you, but sometimes people need more medications to be comfortable, and the medications can cause sleepiness."

"How long do you . . . how long . . ." I could guess what Chris was trying to ask.

"Are you wondering how long Alice will be alive after we remove the tube?" I asked gently. He nodded, wiping his eyes. "Elaine, this can be hard information to hear. Are you okay with me sharing my thoughts?"

She nodded. "Yes," she whispered. "I do and I don't want to know, but we have to be prepared. We'll tell the others all of the stuff you're telling us now."

They need your honesty, I reminded myself. *They will lose her just once.* "Alice has needed a lot of support from the ventilator," I began. "And based on that, I think that she will likely be with us for minutes to possibly an hour or so after we remove the breathing tube." This, too, was a sentence I'd had to practice.

They nodded. "I can't believe this," Chris said.

"No matter how much time she has, Chris, I promise you that we won't let her suffer," I said, telling myself to focus only on my words, not on the emotion of the room, lest it consume me.

I ordered all of the medications Alice would need and discussed the plan with Jackson. "This sucks," he said, and I nodded in agreement. But was it worse than anchoring Alice's body to a world it was trying to leave?

. . . .

Though I'd wanted to be in the room when Alice was extubated, I wasn't paged when it happened. When I went to see her, her bed was empty, the mobile and photographs and cards gone. "I thought someone had paged you!" her nurse said when I asked when Alice died. "She was gone in about twenty minutes." By the time I arrived, Alice's body had already been moved to the morgue.

Because I wasn't in her room when she died, I tell myself that Alice didn't feel any pain or have any difficulty breathing. That the last thing she felt was the love in the room, the love that was big and buoyant enough to grant her wish to fly. I stood in the space where Alice's dialysis machine had been, in the few minutes before a janitor began to clean it. The room was finally, overwhelmingly, silent.

. . . .

It will eventually become second nature to sit with a patient you barely know, a patient like Alice, and help them to understand that they are nearing the end of their lives. You tell yourself to push aside the awkwardness of essentially being a stranger to them, and talk to them as if you *do* know them. You are forced to a place of extreme intimacy, talking to them about the lives they have led up to this point, their fears and regrets, the people they love, the ways they have made sense of loss earlier in their lives, and how they are making sense of loss now, in the days or weeks or months they may have left to live. You must act as if it is normal for a doctor to ask these probing questions during the first or second meeting with them. Because if you act awkward, they will wonder why you are here, why you are asking about their pain and nausea and shortness of breath, about who makes their medical decisions if they no longer can, about what they hope for, and whether those hopes are realistic. You remind yourself to listen to them carefully, to choose your words carefully, because one day you will be on the other side of this conversation, and you will long for someone to listen to you and choose their words carefully.

You will tell them how sorry you are that they are sick, that they have been in such distress, that they have to have a difficult conversation with you. You wonder if being a stranger actually helps you to say what the doctors they have known for a longer time cannot say. They will tell you they have never heard of palliative care. Is that hospice? they will ask, while telling you that they would never consider hospice because hospice means giving up. They try and fail to pronounce the word "palliative." One will ask if you are from the primitive care team. Another will ask if you mean you are a paleontologist.

They tell you how humiliating it is to have gone through innumerable surgeries and rounds of chemotherapy only to be more familiar with their doctors' hands than their lover's hands. They tell you that because of their feeding tube, they haven't tasted real food in more than three years, that they have forgotten the crunch of apples, the tang of oranges. They tell you that in three months, they plan to move to Oklahoma to be near their son; you wonder aloud if they have considered going sooner while trying to figure out how to tell them that three months—maybe even three weeks—is wishful thinking. They tell you that it isn't fair that this is happening to them, because their spouse doesn't deserve to be alone. They wipe their tears on T-shirts that say "Fight On!" or "Miracle" or "Fuck Cancer." They tell you that they know someone who had stage IV cancer and was told by their doctor that they wouldn't survive for six months, but it's been six years and their friend is still alive, visiting them every day, telling them that doctors don't know everything. They show you photos on their phones of themselves with their families on the beach, in the park, at a parade, in a café, and you sometimes have to blink back tears because you know that they are trying to say, "This is the real me! I'm going to be the real me again!" and you fear that cancer will claim their old and new selves, probably before the month is over. They wonder if death hurts, if they will suffocate or die from extreme, uncontrolled pain, but they stop mid-sentence and tell themselves that death is still a long way off, and they mustn't worry themselves with those questions right now. You imagine that each of them wears a necklace of intricate, intersecting circles of loss, grief, anger, fear, sadness, regret. You visualize this necklace hanging at their throats, golden and glistening under the hospital's fluorescent lights, in the moments when their expressions of emotion make you want to leave the room. This is a necklace that you choose to wear, too.

Some will tell you that everything you say is coming from a place of negativity, that they will be the miracle patient to prove you wrong. They tell you that you will never forget them, because they will show you how wrong you were.

You *won't* ever forget them, you think to yourself, no matter whether they prove you wrong or not. You will pray for all of them. You will attend their funeral services, if invited, and place the program on your altar, next to an image of Lord Ganesha. You will ask Him to guide them on their way. You don't tell them this, because you know that what they need more than anything is to search for hope in any way that they can, including by saying that they *know* they will prove you wrong.

There is no script, no training course, that can teach you how to sit in silence, how to listen to them. You either have a deep well of your own suffering—your own intersecting, interlocked circles of loss, grief, anger, fear, sadness, regret—to draw upon, or you have a well of suffering that you have not recognized or are not ready to draw upon. We all have our suffering. Whether you can use yours to connect to the suffering of another is a separate matter entirely.

You want to tell them that their bodies will die, but they won't. That it is their bodies, not their spirits, that are finite, mortal. You want to tell them that you have had patients who have had near-death experiences, who have hovered above their bodies as medical teams performed CPR and experienced the purest joy and freedom they have ever known. You want to tell them that these people described freedom from their diseased bodies as being enveloped in pure, divine love, finally free of suffering. We never wanted to return to our earthly bodies, they tell you later.

You remind yourself that it isn't your job to erase or to justify all of their suffering, but rather to see it, not ignore it. To ease it when you can. And to be there as they move through it, as it passes through like clouds in the sky.

Six

BELIEVE

I was a first-year medical student when my father experienced chest pain for the first time. I imagine that I was probably hunched over a study guide in San Francisco, reviewing how to interpret EKGs, when my father began his morning walk in Los Angeles. About thirty minutes into it, my father would tell me later, a stabbing sensation tore through his upper body, stopping him in his tracks. He struggled to breathe even as he stood still and hunched over, hands on his knees, eyes fixed on the grass below him. Nausea came and passed. The pain had arrived suddenly but dissipated slowly. He sat on the wet morning grass and wondered if maybe his acidity was flaring, or if he had pulled a muscle while pumping his arms as he strode up the steep hill leading to the park. After a few minutes, he took a deep, painless breath and stood up to walk home, deciding that this was probably not worth mentioning to my easily worried mother.

About a week later, another bout of chest pain interrupted my father's sound sleep. He suddenly sat straight up, feeling as though a kebab skewer had been pushed through his chest, struggling again to breathe. Beads of sweat dotted his forehead. A wave of nausea overcame him and he squeezed his eyes shut, willing himself not to vomit on the plush brown carpet below. My mother stirred and then awoke, the sight of my father instantly provoking in her a doctorly response.

His pain lasted longer this time but eventually subsided, taking the nausea with it. My father refused to go to the ER in the middle of the night, but my mother made him promise to see a cardiologist, one of my mother's colleagues, first thing in the morning. As my father walked on a treadmill in the cardiology clinic, the cardiologist closely monitored my father's heart by examining a continuous EKG. Midway through the ten-minute test, he told my father to stop walking; the electrical pattern on the EKG revealed that the right side of my father's heart was not getting enough blood, most likely because of blockage of one of the arteries feeding the right side of his heart. Had my father waited any longer to see a doctor, he might have died during his next morning walk.

Since I was in the midst of studying the heart and circulatory system, I knew more than I wanted to know about situations like my father's, but this knowledge somehow vanished when my mother called me tearfully, telling me details about my father's EKG, details that I suddenly couldn't comprehend. Because it was my *father's* abnormal EKG. I flew from San Francisco to Los Angeles immediately.

My brother and I accompanied my parents to the hospital, where my father would undergo a cardiac catheterization—a procedure in which a cardiologist would thread a thin, flexible tube from a blood vessel in my father's upper leg all the way to his heart, enabling the blocked artery that caused his chest pain and nausea to be visualized and stented open. We huddled together with my mother as my father changed clothes. Tall and occasionally imposing, my father looked uncharacteristically frail in a pale blue hospital gown that masked his round belly and showcased his thin arms and chicken legs. He laughed at my mother's nervous tears and the serious expression on my brother's face: "What's wrong with you two? You look like I've already died!" He fixed his gaze on my mother, barely flinching when the nurse placed an IV in each of his arms. "You all worry too much," he said, shaking his head as my mother wiped her eyes on the sleeve of her white coat. My brother and I wrapped our arms around her. "This isn't funny, Ashok!" she said, her voice muffled and broken.

My mother knew catheterization labs well because in the past she'd provided sedation to patients undergoing pacemaker placements and catheterizations. She had witnessed both the incredible power and the terrifying complications of attempts to fix broken hearts. Sometimes, a heart severely deprived of oxygen by multiple blocked blood vessels might stop before the blockages could be treated; other times, an artery might accidentally be torn by the advancing catheter and the patient would need to go to the operating room for an immediate repair. My mother would place such unstable patients on breathing machines and whisk them away to the ICU or the operating room, where, hopefully, they stabilized. She'd often walked by the nondescript waiting room outside the lab, where spouses and children and caretakers stared at the talk show du jour on the television overhead and leafed through dated, rumpled issues of *People*. But she had never sat there herself, trying to restrain her restless mind from wandering into the tricky territory of worst-case scenarios.

The cardiologist came by again, asking whether my father had any questions before his procedure. My father shrugged and said he had no questions, but my mother had one. "Can I tape this to his chest?" she asked, holding up the picture of Lord Ganesha that she usually kept in her wallet. The cardiologist smiled and put his hand on my mother's shoulder. "Sure, Rita. No problem. But I want you to know that he is going to be totally fine," he said softly.

Amid the uncertainty of everyday life, my mother relied on God. The cardiologist could quote endless statistics to convince my mother that my father's procedure would go well, but what she needed was a blessing from beyond. "I know you will take good care of him, but I need God to take care of him, too. It's okay if you think I'm crazy," my mother replied, her voice unusually quiet. She looked so small to me then. Fear diminished my powerful, confident mother. I kissed the top of her head, which rested against my shoulder. My father laughed again. "Nothing is going to happen to me," he said.

Lord Ganesha, revered as the merciful destroyer of obstacles, glowed in this particular drawing, a gold crown atop his elephant's head, his round body swathed in a pastiche of gold, red, and green cloth. In his four hands, he held both weapons and flowers. One broken and one unbroken tusk flanked his trunk. He sat majestically in the center of a pink lotus. He appeared to be both loving and menacing, peaceful but ready to defend himself if needed. My mother grabbed a roll of hospital tape, the same tape she used to secure a breathing tube in place, and fastened Lord Ganesha directly over my father's heart, kissing the picture before the nurse wheeled my father behind a set of double doors that, this time, my mother couldn't enter.

. . . .

My parents believe in both science and God, and never understood why that might seem strange to people. They were raised in the Hindu and the Sikh faiths, though they would teach my brother and me that all religions are simply different pathways to the same place, that every faith is built around similar lessons: live kindly and compassionately, with regard for the well-being of others. My mother introduced me to human biology and physiology, but she and my father also taught me that the body, imperfect and impermanent, is the home of the soul. And the soul, the eternal spirit within each body, is immortal, indestructible, immune to the cycles of birth and death that our mortal bodies experience. We are not these bodies, my parents would tell my brother and me. We are the souls within. Part of our journey on earth is to learn that birth and death may be the beginning and end of the body, but not of us. And a spiritual practice can help us to remember the truth of who we are, and to recognize the unified quest of all beings: seeking to understand themselves and their own innate divinity. Doctors could treat disease, my mother told me, but only God could shape the soul's journey. This was why some patients survived when nobody expected they would and others died when their survival was assumed. Prayer, my mother told me, was more powerful than medicine, and a necessary part of any treatment plan.

My mother usually met her patients for the first time in the preoperative area, a collection of beds separated by thin curtains, similar to where my father had been prior to undergoing his catheterization. She talked to them about their medical histories, reviewed their lab results, examined them, and answered any questions they had. They wouldn't speak to her again until after their surgeries were complete and they had recovered from the nausea-tinged haze that followed anesthesia. But in the brief period between meeting patients and taking them to surgery, many would share their fears with my mother, worries that ranged from dying during surgery to finally knowing and confronting a diagnosis that surgery might unmask.

Do you pray? my mother routinely asked her patients.

Of course, many would tell her.

Would you like to pray together before your surgery? she would ask, and many of her patients would brighten, nod, and begin to speak to God. Her patients were any combination of terrified, overwhelmed, hopeful, hopeless, desperate, confident, nervous, grateful. My mother pressed her palms together, bowed her head, and listened as they prayed to Jesus, Allah, Ganesha, Guru Nanak, Zoroaster, and the Universe. She observed that everyone, no matter what their religion, prayed for similar things: God's mercy, survival, minimal suffering. And no matter what name they used to call out to God, she told me, what they really longed for was love and protection. God, she would tell me, is not a deity in the sky, looking down upon and judging us. God is pure love.

As my mother wheeled each person into the operating room, she asked for God's blessing. *Please help me to keep my patient well through surgery and anesthesia.* Her surgical colleagues, who eventually learned of her practice, turned to her in moments of frustration during surgery, asking, "Rita, where's your God when we need Him? Call Him right now!" I don't think my mother understood their sarcasm, because she'd answer as though their questions were genuine: "Don't worry, He's been here the whole time."

As my mother told me her stories, I rolled my eyes at what I called her "obsession" with God, yet secretly admired her for believing in both science and spirituality, for considering that both systems of belief were equally true, even complementary. There had been moments in my life when I'd felt the intense presence of divinity: observing flowers turn toward the sun in our backyard, watching migrations of whales across a stretch of the Pacific, even noticing the healing of a bruise or a paper cut. I knew that each phenomenon had a scientific explanation, but they also seemed to share a certain mystery that struck me as divine.

But I hadn't experienced divinity the way my parents had. I had been born into comforts distilled from their sacrifices, which in turn were made possible, in their eyes, by God. Their faith gave them a way to understand both joy and hardship as part of God's plan, and a way for them to grow. God is how they found hope and peace, especially in circumstances as overwhelming as health crises. I wanted desperately to believe the way they did, rather than forcing myself to sit through the hours-long prayers we held in our home on Sundays and Thursdays. I recited every mantra I was taught, sang devotional songs at the top of my lungs, and participated in every community service project our spiritual community organized. And yet, going through the motions of certain rituals and reading translations of holy texts didn't liberate me from my skepticism. I sat with my mother as she recited mantras 108 times. I followed my father around the house every evening as he touched each picture of God on our walls before going to bed at night. Imitating my parents didn't give me instant access to the devotion they'd cultivated over a lifetime. I'd hang out after prayers with other girls my age whose parents belonged to the same spiritual community. We'd scoff at our parents' insistence that we attend prayers; after services ended, we'd sit together and talk about the movies we'd seen and the boys at school we thought were cute.

My parents knew that I didn't share their strong faith. I sensed that this broke their hearts. "Nobody can teach you to have faith," my father told me one day when we argued about why God didn't eradicate poverty, war, and famine if He really existed. Wasn't that God's purpose? "God's purpose is not to erase human suffering, but instead to teach you how to overcome whatever life might bring. If you turn to Him, you can learn much about acceptance and surrender and real joy."

. . . .

About midway through my fellowship year, I met a physician who taught me how to talk to patients about God. A five-foot-tall Vietnamese woman, Dr. Christina Nguyen probably barely tipped the scales at ninety-five pounds even after having three children. She was tiny but mighty, exacting but deeply compassionate in her conversations with patients. She carried around folded camping chairs from REI during rounds so that she could always sit down to talk with patients without having to scramble for chairs from the nurses' station. She kept packets of soft tissues in her pockets during family meetings, offering them immediately after the first appearance of tears. She wore a perpetual expression of peace and tranquility that put even the most squirrelly patients and skeptical physicians at ease with her role. I tried to emulate her expression by twisting my mouth into a gentle half smile, teeth slightly visible. *Perhaps by adopting her expression and mannerisms*, I thought, *I could also channel her presence with patients.* But I couldn't sustain it no matter how many times I tried. Dr. Nguyen's spirit—loving, empathic, and completely present—was inimitable. In trying to emulate her, I missed the more essential point she demonstrated: she was completely *herself* with her patients, not at all preoccupied with the performance of a specific, stereotypical physician authority. As I watched Dr. Nguyen speak with patients, I felt certain parts of myself—frozen in the long hibernation of residency—thaw and reemerge, like blades of grass through melting snow.

I felt my mother's presence, too, when Dr. Nguyen spoke. On rounds, I'd shake my head in disbelief when one of our young patients died of the flu, or a seemingly healthy marathon runner was diagnosed with pancreatic cancer. Dr. Nguyen urged me to look at these situations with a wider lens. "We have plans as doctors," Dr. Nguyen told me as she peeled tangerines from her yard over lunch, "but maybe God has another plan. Could we possibly be open to that? To the idea that we can't control everything?"

If God had a plan for the thirty-one-year-old whom I'll call Jack, I didn't understand it. Jack's parents, both devout Catholics who held constant vigil at Jack's bedside, reminded me of Rajiv's parents. Their lives, like those of Bajwa Ji and his wife, took on a new shape, both smashed and scathed by the explosive tragedy of Jack's illness. Six years earlier, Jack had suffered a massive bleed from his esophagus for reasons his doctors would never understand. He lost so much blood that his heart, deprived of essential oxygen, stopped. Even though his heart began to beat again after fifteen minutes of CPR, his delicate brain never fully recovered. He had remained on a ventilator ever since then, living in a facility specifically for patients on ventilators. He could open his eyes, but could not speak. A feeding tube in his belly provided him with nutrition, the ventilator assumed the work of his lungs, and a Foley catheter in his penis collected his urine. Nurses turned him from side to side several times a day to prevent bedsores, and changed his diapers.

Over the past six years, Jack had shown no signs of neurologic recovery. He was unable to breathe, eat, urinate, or move independently; his survival depended on tubes and machines that predisposed him to recurring infections. His urinary catheter led to bladder infections. Being connected to the ventilator for so long caused several serious bouts of pneumonia. The skin around his feeding tube became blistered and red from recurrent skin infections. The more infections he had, the less effective the antibiotics became. There was now only one antibiotic left that could treat the bacteria causing Jack's latest pneumonia. The medical team worried that it was only a matter of time before Jack developed a devastating infection that no antibiotic could treat. And, according to the resident taking care of Jack, his parents seemed totally unprepared for that scenario.

"We could use your help talking to the parents, because I don't think they get how sick their son is," the resident told me when he called me to discuss this consult. "They keep talking about how a miracle is going to happen and he's going to get better, but soon he's going to get an infection we can't treat. He's resistant to almost every antibiotic known to man since he's been treated with basically each one over the past few years."

"Have you told his parents what you're worried about?" I asked as I clicked open Jack's electronic chart to read through the team's notes.

"Yeah, I've told them he will probably die from his next infection, and his dad talks about how God will pull him through," the resident replied, frustrated. "And the conversation just stops there."

I noticed quotes from his parents, Mary and Steven, in several of the medical team's notes. *Patient's parents say they are hoping for a miracle recovery. Patient's father refused to discuss goals of care, said no need for discussion because patient is doing better. Patient's mother says that God will save patient, declines visit from chaplain.*

And the conversation stopped there. I could understand why. Even though several studies found that patients wanted their physicians to ask about their faith and how it influenced their health, other studies suggested that physicians felt entirely unequipped to do so. Though my mother had openly engaged her patients in discussions of faith, I felt sheepish doing so. In retrospect, there had been times when my awkward silence had probably stung patients who had been trying to communicate a specific type of pain to me.

These patients weren't necessarily terminally ill. There was the young woman who suffered a terrible infection after getting an abortion. *This must be God's punishment*, she told me when I met her in the women's clinic after she left the hospital. There was the accomplished painter with a rare auto-immune disorder who could no longer grasp or lift a paintbrush. *Painting is everything to me*, he told me. *I don't know why God would do this to me.* I asked an elderly patient how he was coping with his new cancer diagnosis. *Maybe this is God's punishment for my years of boozing.*

Do I deserve to suffer from this cancer? What is the purpose of my life in my diseased body? Am I suffering because God is testing my faith? I hadn't considered that these spiritual and existential questions probably caused my patients just as much—if not more—anguish than the surgeries, the cancers, the endless invasive procedures and incremental loss of dignity. What was my duty to my patients in those tender moments? If I was to respond to these questions, where would I begin? And what if I said the wrong thing? These moments of reckoning deserved more than my hasty offer to call a chaplain, which all three patients declined anyway. "Forget I said anything," my elderly patient said. "It's not that big a deal."

Patients in the throes of serious illness clung to the hope that medicine could offer them, but many simultaneously reached for God. Some had never prayed before they'd gotten sick. Others stopped praying when they did. Still others continued the prayers they had always said every day, no matter what their life circumstances. Over the last few months, I'd noticed rosaries, crosses, prayer beads made of sandalwood, and figurines of Buddha on the same tables where patients ate their lunches and kept medications they hadn't yet taken. Some slept with a copy of the Bible under their pillows. Others played gospel music or Gregorian chants or Tibetan Buddhist chants off their phones or computers, drowning out the hospital's daily noise with the audibly sacred. I wondered how Jack's parents expressed their faith, how they reached out for something infinite and invisible.

Jack was just two years younger than me at the time, though he appeared strangely childlike, with innocent but expressionless brown eyes, a smooth face free of wrinkles, and shoulder-length black hair accentuated by a solitary braid woven together by his nurse. His mother, Mary, a short, plump woman with dark hair and deeply etched worry lines on her forehead, bent over him, dabbing his feverish forehead with a cool towel and pulling apart clumps of hair dampened by sweat. "We try to make this room like a home," she told me. Her son's head rested on the pillow from his childhood bedroom, Mary told me, and I marveled at the hand-stitched red-and-blue plaid cover with his initials and birthday stitched in green on one side. Instead of hospital blankets, he had a matching plaid blanket that Mary sprayed with a citrus-scented air freshener to remind him of his favorite fruit. "One day he will have an orange again," she told me, nodding and smiling weakly.

I don't think they get it. I turned over the resident's words in my mind, knowing that I had used this phrase hundreds of times during my own residency, not pausing to think about how unrealistic I must have sounded. Perhaps no conversation, no matter how precisely clear and exquisitely compassionate, would "help them to get" that their child was slowly dying— initially from tragic complications of a medical procedure, and now from medicine's limited ability to outsmart bacterial resistance. There is no freeway between the mind and the heart; a statement of medical facts didn't lead easily to acceptance. *Acceptance is a small, quiet room,* Cheryl Strayed wrote in an essay that I read and reread somewhere around the start of fellowship. I knew that neither I nor anyone else—no matter how skilled a physician—could walk them to this room. It was a place they had to find on their own, though I could support them along the way.

On my drive home that evening I talked with my mother about Jack, looking mostly for her to listen rather than give me advice. My mother remained skeptical that palliative care was a field I could handle emotionally; she was right that I was sensitive, given to feeling too deeply and crying too easily, so I chose my words carefully, talking mostly about the horrible pain I'd see patients endure, and how I'd use many of the medications she used in anesthesia to ease their suffering. Today, I vented about the injustice of young patients dying early. A slew of my recent patients had all been my age or younger; talking with parents about their child's mortality day in and day out weighed on me, though I mentioned that fleetingly to my mother. But she wasn't good at listening without offering advice or solutions. As I spoke about Jack, she cut in.

"I would tell his parents to pray if they believe in God," my mother told me. "There is nothing God cannot heal. We doctors can only do so much but He can make anything possible."

My mother encouraging a patient to pray before an operation was very different from encouraging the parents of a young man to pray for a miraculous recovery from six years of life with a devastating brain injury.

"Yes, but how can I tell them that?" I said. "Don't you ever feel like that's not a doctor's place to say? And why are we talking about this anyway? It's not why I called you."

"Why shouldn't I say that? Why shouldn't you?" she replied, her voice slightly muffled by the screeching of a pressure cooker in the background. I imagined her in the kitchen in her blue hospital scrubs, recently home from work, mincing garlic and ginger while watching the lentils she had placed in the pressure cooker. Just as she had done most days when I was growing up, even right after a twenty-four-hour-long overnight shift. "If you believe it and they believe it, then I think it is good to comfort them in this way."

"But won't that just encourage false hope?" I said, sighing with frustration. "How can I honestly tell them that when the fact is that the kid is just going to keep getting more infections until he dies some horrible death? You think I should just stand back and let them keep praying while their kid suffers?"

"The parents may see their son's sickness as a test from God, and they are responding with more prayer and faith," my mother replied. "I'm not saying that it's right to see it that way, but that may be what they are thinking."

I genuinely believed that Mary and Steven loved and wanted to protect their son. But I also wondered if their reliance on faith and miracles enabled some level of denial about the severity of Jack's situation. And if they did indeed see Jack's every infection and setback as a test of faith, and we saw it as evidence of his slowly dying, whose perspective should dictate the terms of Jack's care? Was my primary responsibility to the patient who can't speak for himself, or to his parents, whose decision making is understandably driven by the unthinkable prospect of losing him?

"Well, screw that way of thinking. They're not going through what Jack is going through. So it's easy for them to sit back and say this is all a test of faith, but how is that fair to him?" Though I'd been hungry when I began my drive home from the hospital, I'd lost my appetite to the anger that overwhelmed me.

"Okay, okay, calm down now," my mother said. "Listen, whatever God ultimately wants for this patient is going to happen. You cannot control the outcome. So you just need to do your job and not think too much about it." I exhaled through my mouth, the hot, quick jet of breath loosening some of the emotion tightening my chest. I saw that I'd been gripping the steering wheel so tightly that my hands hurt.

. . . .

The next morning, Mary, Steven, Dr. Nguyen, and I sat together in a small meeting room with faded blue walls and a gray conference table. Dr. Nguyen introduced herself, pressing both of her hands gently around Mary's right hand. Steven, a stoic man who wore a San Francisco Giants hat, had been living with a rare neurologic disease and moved around in a motorized wheelchair that he was still able to maneuver with his hands. "I never believe everything doctors say," he told me right before I opened the meeting. "It's not disrespect, but I was told by my doctors five years ago that I would live for only six months and I should go on hospice. But I'm still here, by God's grace, and doing just fine."

"That is wonderful to hear," I said, "and you're right—sometimes we don't know exactly what will happen to all of our patients." His words and tone suggested that he knew what our meeting was about, that he'd had this conversation before. I swallowed nervously.

"The doctors taking care of Jack asked Dr. Nguyen and me to talk with you about his condition and to think about how we might take care of him if he were to get really sick," I began, trying, as always, to channel Dr. Nguyen's natural ease. "What have they shared with you so far about the reasons he got so sick?"

"He has another pneumonia, and they said that he is getting better now with the antibiotics," Mary began. "But they haven't said anything about what to do if he got sick again. I hope he doesn't. Wouldn't we just bring him to the hospital and you would give him treatment?"

"You are right that his pneumonia seems to be responding to the antibiotics," I said, nodding. "But since he has had many, many infections, the bacteria that cause the infections are now resisting the effects of the antibiotics, meaning that there is only one antibiotic that can treat his pneumonia at this point."

"But at least there is that antibiotic, correct?" Mary said, and asked whether we could continue to use that one if he got sick again.

"I hope so," I began gently, "but we don't know if that is likely. The more likely situation is that he will have an infection from bacteria that we cannot kill with the antibiotics we have."

"Are there other antibiotics that you can give him?" Steven asked, his eyebrows raised with worry. I had anticipated this question and practiced my response on my way to work this morning. How could I condense the molecular mechanisms of bacterial resistance to antibiotics into plain English?

"I don't think so," I said, pausing for a beat before continuing. "Unfortunately, when patients get sick over and over again from infections like Jack's, and we give them antibiotics to treat the infections, at some point the bacteria are able to evolve so that they can survive even if we give them antibiotics that used to kill the bacteria."

"So what does that mean?" Steven asked immediately.

"Soon, Jack will probably get an infection that we will not have a medication to treat. And we should start thinking about how we should care for him when we have no more medicines to offer." It didn't seem to me that they had known that a great many antibiotics would no longer help Jack. I never particularly enjoyed having to break this sort of news. But what made it bearable, even oddly gratifying, was the honesty of the situation: telling people the truth about their predicament in plain language. I'd sometimes wondered if the more compassionate way to have these discussions was to soften the facts with filler, with long, meandering sentences that blended hope and reality without doing justice to either one. I was learning that honesty sometimes took the form of measured, compact, declarative sentences. I had to be Ernest Hemingway. And this sometimes felt brutal, the exact opposite of compassionate. But the honesty *was* the compassion.

A long pause ensued. In these silences, I searched for what I could still hear: The mechanical tick of watches. The uncomfortable shifting in seats. The tapping of a finger on a plastic hospital chair. The sighs. The quiet sniffles. The vibration or ping of a text message. The world outside moving forward, as the world in the room paused.

Steven broke the silence. "I want to tell you a story."

I nodded, angling my body toward him.

"I was told I shouldn't expect to be alive right now," he began. "Doctors told me that when I got diagnosed with this disease that they don't really understand, I was diagnosed so late that I was . . . what did they say . . . beyond all hope." He smiled, recalling that they told him his only option was hospice.

"But I told them no. I told them I have another option and that option is my faith in Jesus Christ, my Lord and savior." Mary's fist had unclenched, and she looked down at the table, shredding a tissue into feathery bits. A nurse outside raised her voice. "I'm gonna need help with the IV in room four!"

"I was supposed to be dead and gone six years ago," Steven said, turning his head to look me in the eye. "And if I am still alive despite everything those doctors told me, then my son can survive no matter what you say to us. You cannot tell me that medical science is stronger than my faith, stronger than Jesus."

. . . .

Steven's words were familiar to me. Just then, in mid-conversation, I found myself thinking about a scene from years ago, when I was in high school and listening to the story of a different miracle.

After prayers on Sundays and Thursdays, a member of our spiritual community would occasionally share a personal story about how they came to practice their faith, or how they experienced divinity. Eva, a middle-aged Cuban woman whom I'd known since I was eleven, spoke one evening. She'd been diagnosed with colon cancer but refused surgery and chemotherapy, telling her physicians that she knew God would heal her. She described at length her physicians' warnings and frustrations, their conviction that she must be suicidal, and their insistence that she see a psychiatrist. *You are lucky that this cancer was caught early enough that it can still be cured!* they'd say. *Why would you refuse the tried and true therapies we are offering you to live a long life?* My parents had told my brother and me this story many times already, and as Eva continued, I shifted impatiently, wishing she would jump to the conclusion of her story, which everyone in the room knew anyway.

"One night, Lord Shiva appeared in my dream," she began, pausing as she teared up. "And He said, 'I cancel your cancer. I cancel your cancer right now.'"

She awoke in the morning with a sharp, unrelenting pain in the side of her belly where the cancer had been found. She assumed that the cancer was growing, or that a fatal complication was brewing, and went to the emergency room. But on her CT scan, there was no sign of her cancer. Three months after her diagnosis, after she had eschewed medical treatment in favor of prayer and faith healing, it had somehow disappeared. But it did show something: the cancer was gone.

"I knew immediately that He had taken out the cancer, that the pain was all from Him removing the cancer," Eva said, her voice trembling as though she were telling the story for the first time. "The doctors didn't believe what I told them, but of course I knew they wouldn't. They asked if I had a surgery somewhere, but they found no signs on my belly, no stitches, no nothing. But the proof of His miracle was on the CT scan."

My mother, who'd by then been practicing medicine for more than twenty years, fully believed Eva's story. She'd even pointed out other examples of mysterious healings that physicians couldn't explain. There was an Englishwoman with a melon-size ovarian tumor who'd made it disappear simply with prayer and positive thinking. There was another member of our spiritual community who'd cured her breast cancer simply by changing her diet and meditating several hours a day. Yet when my mother told me these stories, I'd argue with her. *How do you know Eva didn't go to another hospital and have the surgery done?* I asked. *What if the first CT scan had been wrong and there was never any cancer to begin with?* Even though she and my father extolled the virtues of medicine and hoped I'd be a doctor someday, they told my brother and me these stories for a different reason. Medicine and science, while great servants of humanity, gave us the illusion that we could fully know and control the vagaries of life. But having faith meant surrender. It meant having trust that you will be taken care of no matter what the circumstance, knowing that ultimately most of life couldn't be understood or accepted by reading books or looking to control what was ultimately unknowable. I think my parents told us these stories over and over again because they hoped that examples of people nearly dying from ailments that God, not medicine, cured would be convincing proof of faith's necessity. Their faith was their bedrock; they feared that, without faith, my brother and I would skid on life's loose soils, collapsing when the earth shook.

But when I heard Eva tell her own story this time, something in me softened. Her cancer had been confirmed through a biopsy; the shadows on the CT scan hadn't been an infection or a benign growth of cells. There had been no stitches or drains or other external evidence of a surgery. I surprised myself by believing that He had indeed canceled her cancer. I scanned her from top to bottom, from the coarse black curls cascading down her back, to her distinct collarbones and lean arms, to her straight back, which had not tired or curved in the least despite sitting cross-legged on the ground for more than an hour. The story she told wasn't tied to my parents' attempts to convince my brother and me of the importance of faith. Yet I turned over my parents' words as I heard her speak, reflecting on the things I couldn't prove or understand or explain, but somehow, at a level beyond emotion and language, felt might be true.

....

I returned to my conversation with Mary and Steven, echoes of Eva's words still on my mind.

"I can understand that God plays a role in all of our lives and can be the source of tremendous miracles," I began. "But I think we should talk about the differences I see between your situation and Jack's situation."

"We are all the same in the eyes of God," Steven replied. "There are no differences between his situation and mine."

"I understand," I continued, intending to say more, but no more words came. The truth was that I didn't understand. What he was saying actually didn't apply in this situation. Yes, we were all equal in God's eyes, but we did not all suffer equally from diseases. We didn't all have the same destiny. I had not anticipated this fierce conceptual gridlock, a face-off between faith and medicine that I'd hoped to avoid. I found myself in the position of Eva's doctors, who must have thought her deranged, insane maybe, for refusing their tested and true treatments in favor of praying to God for a miraculous cure. And yet, He canceled her cancer. I instinctively understood Steven's insistence that God could heal what doctors could not. I was in my own gridlock, caught between having known people including Eva who lived despite all odds because of miraculous interventions, and having cared in hospitals for so many patients like Jack, who never recovered neurologically and instead suffered infection after infection until they died. Usually in the ICU. Often in the company of more plastic tubes and catheters in their veins than visitors. Usually with doctors standing around wondering why the families of these patients insisted that we force the dying body to live, only to have it respond with clearer and stronger statements that, no matter what we did, it was shutting down. I didn't know how to bring the conversation back to Jack, since we had drifted so far from what we'd set out to discuss. But then, perhaps talking about God and medicine was the only way Mary and Steven could manage to talk about Jack.

Dr. Nguyen spoke just then, nudging away the silence with her soft voice.

"Thank you for sharing your thoughts, Steven. Jack is very lucky to have a father who has such deep faith and positivity, and cares so much for his well-being."

Steven nodded, looking at Mary.

"I wonder if you can tell me more about how God has helped you through your own illness?" she asked.

Steven enthusiastically shared that his illness wasn't the first time he had called on God. He had prayed every morning from the time he was five years old, not only because his mother insisted on it but because he eventually found peace and comfort from the ritual, and freedom in disclosing to God what he couldn't share with others. He spoke to God about his ailing father and his failing grades. He prayed to survive to adulthood in a neighborhood known for break-ins and stray bullets. God led him to Mary. God enabled them to conceive Jack when Mary had been told she was infertile. When he was diagnosed with a disease that robbed him of his independence, he saw it as yet another test of faith—if he prayed earnestly, surely God would listen. "And he did," Steven said. "I'm still here. I know God will come through for us again and heal Jack."

"It's interesting how God reveals His will to us," Dr. Nguyen continued. "Sometimes He does test our faith, sometimes He presents us with challenges that He has given us the tools to overcome."

I wondered where exactly she was taking the conversation, hanging on her every word.

"Can you tell me more about Jack and about who he was before he got sick? What did he enjoy doing?" *Ah yes*, I thought. I hadn't even bothered to ask.

"He was a happy boy," Mary began. "He never caused trouble. Let's see . . . he liked sports, he liked playing baseball. He always helped me around the house." She told us a story of the time Jack started cutting school to practice baseball; he'd always wanted to play professionally.

"He also had a very strong faith," Steven added. "He went to church, he believed in God. He was a strong boy."

"And sometimes, no matter how strong our faith is, God has a plan for us that we may not understand," Dr. Nguyen said. "And He reveals His plan to us in different ways. He clearly responded to your prayers, Steven, and gave your body much more time and strength than the doctors thought you would have. But Jack's situation may be different in God's eyes, even when we pray and pray for it to be different."

"Okay," Steven said slowly, his rising pitch tinged with skepticism.

"Jack's body is showing us something different than your body did, Steven," Dr. Nguyen continued, then paused. "Despite all of the care he has gotten from many doctors, perhaps God is showing us, through Jack's body, that He wants Jack home sooner than you want. Sooner than we all want."

I listened, awestruck, to the way that Dr. Nguyen spoke to Steven and Mary authentically and in a language they understood, a language she believed. She said everything I had hoped to communicate, but in a way that they could hear.

"I know my son," Mary said, "and I know that the doctors all see his sick body, but I know he is still in there. He wants to live. Don't forget that he is just a boy. My son." Mary burst into tears, holding her head in her hands, sobbing.

Dr. Nguyen welcomed a spacious silence—one that held Mary's tears and Steven's determined stoicism. "Mary, I can see how much you are suffering. It is so hard to see your own child in and out of the hospital. Do you think that Jack may be experiencing any suffering?"

"Sometimes when I am with him, I see tears in his eyes. Then they fall on his cheeks," she said. "Sometimes I wonder if he is in pain and can't even tell us. I just don't know."

"If his brain isn't working and he can't even tell what is going on, then how can you even tell if he is suffering?" Steven asked Mary, his tone defensive. "Maybe the tears mean nothing."

Steven's desperation was palpable. He barely listened to Dr. Nguyen at times, sharing his thoughts before she finished hers. *My mind is already made up about my son's fate and there's nothing you can say to change it.* I might have stopped the meeting at this point out of anger and frustration, but also for fear of alienating Steven and Mary. Dr. Nguyen found a gentle way to keep going.

"There are different types of things that can cause pain and suffering," Dr. Nguyen began. "Some of those things have nothing to do with the body. They could have to do with losing certain parts of ourselves when we get sick, losing the ability to do the things we love. Things like playing baseball or going to church or just being able to be a young man in the world."

"Yes, obviously because of his condition he cannot do any of those things," Mary replied. "But at least he is still alive."

"One thing that I think would help before we meet again is to really try to think about what Jack would say if God gave him a few minutes to speak," Dr. Nguyen said. "You are right that we have been able to keep Jack alive, but I think we should also talk about his quality of life," she continued gently. "One of the best things we can do for people we love is to try to figure out what they would consider most important to them if they are very sick and we may not be able to get them healthy again."

"We'll discuss this," Steven said shortly.

"Please, please keep doing everything you can for my son," Mary pleaded.

Dr. Nguyen took Mary's hands and smiled serenely. "We are. Part of doing everything for him means having this talk."

. . . .

During those first months of fellowship, I would think back to the fight I'd had with my parents when I told them about my interest in palliative care. *Shouldn't every doctor be able to treat suffering? At that point in their lives, isn't it between the patient and God?* Even my friends outside of medicine assumed that treating patients' symptoms and discussing their mortality was part of every doctor's job. If one is in the business of treating illness, surely one must also have the skills to recognize and discuss debility, mortality, suffering. What had happened to medicine, to medical practice, that enabled us to become physicians without acquiring the skills I was now learning? Were we so blinded by the shiny allure and promise of technology and scientific innovation that we'd convinced ourselves we could defy nature, overlook the common human experience of death and suffering? Were we so focused on learning facts and procedures that we'd forgotten to consider medicine's limits? Had the time pressure to see more and more patients convinced us that we couldn't take on the sorts of discussions we at some level knew were important? Had we built such a strong identity around always being able to offer something, anything, to patients that we prescribed medications or performed procedures out of a sense of professional obligation? Were we so paralyzed by the thought of litigation that we treated patients with procedures they demanded—especially toward life's end—rather than considering the immense harm inherent in these offerings?

As I grew into my role, my field's existence struck me as a sad necessity, thanks to changes in medical practice. But watching Dr. Nguyen speak with Mary and Steven reminded me why our specialty mattered. We weren't around to become other physicians' mouthpieces or to have all difficult conversations outsourced to us. We didn't expect that other physicians would lose the ability to treat pain and nausea and send all patients in the throes of physical suffering to us. But perhaps we practiced medicine with a slightly different understanding of empathy—one that, as Leslie Jamison writes, "isn't just listening, it's asking the questions whose answers need to be listened to. Empathy requires inquiry as much as imagination. . . . Empathy means acknowledging a horizon of context that extends perpetually beyond what you can see."

This isn't to say that other doctors lack empathy, or that we must choose between practicing empathy and practicing medicine. I could understand my friends' confusion, their expectation that all doctors should be able to do this work. But I couldn't envision another doctor having the conversation that Dr. Nguyen led.

"How do you do it, Dr. Nguyen?" I asked when we got back to our office.

"What do you mean?" she replied, laughing as she offered me roasted almonds from her stash of snacks.

"I was getting irritated with them, but you kept your cool the whole time!"

Dr. Nguyen shrugged. "I was sometimes frustrated with them, but then I reminded myself of how many times they must have been told that Jack is going to die and didn't, and how much they must hate these conversations. So I thought, what can I do to make this conversation different? Is there another way to approach the situation that would give them permission to understand things differently?"

"And asking about Steven's beliefs was a way for you to understand how he and Mary were making sense of Jack's situation?" I asked.

"Yes. Before we went and met with Mary and Steven, I had to remind myself that our first obligation is to understand their perspective on Jack's care. Only then can I help them understand the medical team's concerns. If we don't try first to understand Mary and Steven, then we can't help Jack."

I nodded and started to type my note documenting our conversation with Jack's parents. As I wrote, I wondered what we would discuss at our next meeting, especially if Mary and Steven insisted on treatments that we all felt might not benefit Jack. "Dr. Nguyen, what if at the next meeting his parents say again that they want everything done for Jack? How would you handle that knowing what you know about them?"

Dr. Nguyen sighed. "I am hoping that they will think about what will really help Jack to find peace, but you never know. If they ask for treatments like CPR, I think it's then up to us and the medicine team to think about whether we should offer it."

Throughout my training, I'd heard the opposite. I'd felt obligated to describe all treatment options available to a patient and let them choose whichever one they wanted. I thought I was honoring patient autonomy, empowering patients to make decisions they felt were best for their lives and bodies. But I wondered why I sometimes offered patients treatments that I wished they'd decline. Deep down, I knew I wanted them to assume responsibility for making tough choices. When patients asked what I would recommend, I felt obligated to turn the question back onto them, asking them what plan they felt comfortable pursuing. "I don't think I can make that decision for you, but I can give you the information you need to make a good decision for yourself," I'd say, silently hoping they would pick the option I would recommend if I felt empowered to. We didn't ask patients to choose which antibiotics we should use to treat an infection. But we handed over responsibility for the most consequential decisions, especially toward life's end, to patients and families. Yet patient autonomy—the power to choose the type of care that was most in line with one's goals and values—hinged on a clear understanding of how the therapies we offered might or might not benefit a patient. When we'd offer dialysis or third-line chemotherapy, we'd frame these interventions as possibilities. We were more opaque about how these possibilities may or may not be helpful. Sometimes, I felt like nothing more than a waitress taking an order. *Okay, so we're doing the dialysis and the pressors and, if your heart stops, you want the chest compressions but not the shocks?* Making a recommendation, especially against a life-prolonging therapy, felt off-limits.

"Are we even allowed to tell them that we won't do CPR for Jack even if they insist that we do it?" I asked Dr. Nguyen curiously. "I always thought we had to honor a family's wish since it's a matter of life or death."

"Well, let me ask you this. Do you think that CPR will save Jack's life?" Dr. Nguyen asked, crunching on more almonds.

"It depends what you mean by 'save his life.' There's a chance we could get his heart started again, but I don't think it will prevent another infection or make his quality of life any better, only worse," I said.

"So would you recommend CPR as an option for Jack?" Dr. Nguyen pressed me.

"Well, no. If I were the one doing CPR on Jack, I'd hate myself. I would have no idea what I'd be trying to do for him. I'd feel like the family was asking me to torture him."

Dr. Nguyen nodded. "So here's the thing. We are trained to let patients decide for themselves what they want us to do for them. Which is fine in some situations, but not always when patients are as unstable as Jack. That's when we need to rethink the strategy of presenting all possible options and asking a patient to choose."

"So you choose for them?" I asked, confused.

"No, but we seriously consider what options we *should* offer. This happens all the time. Surgeons won't take a patient to the operating room if they really feel the patient would die during the surgery. Oncologists will say a patient isn't physically strong enough to get harsh chemotherapy. CPR is a medical intervention, just like surgery or chemotherapy. My personal theory is that we aren't as confident recommending against CPR because we ourselves can't face the fact of a patient dying without trying something, anything, to keep them alive." I nodded slowly as she spoke, taking in her perspective. "And families feel that they want to give their loved one every chance to stay alive. But we shouldn't put a patient through an uncomfortable procedure with no payoff."

Dr. Nguyen was right. I sheepishly thought back to residency, when I'd cared for a man I thought was crazy for choosing dialysis when his kidneys were failing because of his widespread cancer. In reality, I'd been the crazy one for offering dialysis and hoping he'd say no. I'd tried to dissuade him from choosing dialysis by reciting lengthy lists of the many discomforts it could cause—bleeding and infection from the large IV I'd need to place, nausea and fatigue from the dialysis itself. I'd even gone so far as to ask him, "Are you sure you want me to do this?" when he'd made his decision.

"And you are absolutely right," Dr. Nguyen continued. "CPR might restore Jack's heartbeat, but getting to the point where he'd need CPR would be the strongest evidence that he is dying despite everything we have done."

"How are you going to tell them this?" I wondered aloud.

"It depends on how the conversation goes. They may have already come to the conclusion that Jack should simply be allowed to die a natural death. But if they ask for CPR, I will have to make a recommendation against it. It all rests on bringing them to the same sort of understanding you and I have about CPR in Jack's situation." Dr. Nguyen smiled and nodded. "I know this is a very different perspective on family discussions. But I think we've become afraid of making recommendations to patients, and they need our recommendations the most in situations like Jack's."

This, too, is a reason why our field was so necessary, I thought as I drove home. Even the smartest, kindest physicians who trained me in residency would probably offer Jack's parents the option of CPR and respect whatever decision they made, while secretly dreading the prospect of compressing his chest if his heart actually did stop. Offering every possible option might spare us litigation or quiet angry families who wanted "everything" done for a loved one. And each of us carried within us a handful of stories of patients who had survived and left the hospital even when we had told their families it was time to let them die peacefully. The fear of condemning a potential survivor to death haunted us, distorted our decision making. After all, we'd never know what was possible unless we tried. But did shaping our medical practice around these perspectives really empower patients? Or did it just cause more suffering not only for patients and families but also for the doctors and nurses who cared for them?

....

In our next meeting, Mary and Steven told us that they had talked with their priest about Jack's condition. They told us that the priest advised against CPR, which surprised them. You must think about the quality of his life, their priest had said. Catholicism affirms life, but not when preserving life comes at the cost of immense suffering. It is okay to let Jack go when it is his time, he'd told them. Though Mary and Steven felt relieved that their church would support a decision against CPR, they also thought making that decision meant giving up on their child, which they couldn't bring themselves to do. "Our decision is to let God make the call," Steven said. "So we think it is best for the doctors to do everything in their power, including CPR, and if it is Jack's time, he will die no matter what the doctors do."

Dr. Nguyen nodded. "I am so glad that you were able to talk about this with your priest. These are very hard decisions to think about. CPR can be a good treatment for some patients who are otherwise healthy and who we expect to fully recover. But for Jack, CPR would not fix the reasons why his heart would stop if he had an infection we can't treat. It would only prolong his dying. It wouldn't give him the life you hope it would."

"But how do you know for sure, Doctor? You aren't God, so all you can do is provide for Jack what you would provide for all patients and leave the rest up to Him," Steven replied calmly.

"That is exactly right, Steven," Dr. Nguyen said. "The doctors taking care of Jack, we're all human. I wouldn't offer CPR to a patient as sick as Jack, simply because it would not fix the reasons he is so sick. Needing CPR would show us that all our attempts to head him hadn't worked."

Steven and Mary looked at each other. "How can you as a doctor say you won't try to save our son?" Mary asked, confused.

"It's not that we don't want to save your son. But we as doctors cannot save every patient. Only God has that power. We are all very worried that we cannot save Jack. Our duty to him is to make sure he doesn't suffer from his condition just because we can't save him."

"Only God has that final say," Steven said firmly.

"What do you think happens when God calls us home? What might that look like for Jack?" Dr. Nguyen asked gently.

"I don't want him to suffer, no pain or anything," Mary said. "When it's his time, we will know and we will let him go."

"Nobody would want their child to suffer," Dr. Nguyen said. "I have an idea I want to share with you that may prevent Jack from suffering when it is his time, and an idea to shift our focus, then, to his quality of life for the time that God gives him."

"You mean, we should just let him die?" Steven said indignantly. "Is that what doctors do now? Tell families that there's nothing left to do?"

Steven's desperation was palpable. Though his words angered me, they also made me sad. He was a father losing his son slowly. Of course it wasn't easy for him to hear what Dr. Nguyen had to say. But hearing him argue with Dr. Nguyen also exhausted me.

"Doctors are human, Steven," Dr. Nguyen said, unfazed. "We can do everything in our power for patients, but we also have a duty to tell you when we are approaching our limits so that we can figure out how to care for Jack if we cannot fix or cure him. I know this is very painful to talk about. But for Jack's sake, I do think we need to discuss it."

She is not backing down, I thought. *Yet there is nothing adversarial about this conversation from her end. This is grace.*

"Why are we talking about the end of his life right now?" Steven said. "He is still alive! Last time you said the antibiotics are working!"

Dr. Nguyen took a deep breath and paused, a technique she told me she drew upon to allow strong emotions—both hers and others'—to disperse before making her point. "Remember what Dr. Puri mentioned, Steven? She said that all of us taking care of Jack just want to talk about the best way to care for him if he gets sicker, which we think that he will sometime soon. It might not be now. But we need to have a plan when this happens. It will be so hard if we don't."

"So what do you suggest?" Mary asked.

"When the time comes that Jack has an infection with bacteria that are stronger than our best medications, then our putting him through the types of treatment he is getting now will not fix the infection. If he gets so sick that our worldly treatments cannot fix him, that is how we might know that God is calling him. Stopping the heart is God's call. And I think we should respect that call, knowing that we have done everything we can to try to save him." Dr. Nguyen was kind but firm, and then silent.

God's call. A tiny phrase I had never heard in a medical conversation. Two words that said something enormous, eternal: dying is spiritual, not just medical. The moment of death can be sacred.

"So what would you do then?" Mary asked.

"We would give him medicines to ease any pain or difficulty breathing he might have, or any other symptoms of distress. We would do this knowing that unfortunately his body may no longer respond to any antibiotics. Our focus would be giving him quality time with you, until it is time for him to return to God."

"But Jesus can perform miracles. We believe this. We believe our son will recover miraculously. That is what keeps us going, helps us to survive," Mary said.

"Mary, tell me what a miracle would look like to you," I said, inviting myself back into the conversation.

"It would be Jesus healing my son so he could talk and walk and be himself again," Mary said, adding, "It pains me to see him the way he is. No mother would want this for their child. Any mother would pray for this same miracle!"

"We all hope for miracles, all the time," I said slowly. "But I sometimes have to remind myself what a miracle really is. It's something truly unexpected, something that usually does not happen. It's something really exceptional. Which is why it's a miracle. I completely understand why you are hoping and praying for a miracle. I would do the same. But I also want to make sure we have another plan in place if the miracle isn't part of God's plan for Jack." I spoke the words I'd written down recently in my journal as I thought about Jack's case and Eva and my parents and the nature of miracles.

Mary cried. I felt horrible, unable to say anything reassuring or comforting, because, truly, there was little in this situation that could be reassuring or comforting.

"We don't want him to suffer," Steven said quietly. Mary continued to cry. He reached out to pat her hand, fingering the golden cross just below his throat. "We are just parents, wanting the best for our son."

"Maybe then what you are saying makes sense," Mary said, shaking her head. "If he isn't going to live no matter what you do, if his heart stops, then the best we can do is just let him go in peace."

I thought then of the other musings I'd written about in my diary, the difference between Eva's miraculous recovery and Steven's miraculous survival, and the smaller, everyday miracles that humans themselves were capable of. *Could it be miraculous when people keep going even when the odds are stacked against them? Could it be miraculous to accept a situation no matter what the outcome?* I'd written.

Though we'd actually hoped to talk about issues aside from CPR, this felt like the right time to close the meeting. "I think you are making a good decision for Jack," I said quietly, acknowledging how difficult this conversation had been. "We can still hope for the miracle of him waking up and being himself again. But it is also a miracle that he is still here with us after everything he has gone through. And I'm not sure that would have happened without your love."

Steven avoided my gaze. "Thank you," he whispered.

. . . .

My father returned from the catheterization lab groggy but smiling. They had discovered a 90 percent blockage of one of his coronary arteries, which was now held open with a stent. "He was joking with us almost the whole time," the cardiologist told me. "We had to tell him to stop so that we could focus on his heart." My father looked up at him just then and asked, "Hey, are there free refills on the morphine?"

My mother wiped her eyes and placed her hand on his chest, right over the photograph of Lord Ganesha. "Thank you," she said to the picture, pressing her hand into his chest and closing her eyes.

"I saw my heart," my father told me. "I saw all the images after they put the dye in me. It was so beautiful, beating there on a screen. I even saw where the problem was. It was just a blocked-up pipe and they unclogged it."

My face crumpled, eyes squeezed shut, mouth tense and breath held, exhaling as tears of relief spilled onto my shirt. I shooed away the thoughts that had filled my mind when he was in the catheterization lab, preparing me for the possible reality of life without my father.

"But weren't you scared? How could you have been joking with them?" I asked between sobs.

"Nope," he said. "God was with me the whole time." He patted the photo of Lord Ganesha. "Nothing would go wrong."

"But what if it had? What if something did go wrong?"

My father looked at me, laughing again. "If He had wanted to take me, I would have been gone when I first had the chest pain. Instead, the chest pain was His warning, and now I am fixed," he told me. "But if this was my time to go, then it would have been okay. He would have made sure to take me fast, not let me linger around here," he said, pointing to the ceiling.

"But I wouldn't have been okay. I would never be okay again if you were gone," I said through my tears. *How is it so easy for him to say this, like his death wouldn't be a big deal? Why does he think that rationale and logic could somehow make loss more bearable?*

"Well, then you would only suffer more if you couldn't find a way to accept rather than fight against reality, and I wouldn't want you to suffer like that," my father replied, again using his Mr. Socrates voice. "It doesn't mean giving up or giving in. But it means that you see what you can and cannot change, and learn to be okay with that. Acceptance is really a spiritual lesson. It's something we need God to help us with."

"Okay, Ashok, no more talking about this," my mother said, pulling his blanket up to cover his chest. "You need to rest."

"My manager has spoken," my father said, smiling. "See? I have even learned to accept that I have to do what she says."

. . . .

After our conversation, Jack's parents watched over the next five days as he got a bit sicker before getting better, watching his blood pressure and heart rate, looking for signs that he might try to speak. I examined Jack every day to make sure he was comfortable. The morning before he was discharged back to his facility, Mary asked if she could talk to me.

"You and Dr. Nguyen told us things nobody wants to hear and I was very angry at you both," she confessed. "But I talked to my family about it. I guess I understand now that if I told you to put him through those things, like CPR, I think he would only get hurt, not get better because he is so weak."

"It is really hard to come to that realization," I said. "Especially about your own child."

"Yes," she said as she stroked Jack's face. "But I just have to accept whatever God's plan for him is."

"My father has always told me that learning acceptance is one of the hardest parts of living," I said, thinking back to our conversation after his catheterization. "And accepting this awful situation has got to be some of the hardest work you've ever done."

"Your father is right," she said, wiping her face. "And it is hard to know what you should accept and what you should fight. That is where you let God guide you."

And maybe this is what faith is all about—having a way to understand and accept and endure the most incomprehensible things that happen to us. Having faith didn't have to mean subscribing to a certain set of religious beliefs or praying to a deity or going through elaborate rituals in a church or temple or mosque. Maybe it meant surrendering the complete control we assume we have over our lives, and instead opening to the idea that another force, benevolent and mysterious, looked after us. Maybe it meant practicing acceptance of whatever life brings our way. And maybe it also meant remembering that our sorrows and joys, just like our bodies, were temporary.

I watched Mary redo the braid in Jack's hair and spray citrus air freshener on his pillow. His eyes looked watery. I wondered, as she did, if he was crying. I asked her if we could fill out a form called a POLST (Physician Order for Life Sustaining Treatment) that would travel with Jack back to his care facility. The form was a way of letting Jack's caregivers and emergency responders know that when Jack died, we would focus on keeping him pain free and comfortable rather than performing CPR to jump-start his heart. "Can he still come to the hospital if he gets sick?" Mary asked. "Yes, of course," I told her. "But it is important to keep in mind what we talked about. We may not have the tools we need to help him fight another infection here, but even if we do not, he can always come back here and we will do whatever we can to keep him comfortable and well cared for."

Mary nodded. "Doctor, will you pray for him?" she asked timidly. I willed myself not to tear up. She was asking me to care for her son—and, indirectly, for her—in a very specific way, one that drew on my humanity, not my profession. She was asking me to remember him after he left the hospital in a few hours. Her request felt more serious than requests patients and families had made of me in the past; this wasn't a request for Hail Mary chemotherapy or another CT scan to identify a problem. This was a request for a blessing.

"Of course I will pray for him and for you and Steven," I said, giving her a hug. I felt the stiffness of her hairspray-lacquered bob against my face, and inhaled the scent of the citrus spray on Jack's pillow. Later that day, the *Gayatri* ran through my mind as I watched the paramedics transfer him from his hospital bed into a transport gurney, careful not to dislodge his feeding tube or his tracheostomy. That was the last time I'd see Jack and his parents. One of the hardest parts of seeing patients in the hospital was that I rarely knew what happened to them once they left, especially when I rotated from one hospital to the next. *Please protect Jack and give his parents the strength to let him be at peace when it is his time to go*, I wrote in a letter that I kept on my altar that night, right next to a figurine of Lord Ganesha and an illustration of Goddess Durga that my grandmother had given my mother, who'd passed it on to me.

....

I would run into Dr. Nguyen about a month after Jack left the hospital, when I had moved on to another rotation. We attended a lecture at the Stanford campus and caught up afterward. She would tell me that she had learned that Jack had died recently in the emergency room. He had contracted another infection shortly after returning to the nursing home. His temperature rose and his blood pressure plummeted. The nursing home staff called the paramedics, who'd reassured Mary and Steven that Jack would get better once he got antibiotics and fluids at the hospital. But as they lifted Jack onto a gurney, his heart, initially racing at a rate of 120, suddenly slowed to the 30s. Jack's heart stopped, and Mary and Steven asked the paramedics to do whatever they needed to do to save their son. One of the emergency room notes mentioned that Mary had torn up the POLST we'd filled out and signed together.

The team of doctors and nurses in the emergency room tried for an hour to restart his heart with chest compressions, shocks, and doses of epinephrine pushed through his IV. He died there in that room, several floors below the ward where Dr. Nguyen and I had discussed how little benefit and how much suffering CPR would cause him.

I imagined Jack's wrinkle-free face, his braid, his pillow and quilt, covered with the necessary clutter of emergency situations: IVs and their sterile wrapping, smatters of blood from the placement of central lines or collection of labs, wires dangling from cardiac monitors and the ventilator. I winced as I thought of what he went through, of what must have caused his mother to tear up the form meant to protect him from exactly this situation. I wished that he'd died in the middle of the night, in between nursing shifts, so that he could have gone in peace. I hoped for his parents' sake that they would remember him by how he looked the day or week before he died, not how he looked at the end.

"Why would they put him through that?" I wondered when Dr. Nguyen told me the news. "I really thought we'd helped them to make the right decision."

"It's hard to say. People panic. Parents panic," she told me. "But you should remember that we did help them, even though the outcome wasn't what we hoped for him. It's like doing a surgery that didn't fix a patient. The work was still important."

I didn't find comfort in Dr. Nguyen's words. I couldn't understand how she was so calm and collected about this. All our work ultimately didn't do a thing for Jack, I thought angrily. It was as though we hadn't been involved at all. What had all of those conversations meant if Jack's parents stuck to their original plan? I longed for the days when I could diagnose cirrhosis or lymphoma, treat pneumonias and heart attacks, even if it meant that this was all I did for thirty hours straight every third or fourth night. Though I'd sometimes felt ambivalent about my work, I at least felt useful. These days, I felt like I could throw myself into conversations with patients and the outcome wouldn't necessarily change. What was I supposed to take away from this?

"Remember what we talked about early in your rotation?" Dr. Nguyen asked when I ran into her again the following week. "We have our plans as doctors. But what if God has another plan for our patients? How would you feel if you could say to yourself that you did everything you could but you couldn't control what ultimately happened to Jack?"

I thought about Dr. Nguyen's words that evening as I boiled capellini and stirred a pot of tomato sauce I'd made from scratch. It struck me that I might practice palliative care, but I was just as vulnerable as my colleagues in other fields to the illusion of control over the outcome of every situation I encountered. If other doctors believed they could fix a situation no matter how dire, I thought I could get patients to make and stick to the "right" decisions about the most tender time in their lives. I thought of my father's words, and of Cheryl Strayed's essay. Perhaps here, by way of my chosen subspecialty, was the opportunity to learn more about surrender and acceptance, and to see that our belief in control was a false story we told ourselves to make life and its unexpected sorrows survivable. Yet acceptance wasn't acquiescence. Could there be salvation, comfort, in relaxing my tight grip on life, letting it unfold as it would both for myself and for my patients, knowing that I'd played my part? I reread what I'd written about the nature of miracles and practiced saying to Jack's parents: "Could it be accepting a situation no matter what the outcome?"

And I realized that, in order to keep doing this work, this applied to me, too.

Seven

GASP

On Monday mornings in fellowship, I had a welcome break from seeing patients in the hospital. Instead, I saw patients in our palliative medicine clinic at the Palo Alto veterans hospital. Our clinic was on the second floor of a cream-colored building. I'd see patients in a nondescript exam room furnished sparsely with a gray examination table, desk, and computer. There might have been a lone poster of the human body's anatomy on the white wall. In this sterile space, I'd talk with my patients about the messiest of their emotions, the way their symptoms contaminated and constrained their lives.

The list of patients we saw was small but growing. Unlike many of the patients I saw in the hospital, many of my clinic patients were still able to walk and talk and be themselves. We spoke when they wore their own clothes instead of hospital gowns. I treated their pain before it was so severe that they ended up in the hospital. I talked with them over time about life with their illness and their desired goals and quality of life should they suddenly become sicker. By the time I was called to care for patients in the hospital, many were close to dying from cancer or heart failure or liver disease. But my clinic patients—who were sick, but not sick enough to require hospitalization—needed my help living well.

I met Dave on an August morning, about a month after fellowship began. Dave had emphysema—a chronic, irreversible lung disease caused by years of smoking. He suffered from terrible shortness of breath, despite the inhalers and medications he took religiously. As his breathlessness worsened, his appetite waned and he became more fatigued, sleeping through his alarm and sometimes going to bed well before dusk. His primary care doctor referred him to our clinic hoping that we could help ease the sensation Dave called "that feeling of drowning on land." The electronic referral request also mentioned that his doctor had tried unsuccessfully to talk to Dave about what he would want for himself as his emphysema worsened; he wondered if we could assist with that conversation, too.

While most patients feared excruciating pain, there was something about air hunger, that sensation of breathlessness, that struck me as a different form of profound suffering. Seeing a patient panting, mobilizing sinewy neck muscles to gasp for the largest breath possible, is a struggle for me. My internal medicine training kicked in as I scrolled through Dave's chart: Could his heart failure have contributed to his struggle to breathe? Did he have a blood clot in his lungs because he had been more sedentary recently? Should I order a CT scan of his lungs and an ultrasound of his heart? I wrote down my preliminary thoughts just as I had in residency, reminding myself that in order to be an effective palliative care doctor and treat his symptoms, I needed to understand and treat their causes.

Dave thought I was much younger than I am, and addressed me with the affection of a father: "You must not even have been born when Bush Senior was president! No way you could know much about the Vietnam War, but I fought there, and they would give us cigarettes. I loved my cigarettes. Still do, but no, I haven't had one in the last few years, don't worry, Doc!" Dave hissed when he laughed, his upper chest convulsing and the oxygen tubing falling slightly out of his nose. He stopped laughing and placed his hands on his knees, sucked in a deep breath through his mouth, and looked at me, smiling. He carried his oxygen tank in a zipped black canvas bag, which also contained his inhalers and plastic bags full of his medications. His fingers were thin and knobby from arthritis, and his nails were tinged blue from the chronic lack of oxygen that emphysema caused. Dave was seventy years old, but looked ninety to me.

"You know, Doc, my breathing seems to be getting worse even though I'm taking all of my medications and my inhalers, everything," he said, pausing for a breath after one sentence accentuated by hand gestures and shrugs. Donna came to mind, and I thought of how having a conversation tired her in the way a long run might exhaust me. I didn't need to look at the notes in his electronic chart to see that his emphysema was end-stage. "I'm working on some important family stuff, so I need to be able to at least walk to my truck, drive, and get home again. But it's been at least two weeks since I could do any of that without getting very winded," he told me.

I examined Dave thoroughly and found no obvious signs that his heart failure had worsened or that he had a blood clot in his lungs. He convulsed with coughs when I asked him to take a deep breath. I felt the sharp borders of his shoulder blades and each of his vertebrae as I rested my stethoscope on his back. His lungs whistled emphysema's distinct wind song.

"I have a couple thoughts for you, Dave," I said as I folded my stethoscope and placed it on the desk. I told him that a small dose of morphine might help ease the breathlessness he suffered even after taking his inhalers and other medications. I braced myself for a strong reaction; the word "morphine," much like the word "hospice," could provoke fear in patients who interpreted its prescription as a harbinger of death.

But Dave didn't react to my suggestion. He'd seen morphine work very well for his mother, who had died years before from ovarian cancer. Morphine might bring great relief, he told me, but he objected to the drowsiness he knew it would cause. "I've gotta be able to drive myself and be clear of mind," he said quickly, shaking his head when I inquired whether he would consider public transport or getting rides from friends. "My brother just died and his house is a mess, so I gotta go up there and get it in order so that my son can live there. The house is up in the mountains, so I can't ask anyone else to drive me there all the time. And I gotta go to the bank and deal with his financial mess."

"That's a lot to take on by yourself," I said, genuinely surprised that Dave was using his declining reserves of energy to undertake such mammoth tasks. "Can your son help out at all? Maybe he can give you lifts?"

"He's out on parole, Doc," Dave said, and took a puff of his inhaler. "Probably best if I keep some distance from him."

I nodded, hoping that Dave would offer more, but he didn't. He had just used his inhaler, but he stopped again to suck air inward through his pursed lips, raising his shoulders, exhaling softly.

"How about this," I proposed. "Why don't you have a think about trying the liquid morphine? I'm talking about an incredibly small dose, a baby dose, because that might be all you need to get some relief. We can talk about it some more next time if you want. I could even print out some information for you if you want to read it over."

"Sure, I'll think about it," Dave said. "No need to print anything out right now."

I nervously watched Dave gather his oxygen tank and adjust his nasal tubing, pausing for a sharp inhale before he got up and exhaled, inhaling again before he got to the door. How was he managing at home? I wondered after he'd left, realizing that I'd neglected to ask about that huge, essential part of our conversation because I'd been so focused on getting him feeling better. As I wrote my note in his chart, I added a reminder to ask the questions I hadn't at our next appointment in two weeks.

. . . .

I moved through the rest of my day feeling unsettled, and it took me until the evening to understand why. Dave's breathing pattern reminded me of my grandmother, who had died of emphysema thirteen years earlier, in July 2000. It wasn't cigarette smoke that stiffened her delicate lung tissue, rendering it unable to stretch and accommodate the tides of breath she gasped for. It was just the air in Mumbai. Breathing it daily for many years made her sick, my mother told me. She had survived the violence of India's independence only to settle in a city whose air would take her life.

My grandmother enjoyed stretches of respite from Mumbai's air only during her trips to Louisville, Kentucky, when she visited my mother during her residency. Without speaking a word of English, my grandmother had somehow secured a visa and passport and made her way from Mumbai to New York, catching a connecting flight to Louisville. She clasped a note that my mother's brother, Uncle Raju, had written in English to help airport staff in New York direct her to the correct gate: "Please help me find my flight to Louisville. I do not speak any English."

After my birth, she witnessed my mother's struggle to balance caring for me, her first child, during an unforgiving residency that allowed her only two weeks' worth of maternity leave prior to returning to a grueling training schedule and her looming licensing exam. Watching my mother's fatigue grow, my grandmother offered to take me back to Mumbai and care for me until my mother completed her exams.

One week after this discussion, my mother covered me with kisses and tears, watching from the window of our tiny apartment as my father drove my grandmother and me to the airport. She wondered if this was migration's jagged edge, the price she must pay for leaving Mumbai: that her daughter, new to this world, would spend eight months in the old world without her mother.

I was just six months old. While I don't remember much about the eight months I spent with my grandmother, black-and-white photographs from that time suggest that I was happy: I slept next to my grandmother in a small bed in my uncle's flat, where she now lived. She fed me the rice and lentils she had fed my mother, and I would clap my hands and smile afterward. She had me vaccinated against tuberculosis by a local pediatrician. The characteristic imprint of the BCG vaccine on my left shoulder—an imprint that marked my parents and many immigrants at that time—is my only reminder of our time together.

I saw her five more times over the next twenty years during trips to India I took with my parents and, in college, by myself. Between trips, we spoke during brief phone calls, though we struggled to hear each other because of the crackling static of the phone connection and the gradual worsening of her cough and raspy voice. My mother was the only one of her siblings who lived overseas. She saw my grandmother on her trips to India, many of them taken alone, when she volunteered as an anesthesiologist at several different hospitals. "The time you spent as a baby with your grandmother was very special to her," my mother told me once. "When you were with her, it was like I was there, too."

The last time I saw my grandmother, in 2000, I'd chosen to spend the summer in Delhi working for a nongovernmental organization. I'd seen her the summer before as well, but in just a year her slender body had become skeletal, her ribs visible underneath her sari blouse. Her hands, which had previously held, comforted, and fed me, were cold to the touch, her fingernails blue from her body's chronic struggle for oxygen. Her face, bloated from taking steroids to ease her breathing, seemed misplaced atop her shrinking frame. She required constant oxygen, just like Dave, and could no longer cook, bathe, or dress herself without help from my uncle Raju and his maid, Anu. He and Anu bathed and powdered her every morning. I watched him tenderly feed her spoonfuls of *daal*, rice, and mixed vegetables with the same tenderness I imagined she had fed me.

When she took naps, I sat or lay down next to her, watching her breathe, alert to signs of danger. In the afternoons, we'd sit together on her bed and look out her window. She pointed at the families of white cranes in the trees across the street. Several females, long-legged and with pristinely clean feathers, jumped from branch to branch, bringing food to their peach-fuzzed young. "*Bagala*," she said when I asked my grandmother the name of these birds. They seemed oblivious to Mumbai's cacophony. Bicycle bells sounded as they weaved between cars and large trucks adorned with colorful decorations and "HORN PLEASE" painted on their bumpers. Thin men pulling wagons full of brick yelled at one another across the street. Hindi film music blared from a chai stall, where two teenagers swayed their hips as the *chaiwalla* poured steaming tea into small steel cups. Two cows huddled together in a patch of shade and mooed at each other. My grandmother laughed at the cows' loud conversation and quickly grew breathless. She took a puff of her inhaler and her breathing became more regular. I asked her repeatedly what I could do to help her feel better. She told me she felt fine, that I worried too much, just like my mother.

How are your studies? she asked me. She'd alternate speaking to me in delicate, precise Hindi and rougher-sounding Punjabi. I joked with her that I was getting married soon, and she grabbed my hand and said, *No! You must finish your studies first!* This was an unfathomable response for a woman of her generation. I suddenly teared up, moved by how her progressiveness had enabled my own life, knowing that she had encouraged my mother with the same words.

Though I watched her shrink and gasp for air, I couldn't admit to myself that she was dying. I avoided the subject with Uncle Raju, though I did ask whether she should see a doctor. She wants to stay at home, he would tell me. Trying to take her to a clinic at this point would simply tire her. I pressed him, telling him I was worried when I saw her gasp for air. Did she need a different medicine? A more powerful oxygen mask? *It passes when she takes the medications she has*, he told me. He took mild offense at my suggestion that a nurse or caregiver should help take care of my grandmother; taking care of his mother was a duty and privilege he wouldn't dare share with anyone outside the family. But, he admitted, sometimes he didn't know what to do for my grandmother when she became breathless even when she used her oxygen and inhalers and steroids. He and Anu would sit with her, giving her extra doses of medications and praying, waiting for these stretches of breathlessness to pass. I'd pull myself close to her thin frame when she gasped at night, wishing I could give her my lungs, my breath. When I took showers, I'd let myself cry, my tears mixing with the water my uncle had warmed on the stove and placed in a bucket. I'd use a smaller plastic bucket to scoop water from the bigger bucket and douse myself, rinsing away my shampoo and my tears. I scooped and cried, scooped and cried, and emerged with puffy eyes and red skin that I'd blame on the warm water. I was overwhelmed by my powerlessness to ease my grandmother's suffering when she'd eased and prevented my mother's, and mine.

....

Dave missed his next appointment with me. Worried that he had been admitted to the hospital, I called him. I didn't usually reach out this way. I was accustomed to patients' missing clinic appointments with me in residency, but I didn't know Dave well enough to guess at the reason that could justify his absence. Had he simply been too busy that day, or had he forgotten, or gotten sicker? The phone number listed in his chart rang endlessly but didn't lead to voicemail. He had no other number, and his emergency contact turned out to be his brother, the one who'd recently died. Surprisingly frantic, I checked the roster of hospitalized patients at the veterans hospital, looking for his name. I wondered if I'd missed a sign of something serious; should I have admitted him to the hospital when I'd seen him?

It turned out that he'd rescheduled his appointment for the following week, and the clinic staff had simply forgotten to tell me. When he arrived, he told me he'd had to miss our appointment because he'd been called to his brother's house to meet a contractor. "I'm sorry I worried you, Doc," he said, and my brief annoyance with him dissipated.

Dave told me he didn't have a cell phone. And his landline didn't go to voicemail because it wasn't really a landline. "I live in . . . well, an unusual place," he said. "It's not exactly a home."

Confused, I asked him if he could tell me what he meant. "I basically rent a part of a warehouse," he said, "and the landline I have is kind of the back line to where the workers are in the mornings. Landlord checks up on them by calling that number, so there's no voicemail."

Dave described his home as a spare room he rented for somewhere around $500 a month, the most he could afford to pay in the pricey Bay Area. But it didn't sound like a spare room to me. Dave told me he slept on a green cot that he folded against a wall. When he awoke in the morning, he took a shower in a tin basin after filling a bucket with water from the sink. It took more than ten minutes for the water to warm, and because he didn't want to waste water, Dave took cold baths. There was a toilet right next to the sink, and each night Dave unfolded his green cot a few feet away from the toilet so that he could use it without walking too far and tiring. There was a partition separating the toilet from the rest of the room, but no other furniture or closet. He stored his clothing in the back of his truck, where he often ate. He went to coin laundromats when he needed to. "The owner, he's pretty nice. Understands my situation and lets me be. But I don't want to stay there forever. Right now, it's working out pretty good."

Dave's room wasn't designed to be anyone's home. Nobody called or stopped by to check on him. His breathlessness dictated the circumference of his living space. His cot and toilet were only a few feet apart. But there was at least fifteen feet—an increasingly intolerable distance—between his cot and the doorway. This morning, his bath had taken an hour. He'd walked from his cot to the sink, filled a bucket, carried it back to the tub, bent down to scoop water, and stood up to sprinkle it over himself, all while making sure his oxygen tubing remained in place. When I asked, he told me he didn't have a rail to stabilize him if he felt dizzy, and couldn't sit down in the tub because it was too small.

Still, he insisted he was managing. He knew that he could fill the prescription for morphine that I had given him, but remained ambivalent. He still had so much to do, he explained, and didn't want the morphine to slow him down. He repeated what he'd told me last time—that he'd think about using the morphine when he really needed it. I told him that we needed to update his emergency contact since his brother had passed away. Did he have another person in mind? "I'm afraid I'll have to think about that, too," he said. "Is your son a possibility?" I asked. I sensed that their relationship was tense but naively hoped for an olive branch.

"I wish he could be," Dave said. He told me that he didn't know which came first for his son, the drugs or the mental illness, the outbursts of anger or the street fights and arrests. Soon, Dave became a victim of his son's increasingly unpredictable behavior. "He thought I was out to get him or something, and he tried to strangle me when we were at the park one day." A passerby called the police, who arrested his son. Dave hadn't wanted him arrested; he did not believe that his son intended to kill him. But precisely because he was unpredictable and now out on parole, his son didn't know Dave's address or phone number. Dave called his son from his landlord's cell phone, blocking the number first. But even though he feared his son, he remained focused on fixing his brother's house so his son would have a place of his own. "He may be a sick kid, but he's still my son. Looking out for him will always be my responsibility." Dave wiped his eyes as we spoke. It was the first and only time I'd see him cry.

Many of Dave's friends had died, so he wondered if he might ask his landlord to be his emergency contact. He felt secure in his warehouse, though I wondered if he had ever considered living in a place with more support—a place I instinctively knew he'd refuse because it didn't seem like he was ready to accept just how bad his emphysema was. Still, I tried.

"Have you ever considered living in a home where nursing staff and others can help care for you? You'd get help with bathing and cooking and the staff would look out for you in case you got sick or your breathing became a big struggle or you fell."

"An old persons' home? No. I'm not there yet, am I, Doc? I need my own space and my independence," he said firmly. "I really appreciate the idea, but I think I'll know when it's time for that. Right now I can still manage on my own."

Another idea came to me. "What if we could get a team to visit you who could check on you once a week or so, and make sure you are feeling well between your doctors' appointments?"

He paused to consider this. "Yeah, like a visiting nurse or something? I had a friend who had that."

Home-based palliative care, like the palliative care clinic, gave patients access to palliative care services outside of the hospital, when they were still living in their homes. Yet because both were also far less commonly available than palliative care services in the hospital, not every patient who qualified for these services could actually receive them. Not every health system had palliative care specialists, and not every health insurance covered home-based palliative care. I hoped that I'd be able to get Dave into a home-based palliative care program, but needed to be sure he had access to this service before promising it to him.

"I'll look into the home program, and you'll talk with your landlord about being your emergency contact, and you'll also try the tiny dose of morphine one night," I said, recapping our discussion.

"If I do the home program, could I still come to the clinic and see you?" Dave asked.

"Of course," I told him. "I wouldn't recommend it if I lost you as a patient," I joked.

"I wouldn't do it if I lost you as a doctor!" he said, his laughter giving way to loud coughs.

. . . .

I brought up the question of home-based palliative care for Dave when I spoke with my supervising physician that day in clinic. I worried it would be a long shot, but the answer I got was still unexpected. "You say he lives in a warehouse?" she asked. "I don't think he will qualify for the program. You have to have a residential address. You may want to check with the social worker, but I don't think we've been successful in the past in these situations."

Our clinic social worker came by shortly after I called her and explained Dave's situation. "I think a home program is a great idea for him. What's his home address? I see only a P.O. box here," she said, opening his chart and trying to find out which home programs might cover his neighborhood. "Well, he lives in a part of a warehouse that the landlord rents out to him," I said, scouring my notepad to see if I'd gotten his address.

"Uh oh," she said, removing her glasses. "Well, this will complicate things, because the agencies we contract with can go to the patient only if he has a residential address. And a warehouse wouldn't qualify. At least I don't think it would. I can call and ask."

It took me a minute to wrap my head around her words. Just a year ago in residency, I'd known of homeless patients at the county hospital placed in shelters or temporary housing while they received chemotherapy. If our system could find a way to house a homeless patient undergoing chemotherapy, wasn't it possible to arrange for a visiting team to treat Dave's shortness of breath so that he could drive his truck, walk more comfortably, and work on fixing up his brother's house for his son?

"If we can't do home palliative for him, are there other things you would suggest?" I asked, convinced that there must be *something* we could do for Dave. "I did offer the option of a nursing home but he wasn't having it," I said.

"Why don't I help you out and meet with him?" she asked. "He definitely needs a social worker."

"That would be amazing," I said. "I feel weirdly torn up about his case. He's doing all this legwork for a son who tried to kill him, when he's clearly stressing his body trying to do it all. And I don't think he has much time left. I just wish he would use it to take care of himself."

"You are so adorable," she said, grinning at me. "You are so green and new that I kind of want to pinch your cheeks! Wait till you're twenty years in and you'll have some peace around what you can and can't change for people."

. . . .

My grandmother died three weeks after I saw her, in August 2000. I hadn't spoken with her since I'd left Mumbai. After I wrapped up work at my internship one afternoon, I'd returned to my aunt's flat, where I was staying in Delhi. She was nowhere to be found, but had left a note telling me that my grandmother had died, and that I should take the airplane ticket next to the note and fly immediately to Mumbai. My aunt had left an hour earlier. I stared at the note. I read and reread it. *I should have called her,* I thought. *She was much more important than this stupid internship.* I could have called her more often for twenty years but I didn't. There was always something more important, usually something related to school or work, something that I should've seen was less important than the woman who had helped to raise me. My hands trembled. I crumpled the note, stuffed a few pairs of clothes in my backpack, and ran outside. August in New Delhi was all heat and dust, and I stood outside my aunt's flat squinting at the late-afternoon sun, utterly paralyzed, unable to move until a neighbor noticed and put me in a cab to the airport so that I wouldn't miss my flight.

Did my mother know? My sobs intensified and the cab driver, an elderly man with kind eyes, glanced at me in the rearview mirror, hesitating slightly before asking me what happened. "*Naniji,*" I said, the only word I could manage. My grandmother. He shook his head and told me he was sorry. That he reminded me of my grandfather, who also struggled to make a living driving taxis, doubled my sorrow. *How is my grandfather? Who told my mother? How can I reach her? I must reach my mother right away.* My thoughts raced quickly, becoming as blurry as Delhi's cityscape, which I caught between tears: the cows whose tails swatted at endless hordes of flies, the red-yellow-green-blue storefronts with painted advertisements for Lay's potato chips and Thums Up cola, the clouds of exhaust emitted by the trucks and rickshaws and motorcycles and taxis that battled one another for road space. *My grandmother was my mother for half of my first year in this world and I saw her only five times after that and now she's gone.* I thought of the last time I saw her, the way her cold hands startled me when she hugged me close, how I'd pressed my face against hers, feeling the outline of her cheekbone and jaw. As always, she'd smelled of coconut oil and mustard seed and Tiger Balm. The flight from Delhi to Mumbai seemed endless; I thought only of her face, the one I'd seen three weeks ago and the one I'd seen in photographs when she'd held me close in my infancy.

After the flight landed and I gathered the few belongings I'd managed to bring, I hailed another taxi. I winced as the taxi driver drove up to the apartment complex where my grandmother had lived with Uncle Raju. Everything familiar felt completely different. I couldn't bring myself to step into the elevator that you could access only by pulling back a creaky metal door and stepping into the narrow space inside. I headed for the stairwell, dank and dark, smelling faintly like a pile of wet towels. Paint peeled off the light green walls, which were covered with red splotches that, when I was younger, I fearfully assumed were blood. My mother explained that the red streaks were there because people chewed and spit out betel nut (*paan*) over the many years my grandmother had lived here with Uncle Raju. I looked at the walls now, wishing it was 1988, when I'd climbed the stairs for the first time, unable to tell the difference between blood and *paan*, frightened by the darkness of the stairwell but thrilled to be bounding up to meet my grandmother at the door, her thin arms wide, her cotton sari soft, her embrace indistinguishable from my mother's.

Soon, she would be dust. Her cremation, Uncle Raju told me, would be the very next day.

"Mama won't be able to get here in time!" I objected, incensed at the thought that the cremation had been planned without taking into consideration my mother's need to travel.

"She said that if you are here, it's like she is here."

We called my mother together. I could tell she was trying very hard to hold back her tears. "They shouldn't wait for me," she said. I couldn't believe that my mother wasn't bothering to drop everything to try to be at her own mother's cremation.

"It's just her body, Sunita, it's not her," she reminded me gently. "She's with God now." She began to cry softly then. She told me that Uncle Raju had called her in the middle of the night. Calls from India in the middle of the night were always emergencies, and she had awoken, startled but immediately bracing herself for terrible news.

Uncle Raju told my mother that my grandmother was breathing so rapidly that she could barely take in one breath before gasping for the next. She was sweating and her lips were turning blue. *Should we take her to the hospital?* my uncle asked my mother. The last time she'd been hospitalized, my grandmother had required the support of a ventilator to treat a terrible flare-up of her emphysema. She was on the breathing machine for six days, after which she told Uncle Raju and my mother, "Never do that to me again."

"It is the hardest thing to be a daughter but also a doctor," my mother would tell me months later. My mother knew what another intubation would mean: a breathing machine in the ICU, possibly a tracheostomy if my grandmother even survived, with a slim chance of her ever coming off a ventilator because ultimately her emphysema would never heal.

My mother knew everything about these situations. She knew about the frenzied, tearful eyes of daughters like her, having to make a decision like this. She knew how to push medications that would relax the patient she hovered over; from the head of the bed, she watched their breathing slow, their face go slack, their body relax after the tremendous work of breathing forty times per minute, trying to sustain life. She would go on autopilot, she told me, having opened thousands of patients' mouths, searched for their vocal cords with a laryngoscope, and slid a breathing tube down their trachea until their chests would rise and fall to the rhythm of the ventilator. Then they were peaceful, appearing as though they were simply sleeping. The daughter might be outside the room, watching, wondering if she had made the decision her mother would make, fearing that she wouldn't be able to live with the sadness of her mother's death and her own guilt if she had refused to have her mother intubated. My mother would pull out her stethoscope, the same one she used to help me listen to my own heart and then hers, and listen for tides of air moving through both lungs. Her job was done. Crisis averted. But perhaps another crisis loomed—that of the patient being unable to survive without the ventilator if her lungs simply couldn't recover.

My mother told me she didn't cry when Raju first called. She listened. Doctorly. She imagined her mother on a ventilator, knowing all of the risks intimately. *No*, my mother told Raju. *She wouldn't want this. She's told us once before. Give her sacred ash. Give her inhalers and make sure the oxygen tank is on. Pray.*

My mother still cannot describe this phone call in detail to me without asking me angrily why I feel the need to know this information, to force her to remember that painful night. I have pieced together what I am writing here from the moments over the past fifteen years when she described a glimpse or two of that night. She hung up with Uncle Raju and went to the room in our home that she and my father had made into a prayer room. Pictures of deities surrounded her in the midnight stillness and silence. She lit a candle and bowed deeply, feeling the carpet beneath her knees and hands and sobbing into it, praying and begging for God either to take her mother quickly and painlessly or to heal her spontaneously. *I had to remember that she didn't want the machine. She told us that. And even if she had, and we had put her on it, she would have never made it home, where she wanted to be.*

Her cheeks brushed against damp carpet and the flame flickered, moving the shadows of Lord Ganesha's and Lord Krishna's figurines ever so slightly across the wall. She imagined she was with her mother, and that her mother looked just as she had one year before, when she had last seen her. She imagined pressing her cheek against her mother's, holding her through her breathlessness, saying the prayers that she said now, at a distance of nearly nine thousand miles, over and over again through her tears and trembling. *I implore you, Lord Shiva, please ease all suffering, and free us from the cycle of birth and death, leading us to immortality.*

त्र्यम्बकं यजामहे सुगन्धिं पुष्टिवर्धनम्
उर्वारुकमिव बन्धनान्मृत्योर्मुक्षीय माऽमृतात्

tryambakaṃ yajāmahe sugandhiṃ puṣṭivardhanam
urvārukamiva bandhanānmṛtyormukṣīya mā'mṛtāt

Over and over and over again, as the candle flickered and the shadows moved and the carpet dampened and the phone finally rang again, and she knew.

Loving my grandmother meant letting her go.

. . . .

In Dave, I saw a second chance to care for my grandmother. He resembled her more every time he visited the clinic. I still cry at the image of my grandmother struggling for air, and struggle myself to make peace with the idea that all I know now came thirteen years too late to benefit her. She didn't have the option of a home palliative care or home hospice team to visit her. And in India, morphine, which could have eased her difficulty breathing, was difficult to obtain because of the stigma associated with the use of opiates, the fear of misuse and addiction. But she did have Uncle Raju and Anu, and for that I am grateful.

I'd been shocked to learn that although Dave lived in a rich country, he still couldn't access home-based palliative care simply because of where he lived. And though he did have access to morphine, he remained hesitant to use it. As I watched his oxygen requirement increase, more frequent gasps punctuate his sentences, and his face grow puffier from the increasing doses of steroids he needed to use, I pushed him harder. He'd told the social worker exactly what he'd told me. *No home for me. I need to set things up for my son. Not ready to die yet.*

"Hi, Doc, sorry I'm late," Dave said as he ambled into the clinic room and shook my hand. The new coolness of his hand startled me. I noticed his paler palms and bluer fingertips. He sat down and sucked in air, hands on his knees, smiling, eyes ringed by darker circles. I glanced at his vital signs. When he was resting, his oxygen saturation hovered around 88 percent despite a recent increase in the amount of oxygen he needed.

"How's it going, Dave?" I asked, my concern apparently quite visible. Over the course of my education, I'd come to sense when patients' bodies were starting to decline more rapidly. Something would nag at me. By the time I was nearly finished with residency, I'd learned to listen to my intuition, though I never understood what triggered this inner alarm. Perhaps it was something about the way *the patients looked*, apart from how their lab tests and CT scans looked. Now, in fellowship, I'd discovered the same inner guidance alerting me to patients whose bodies were failing faster than expected. Was it the shadows behind his eyes? I wondered. Was it the way his gasps appeared sharper?

"No need to look at me like that, Doc, I'm doing just fine." *Sharp gasp.*

"It looks like you might be a little bit more out of breath than before," I offered, looking at his oxygen tank.

"I think it's because I was rushing here," he said. "I had to drive back from my brother's house." *Cough.* "So, how's things with you? Your job search going okay?"

At our last clinic appointment, I'd shared with Dave that I'd started to look for jobs in the Bay Area. Since palliative care fellowship was only one year long, it felt like my job search started just as I'd finally settled into a routine. "Thanks for asking. It's going okay, but I'm still not sure where I'll end up."

"You know, this really strange thing happened the other day, Doc," he said after I asked him how he'd been. "I got up, and I was breathing hard, but then I looked outside my window and I swear to you, I thought I saw a horse pulling a buggy. It was the strangest thing."

When the brain is deprived of enough oxygen, patients can start to hallucinate. "Wow, that must have really startled you," I said, choosing my words carefully to modulate my concern.

"It really did! At first, it was kind of a pleasant sight, but then it wouldn't go away. I mean, a horse and buggy outside a warehouse? Doesn't make sense."

"Were you dizzy or out of breath at the time?" I asked.

"No. In fact, I'd just taken my inhalers and all my medications. I was just getting ready to leave my place. It was like a scene out of an old movie, and then it was just gone. Do you think it means something?"

Dave might have hallucinated for several different reasons, but because he struggled to breathe at the time, I worried that his oxygen levels might have been dangerously low.

"I do think it means something," I replied slowly. "When the amount of oxygen in the blood gets pretty low, sometimes people see things or hear things that aren't really there. That would mean that maybe you saw a horse and buggy because your lungs are having a harder time getting enough oxygen to your brain."

"Oh," Dave replied. "So I'm really getting worse."

"I'm worried about you, Dave," I said. "Have you given any more thought to what we talked about last time? I think we're seeing signs that you really do need more help."

Dave sighed, exasperated. "I talked to the social worker. She told me that nobody can come help me at home because I live in a warehouse and that's not the type of place those teams go."

My anger over this injustice persisted, but sharing my indignation with Dave wouldn't change the situation. "I don't understand why, but apparently that's the case, and I'm really sorry," I began. "Dave, I know you told me that you're not open to staying in a facility, but I'm worried that you might need more help just to take care of yourself in the coming months. To finish the things you're working on, you might need some help taking care of yourself."

Dave smiled, a flash of his yellowing teeth against his cracked lips. "I knew you'd bring this up again," he said wearily, hands again on his knees, his sentence chased with a deep breath. "I'm just not ready yet. I still have work to do on the house."

As I'd gotten to know Dave, I'd come to understand how fiercely he raced against a ticking clock to ensure that he left his son in the best possible situation. He persisted despite his son's behavior, despite the fact that continuing to drive limited the medications I could give him to relieve his worsening gasping. Because I admired him and possibly because I was secretly hoping he'd outlast his prognosis, I hadn't actually had a forthright conversation about how his disease was progressing. The thought of doing so made me feel as though I would lay waste to the meaning he still hoped was possible to make of his remaining time. I hesitated before I spoke, understanding first-hand why it was so difficult for oncologists and other specialists who had built relationships with patients over time to tell them the difficult truth of how sick they were, and how they were likely to get sicker quickly.

"Dave, I know you've mentioned to me that you still have things to do. And I want you to be well enough to do those things. But it's clear to me that your emphysema is getting worse. And I wouldn't be a good doctor to you if I didn't talk with you about what you might want as you get sicker."

"You mean *if* I get sicker?" Dave responded.

Doing everything for you means having this conversation. I told myself that if I wasn't honest with Dave, he might not have a say in what happened to him if he took a turn for the worse. He might get treatments he'd never want, suffering in ways that could be avoided just by having an honest conversation with him. *To be his doctor, you must tell him the truth. It might be hard for you. But this isn't about you, it's about Dave and his life.*

"Dave, unfortunately your emphysema is going to continue to get worse until it takes your life at some point. I know that is difficult to hear. It's difficult for me to say, but I have to tell you this because it's important that we talk about what you want for yourself as you get sicker." I held my breath, hoping that he wouldn't shut me out.

He nodded. "Yeah, Doc, I know, I know you're right, but it just doesn't seem like it's my time yet, you know?" Before residency and fellowship, when I pictured a dying patient, I'd imagine someone comatose, lying in a bed, fully dependent on others for care. But dying can be a slow unfolding, rather than a sudden catastrophe. A dying person might still be able to walk, talk, and go about their lives, even when living with a terminal illness. This was why it had been hard for me to accept that my grandmother was dying: she was still in her right mind, still moving around my uncle's flat, still able to eat and interact with us. Dave probably—and understandably—saw himself the same way: managing to live, not incrementally dying.

"I know. You have so much life in you, Dave, and I can hear how hard it is to reconcile your sharp mind with how much your body is struggling." Right now, Dave was clear-minded and relatively stable, rather than critically ill and hospitalized. We could actually have a conversation about topics that would only be harder to discuss when he couldn't breathe, or became confused and disoriented, or suffered from too much pain to talk. It wasn't an easy discussion, but it lacked the occasional awkwardness of similar conversations I'd had with hospitalized patients I'd never met before.

"Dave, do you remember when you were on a breathing machine about two years ago when you had a flare-up of your emphysema?"

"Yeah, how could I forget it? That was a tough time. But I pulled through."

"How do you think you're doing now compared to back then?"

"Not that different, I think," Dave responded.

Spit it out, Sunita. Don't wait for him to say it. "Dave, I actually think you have gotten weaker because your emphysema has worsened. You need more oxygen, you have lost weight, and you are seeing things that aren't there because at times you're getting very little oxygen to your brain. And if you got so sick that you needed to be back on a breathing machine, I'm not sure that it would help you now the way it did then. In fact, I think there's a very high chance you'd never come off the breathing machine." The words came to me easily this time.

Dave nodded and looked down. "I didn't know I might get stuck on that machine next time. But I still feel like it isn't my time. I don't feel that horrible right now."

"And that is what we want to try to maintain," I told him. "I mean . . . it's a great thing that you are not suffering, and I hope that I can help you feel the best you can for as long as possible. But at some point, you won't feel as well. What if you got worse and you couldn't do the things that are meaningful to you, like working on your brother's house? What if you needed the morphine to stay comfortable and that meant you couldn't drive your truck?"

"You mean when I'm dying?" Dave asked bluntly.

"Yes," I replied. "When you are dying. Because if we don't discuss this, I worry that you may get sicker before you have a chance to tell me what you want for yourself at that point. And if we don't know, you may end up getting therapies like the breathing machine that you may not be able to live without because of how severe your emphysema is."

Dave looked down at his hands. "I was worried that they're colder and they have that blue tinge," he said.

"Yes," I said. "I was worried, too."

"So . . . I guess you're asking me what I want if things worsen. Or when things worsen, I guess that's what you're saying. That's a heavy question. I'm pretty sure I don't want to die plugged into a machine. But I need to think on it more. If I couldn't get out of bed and I couldn't drive my truck and someone had to wipe my butt, I don't think I'd want that type of life."

"You should definitely take some time to think about it," I said. "Maybe we can talk more when I see you again in a few weeks?"

Dave looked again at his hands and squinted. "What if you were in my shoes, Doc? What would you do?"

As my months in fellowship passed, I couldn't do my job without wondering what I would want in the situations I confronted daily, so I answered Dave honestly. "I'd think about who I wanted to be with and see, what things I might want to do. I'd think about the types of suffering I couldn't deal with. I'd want to be at home, not the hospital. And I'd want to spend that time with the people I love, doing the things I can manage."

Dave nodded. "I'll think about it, Doc. Thank you for bringing it up. I wouldn't have," he said, laughing and then inhaling sharply, his hands on his knees again.

. . . .

When I thought of my grandmother, as I did so often after seeing Dave, I envisioned her with emphysema. I wish I could remember what it felt like to be mothered by her: How she held me close as we boarded a plane to New York, then Berlin, then Bombay, stroking my head and rocking me gently so that I wouldn't cry. How she cradled me when I cried and gave me bottles of warm milk and slept next to me. How she gave me baths in a small bucket and wrapped me in baby clothes she sewed herself. How she sat me next to her in the small kitchen where she prayed in the mornings, reciting mantras and clapping her hands as she sang devotional songs. I wished I remembered her singing.

I thought about my answers to the questions I asked Dave. If I had a few months to live, I knew I'd want to be at home in Los Angeles, near the ocean where I'd played as a child, with my parents and brother. But my life right now didn't reflect anyone or anything I'd value at my life's end. If I instantly knew I'd want to be with my family at the end of my life, why wasn't I thinking about being with them now?

I hadn't lived near my parents since 1998. I left Los Angeles immediately after graduating from high school and attended college on the East Coast. I went even farther away afterward, moving all the way to Oxford, in England. Although I could have returned to Los Angeles for medical school or residency, I chose to move to San Francisco instead. I love my parents and brother deeply, but for many years I chose to live at a comfortable distance from them. I'd always assumed that I could go back to Los Angeles when my adventures were over, expecting to find my parents in perfect health, waiting for my return. I'd taken them for granted just as I'd taken my grandmother for granted.

I have to go back to Los Angeles. My mind and heart spoke in unison, just as they had when they'd directed me to Connecticut and Oxford and San Francisco. But there was more. I'd started to recognize how entitled I'd been to assume that I would live a certain number of years, that my parents *definitely* had decades left because they were fit and mostly healthy, that my life would follow the expected linear trajectory of marriage, children, old age. In fellowship, I'd cared for so many patients my age or younger who were dying just when their careers were beginning, or shortly after they'd gotten engaged. People older than I was had assumed they would see their grandchildren's births or take an around-the-world trip when they retired, only to be sidelined by an accident or diagnosis. I'd learned a lot of medicine in fellowship, but the most profound lesson I'd learned was that living required both humility and acceptance of the unexpected. At some level, I'd known this all along. And when I asked myself the same questions I asked Dave and my other patients on a daily basis, it was clear to me that my life up to this point bore no resemblance to the life I'd want if my time was short.

While in residency, I'd borrowed two family photograph albums from my parents and recently found myself poring over the pictures as though I were seeing them for the first time. There was a photograph of my brother's high school graduation, my mother in a lime green *salwar kameez*, my father in a black suit, my brother sheepishly smiling in between them. I hadn't been there, opting instead to stay on my college campus and start an internship early. Another snapshot: my mother beaming in a pink sari, my father in an ivory *kurta*, raising a glass of red wine to toast their anniversary. I'd been in residency, too tired to book a flight to Los Angeles to attend their celebration just for that one day. *There's always next year*, I thought at the time.

As I leafed through the albums now, my absence stung me. The years had passed so slowly, and then so fast. I had put my family relationships on the back burner, chasing my dreams (or fulfilling their expectations?) at the cost of tremendous distance between us. I couldn't forgive myself for privileging schoolwork over my relationship with my grandmother; I didn't want to make the same mistake with my parents and brother. I opened my computer and began to search for palliative care jobs in Los Angeles.

....

Despite my many worries, Dave remained stable. Not well, and not improving, but not getting worse. He still gasped, and he occasionally hallucinated, but he began to eat a bit more after starting the appetite stimulant I'd given him. He had a little bit more energy to work on his brother's house and make it to his appointments at the VA. "I tried the morphine one day, Doc, when I knew I wasn't going to drive," he told me. "I think it really helped. I didn't feel like I was struggling when I took a bath. And I finally slept through the night."

"I'm so glad to hear that, Dave. It's great that you tried it, so now we know that it works at this dose!"

"I also thought about what we talked about last time," he said, his face turning serious. "I really think that I'm still strong, Doc. But if it's my time, I just want to go in peace, maybe in my own bed."

I was grateful that Dave broached this subject. "I hope it's a really long time away, Dave, I really do. And please know that saying no to machines doesn't change the many other treatments you can get. Our plan would be to keep your breathing and fatigue under control so you can have the best possible quality of life. But saying no to machines at the end makes sense."

Dave's face softened. "I'm glad to hear you say that, Doc. I was thinking maybe that no machines meant no treatment, no nothing, just letting me die like a dog. But I'm happy you'll take care of me till the end."

I helped him to fill out a POLST form and told him I'd scan a copy into his medical record and give him the original to place on the wall of his warehouse. He promised to share the form with his landlord, who'd agreed to help make medical decisions for Dave if he couldn't make his own.

We discussed when moving into a nursing home might be the safest option for him, and when it might be time to enroll in hospice care. For now, he told me he could live with the shortness of breath and the occasional hallucination since he was still managing to meet his own needs. But if he became mostly bedbound and couldn't get in his truck and drive, he'd interpret that as his body shutting down, and he'd want hospice care, probably at a nursing home if he couldn't stay in his warehouse. "I know that I don't want to be alone at the very end," he told me. Dave acknowledged that it hadn't been fun to have this discussion, but he was relieved to have made his own decisions about what he'd want at that point in his life. "It's so hard, Doc, when your mind is sharp and your body is shutting down. But at least I have a little control over the end since we spoke about it."

. . . .

Exactly one year after I'd moved to Burlingame, I stuffed my clothes and books into two suitcases, filled plastic trash bags with even more papers and books, loaded up my blue Honda, and began driving to Los Angeles. I couldn't believe that my medical training was done. I felt just as disorganized as I'd felt as a resident and fellow, but as of yesterday, I'd become an attending physician—a full-fledged physician who had completed her training. Though I usually blasted a hip-hop mix when I drove down Interstate 5 to Los Angeles, I began this drive in silence. Familiar scenes whizzed by: The water-starved brown fields alongside the freeway. Lines of almond and citrus trees on family farms. The black and brown cows feasting on lone patches of green. I left behind all the years I'd spent in the Bay Area, the years that passed so slowly and then so fast, just like the drive down the 5.

When I parked outside my parents' house, I realized it had been fifteen years since I'd been in Los Angeles in July. I'd forgotten just how oppressive the summer heat here could be. I wasn't looking forward to unpacking my car. I only had energy to bring in one suitcase packed with the clothes I'd need for the rest of the week. The front of my parents' home looked nothing like it had when I last lived here in my senior year of high school. The basketball hoop wasn't atop the garage anymore, and shiny copper wind chimes swayed right above the newly planted succulents and lavender in the front yard. But this isn't a visit anymore, I reminded myself. My childhood home was my home for the next two months, after which I'd move into the heart of Los Angeles and begin my first job as an attending.

I set my bags down in the bedroom and noticed a new voicemail on my phone, even though I hadn't heard it ring, possibly because of the poor reception on the freeway. The message was from Dave. On a whim, I'd given him my cell phone number and told him to keep in touch and let me know how he was doing. Even though I shared my number with a handful of patients over the years, most never called. I hesitated before listening to the voicemail and imagined that any number of scenarios could have prompted Dave to call. I stopped myself from jumping to the worst conclusion, since he couldn't have left a message if he was intubated. I pressed Play. It was as though he were right there, in front of me in the clinic, pausing and gasping and putting his hands on his knees and telling me exactly what he had to say.

"Doc, it's me, Dave. I came in for my appointment today. I just met my new doctor, the one I guess is your replacement. *Gasp.* She's kind of green, I guess. Still learning maybe. *Cough.* I just wanted to say I'll never forget you. I wish you all the best of luck in your career. Thank you for everything you did for me. *Cough.* You don't need to call back, I just, you know, wanted you to know."

I saved his message and pressed my phone against my heart. I looked out the window of my childhood bedroom at the guava tree and tomato plants and patches of wildflowers in my mother's small garden. I listened to the pressure cooker hissing in the kitchen below, inhaling the scent of the garlic, ginger, and onion that my mother had chopped and stirred into my favorite *daal*. It was as though I were back in high school, just on the verge of leaving for college. Nothing had changed, though everything had. I wondered if I'd be here right now if I had not met Dave. I pressed the phone harder against my heart and wished I could thank Dave for everything that *he* actually did for *me*.

Part 3

....

INFINITY IN A
SEASHELL

Eight

BEGIN

I'd taken my first job as an attending physician at a hospital that was both new and familiar. A brightly lit, gray building with a large courtyard, the hospital rose above a busy Los Angeles intersection. It was part of the large medical group that my mother had joined when we moved to California in 1986. Though my mother had never worked at the specific hospital I joined, the hospitals in the group share similar architecture and furniture. The hospital's motto, its logo, and the font of the signs pointing to the pharmacy and radiology remained unchanged over the years. I calmed my nerves by reminding myself that, nearly three decades ago, my mother walked into a nearly identical hospital for the first time, and it quickly became her professional home.

Meg, a kind woman from the human resources department, had shepherded me through the process of applying and interviewing for this job. After I had mulled over and finally accepted the offer, she said, "Maybe this is a long shot, but a long time ago I recruited another doctor whose last name was also Puri. She was an anesthesiologist. Any relation to you?"

"Yes! She's my mother," I said proudly, a wide smile on my face.

"I remember your mother so clearly," she exclaimed. "This was back when it was really hard to find a well-trained anesthesiologist, and I remember thinking we had to nab her!"

Anesthesiologists were once in short supply and high demand, just as palliative care doctors are now. "Does she still have that long, beautiful hair?" Meg asked. I envied her memories of my mother, who'd cut her hair chin-length when I was young. I'd only seen her long hair in snapshots from family albums, generally from years I didn't remember. "She cut it a long time ago," I said. "Well, I am sure she is just as beautiful as she was then," Meg responded before describing the details of my orientation day.

I could feel my mother with me as I walked around the hospital lobby, studying the signs to the laboratory, radiology, primary care clinic, and cafeteria. I stopped by the cafeteria and found a breakfast station offering scrambled eggs and potatoes, no Grandma's brownies or ice cream machine. I imagined that the overnight call rooms now had more comfortable beds, updated televisions, and computers, since all charts were now electronic rather than paper based, as they'd been when my brother and I visited my mother's call room.

When it was nearly time to meet my new team, I stopped by the bathroom for a few minutes of solitude. I inspected myself in the mirror.

My dark hair, freshly washed and slightly wavy, fell around my shoulders. I wore an orange shirt with a floral pattern that you could see only if my white coat opened just a bit. The coat itself was pristine. I hadn't yet had the chance to speckle it with the coffee stains or pen marks that always found their way onto my white coats in medical school, residency, and fellowship. I'd retired them all in one corner of my closet, my ID badge from each stage of training still clipped to its respective coat. The badge I wore today was the first one that didn't list a year in training.

"Congratulations," my mother said when she called me on my way to the hospital an hour ago. "It's a very big day. The beginning of your career."

9:00 A.M.

I meet my new team in a basement office lined with three workstations. Candy has been a palliative care nurse for several years and works closely with Brittany, the team social worker. I spend my mornings seeing patients with them here in the hospital, just as I did throughout my training. But I spend my afternoons driving to the homes of patients enrolled in hospice or home-based palliative care.

Candy and Brittany welcome me graciously, pointing out a pile of snacks atop the small refrigerator in the office, as well as the bathroom around the corner. There are five new patients to see, Candy tells me. "Doctors here place the orders for a consult electronically rather than by paging us," she says, "but you are free to call them and get more information about the reason they need our help."

Candy suggests that since I'm here only for the morning, maybe we should split up and she can see a few patients while I see a few patients. We could regroup after that. She and Brittany give me their cell phone numbers so that we can keep in touch throughout the morning. They tell me to concentrate on seeing the new referrals over the next three hours, reassuring me that they will see the other patients on our list.

There are no typical days, I discover quickly. But an average day goes something like this:

9:30 A.M.

Maddy is my first patient. She's sixty-eight, with metastatic pancreatic cancer, Dr. Lee, the hospitalist this week, tells me over the phone. I hear her pager go off several times in the first two minutes of our conversation. Maddy was admitted last night for fevers and chills caused by bacteria that had moved from her gut into her bloodstream. "She's getting sicker as we speak. Her blood pressure is marginal. We could send her to the ICU, but given that she's got metastatic pancreatic cancer, I don't think that's a good idea but haven't been able to sit down and talk that through with the daughters. Everything happened so fast and I barely know the patient. Can you come soon? Her daughters are here."

I stand outside Maddy's door at first, noticing a certain type of chaos unfolding, the type that begins when a patient's blood pressure is dropping and her breath becomes shallow, her consciousness slipping away. Maddy is thin and jaundiced, her brown eyes open but blank, faraway. She has one tube draining green bile from her abdomen and another collecting brown-red urine. Respiratory therapists and nurses are gathered around her bed and a young man with bright blue eyes and a mop of dirty blond hair rushes past me with a central line kit under his arm. Her blood pressure cuff, which automatically cycles every few minutes, hums in the background while all of us await its red-numbered verdict.

89/54. A series of red blinks and a warning alarm. Her oxygen saturation on the monitor also blinks: 88 percent.

Blue Eyes surveys the situation and speaks: "Dr. Lee called for me to put in a line."

I respond. "She also asked me to stop by to see the patient. I'm Dr. Puri, from palliative care." I am so fixated on the blinking red numbers that I almost forgot to introduce myself to Blue Eyes.

"Nice to meet you. I'm Justin, one of the physician's assistants from the surgery team. Why don't you talk with the family. I'll be over at the nurses' station." He gives me a look I'd seen many times—raised eyebrows and pursed lips that suggest he would rather *not* put a central line in Maddy.

I turn to introduce myself to Maddy's two daughters, Molly and Beatrice, both with tear-streaked faces and red eyes, huddled near the door. I have just a few moments to explain my role in their mother's delicate situation. I guide them just outside their mother's increasingly chaotic room into the hallway. I position myself so that I can glance over Molly's shoulder to watch Maddy's vital signs on the monitor.

Fluorescent light floods the hallway. The floor, recently mopped, glistens. "I am so sorry that your mother has taken a turn for the worse," I say, "and my role is to help you make some decisions about her care since she's quite sick."

"Okay," Molly says. "Her doctor called me and said she needs to go to the ICU but she didn't say what was going on. I drove right over. Why can't my mom talk to me?"

"She has a blood infection," I begin, keeping an eye on the personnel going in and out of her room, "and her blood pressure is very low because of that, which is why she's having a tough time communicating with you."

"Can they fix her in the ICU?" Beatrice asks.

"We are trying to treat the infection with antibiotics, but it's already caused such damage to her body that she may need a breathing tube and medicines to maintain her blood pressure. Sometimes, people can get better with these therapies. But since your mother has a very advanced cancer, it may be harder for her body to fight the infection, even with all of the help we can give her in the ICU."

"No," Molly says, shaking her head and tearing up as she cuts me off. "No, she said she would never want that again."

"What are you talking about, Molly? We're talking about her *dying* here! We are not giving up on her!" Beatrice argues.

"Do you remember what happened the last time she was in ICU? Don't you remember she said she'd kill us if she woke up with a tube in her throat? She said she would never want that again," Molly pleads.

83/47. Red numbers blink. 86 percent. The monitor beeps. A respiratory therapist places an oxygen mask over Maddy's face.

Molly turns to me. "What will happen if we don't do the tube?"

"If we don't use the tube, we can give her oxygen through a mask and medications to prevent her from feeling breathless. But going that route and focusing just on her comfort would mean that she might die within hours based on how sick she is right now." I speak slowly, enunciating each word carefully, as though the spaces between them would soften their blow. I wonder if Maddy had written down her wish not to be reintubated so that the decision wouldn't fall to her daughters. Though I'd wanted to be helpful, I wonder if I should have told Dr. Lee that it may be too late to attempt this discussion when Maddy's condition is so tenuous.

"That's what she wanted, sister," Molly says, crying as I speak. "I know you don't want to hear it but you don't live with us, you don't see her suffering like I do." I ask if Maddy had ever written down her wishes not to have a tube. She hadn't.

"Yeah, but she's got nine lives! She's been this sick before and she got better. She didn't know what she was talking about when she said that thing about the tube. That was the pain meds talking, that stuff they give her here!" Beatrice insists.

"Let's ask the doctor," Molly says, wiping her eyes. "What would happen if she goes to the ICU?"

"Well, we would put her on a breathing machine and keep treating her infection and blood pressure. We'd watch for signs of recovery, which would include her coming off the ventilator and not needing medications to support her blood pressure. But patients with an advanced cancer and a serious infection have a very high chance of dying because their bodies are overwhelmed and weak," I say. I wish that someone could have had this discussion before this point of crisis.

"So then, what? You let her die here instead of going to the ICU and trying to save her?" Beatrice asks.

Before I have a chance to answer, I see the respiratory therapist and two nurses wheeling Maddy out of her room. A third nurse pushes along the IV pole and watches the portable gray monitor that was on Maddy's hospital bed, the green tracing of her racing heart peering at us as she left. His central line kit under his arm, Justin trails after the group, pausing to tell me that Dr. Lee has decided to send Maddy to the ICU, where perhaps she can stabilize.

Beatrice follows her mother while Molly turns to me. "I couldn't even keep my promise to her," she said as she cries in the hallway.

10:20 A.M.

Marco has end-stage pulmonary fibrosis, Dr. Fong, the ICU attending, starts to tell me. This ICU is identical to all the others I've visited throughout my training: the same large rooms, the same sliding doors, the same monitors, the same beeps of the same machines in the same cadence and sequence.

Beep-beep-beep-beep-beep! the ventilator screeches.

Ding—ding—ding—ding! the blood pressure monitor sings.

"I can tell you his story," Dr. Fong says, adding, "but you can see him tomorrow since his family isn't here today."

I write down Marco's name and medical record number and begin to take notes as Dr. Fong tells me the history.

End-stage pulmonary fibrosis, on ventilator for fourteen days, not getting better, wasn't really waking up off sedation, CT scan of head found large stroke, unlikely that he will ever wake up again, but family demanding tracheostomy and feeding tube.

"One question—what has it been like talking with the family?" I ask.

He squints at me, as though my question takes him aback. "Well, I basically told them what I told you. He won't recover from this large stroke on top of this terrible lung disease and I didn't think it would make sense to do a tracheostomy or a feeding tube, but they kept insisting that we do both."

"Did they explain why they felt that way?" I ask as I continue to take notes.

He lets out an exasperated sigh. "Isn't that your job?" he says. "Most of the time, you guys handle those types of conversations."

I was clearly annoying him, and I wasn't about to anger a new colleague. "Sure, happy to help. I'll give them a call to set up a meeting for tomorrow," I say, forcing myself to smile.

"Thanks," he says distractedly, looking back at his computer. The ICU was full, every bed occupied by a patient with an uncertain future. As I leave, I notice Maddy in one of the beds, her eyes closed, her chest rising and falling to the rhythm of a ventilator.

11:00 A.M.

From the entrance to her room, I can tell that the lady in the hospital bed is all bony edges and sharp angles, from her cheekbones to her elbows to her knees. Tiny white curls cover her head except in a few patches where, I would learn, she has apparently pulled them out. Her caregiver, a plump Asian woman wearing pink scrubs, is reading a magazine and waiting for me to stop by.

I walk into the room, which she shares with another patient, someone on the other side of the curtain who is playing Bob Marley. "Hello," I say softly to the caregiver, who is startled and drops the magazine. "Oh, I am sorry, Doctor!" she says, retrieving the magazine and shaking my hand. "I am Anna, Miss Jones's caregiver. Are you from the hospice group?"

"I'm Dr. Puri, from the palliative care team. It's very nice to meet you, Anna," I say, shaking her hand and looking at Miss Jones. She has the faraway gaze that so many patients with dementia have. Her eyes, faintly brown, now appear ringed with blue. I wonder what she sees when she looks around. She makes a soft sound that reminds me of an infant. *Bababa-bababababa*, almost a whisper. *Babababababababa*.

"I think she's trying to say hello to you!" Anna says cheerfully. "Aren't you, Miss Jones?"

I sit at the edge of her bed and hold her hand, easily able to feel its delicate architecture of bones and ligaments as it rests in mine. "I understand Miss Jones came in because she continues to aspirate when she's eating, and that you were thinking maybe about putting a feeding tube in her?" I ask.

"Yes," Anna says, "and she isn't eating much anymore. When I feed her, she swallows one or two bites but then she just keeps the food in her cheeks. Then yesterday she swallowed and started coughing, having a tough time breathing, so I brought her here."

I listen to Miss Jones's lungs and hear the crackles that signify either a brewing pneumonia or irritation of the lung tissue from food that had made its way into her windpipe and then her lungs. She breathes comfortably, and doesn't sweat or grimace as I examine her.

"She's lost fifteen pounds over the past two months," I say, referencing what I'd seen in her chart.

"Yes," Anna says. "One of the doctors mentioned that maybe it is time for a feeding tube, but . . . I don't know if that is good for her."

This was the reason I had been asked to see Miss Jones. Even though feeding tubes sounded like a good idea for patients with dementia who weren't eating or cancer patients who had no appetite, they can actually cause significant harm.

"When a patient like Miss Jones has advanced dementia, I think of losing appetite as the body demonstrating that it cannot use food as it once could," I say, adding that feeding tubes in patients with advanced dementia won't necessarily guard them against aspiration and could cause infections. Elders with dementia can also tug at a feeding tube, dislodging it and causing bleeding and pain.

"But would that mean she would starve?" Anna asks, her voice shaking.

I reach again for my tissues. "I cannot starve her, Doctor. I could not live with myself."

I motion to Anna to sit down. "You are saying exactly what most people say when I talk with them about feeding tubes," I reassure her. "It means that you love and care so much for Miss Jones, and you really want to do the right thing for her."

Anna nods, her features scrunched together by a spasm of sadness. "But when patients stop eating on their own or start pocketing food, it is actually a sign that their bodies are getting sicker from the dementia. Just like we have heart failure or kidney failure, dementia is a sort of mind failure. And we know from studies that putting feeding tubes in patients with very advanced mind failure may not help them to feel better or get stronger."

Anna's sadness reminds me of the many caregivers I meet who consider their patients to be family. Sometimes, caregivers were the only companions that patients had, and their attachments to patients ran deep. Clearly the attachment was mutual: in her advanced directive, which she completed five years ago, Miss Jones had listed Anna as her medical decision maker, the person she felt knew her well enough to be her voice when she could no longer speak.

"Let me ask you a question, Anna," I say. "What do you think Miss Jones would say about this decision if she could speak to us? You know her better than anyone in the world."

Anna fingers the tissue in her hands. "I know she would not want it," she says quietly. "She has a directive saying that she doesn't want any tubes. But I can't . . . I can't be the one to say okay, no tube." She begins again to cry. "I know I am her caretaker but she feels like a mother to me."

She needs space, I think to myself. Space for her tears and grief. I sit with her, allowing her to cry, imagining how painful it must have been for her to watch Miss Jones deteriorate, how much strength she must have needed to continue to care for her as she grew bony and mute.

Her tears slow to sniffles, and I ask her if she wants to stop for now or keep talking. Either was fine with me. This wasn't a decision we had to make right this second. *We can keep talking*, she tells me.

"What strikes me as such a gift, and so powerful, is that Miss Jones has really made her own decision about this," I remind her. "She wrote it out for you in the directive. I'm not saying that the directive makes this situation better or easier, but you wouldn't be starving her, Anna. You would only be honoring her wishes."

I have learned that, for family members or caregivers, following a directive could provoke just as much guilt and sadness as making a decision without the guidance of a directive. Anna looked at Miss Jones and massaged her tiny arm. A piece of paper doesn't soften the blunt force trauma of loss.

"It's so hard for me, but I cannot be selfish," she says. "I know what she would say."

Not all conversations about feeding tubes went this smoothly. Many, like my conversation with Masaki's family on the first day of fellowship, provoked emotions on the continuum between surprise and anger. A devoted son wondered, as Anna did, whether his father would starve without nutrition. A loving wife wondered if forgoing a feeding tube would expedite her husband's death. Almost everyone wondered how food could cause harm.

Anna has questions about how to recognize when Miss Jones is hungry or thirsty. She wonders how long Miss Jones would live at this point. She herself asks about hospice. She asks all the right questions despite her emotions.

"I have to be her voice."

11:45 A.M.

I step into the elevator, trying to find my way back to my office in the basement, and a young woman smiles at me. She is tall with shiny dark hair that reaches past her shoulders, and wears a stylish blue top with knit brown pants and small heels. One pocket of her white coat is stuffed with what appear to be printouts of notes from patient charts and a prescription pad. She has curled up her stethoscope and placed it in her other pocket. I notice her glancing at my name tag, something I'd often done when standing next to colleagues in elevators, trying to guess their specialty. "Oh, you're our new palliative doc! I'm Daria Lee! We spoke on the phone about the lady who went to the unit!"

"It's so nice to meet you, Daria! I'm sorry I couldn't help more with that patient. It was . . . a tough situation."

"Don't worry about it, I'm just glad you're on board. We'll keep talking to the daughters," she says. The elevator dings. We are at the first floor. "Are you here full time?" she asks as she starts to step out.

"No, just in the mornings. In the afternoons I do home visits."

"I actually have another consult for you," she says, "and I feel bad because I know you have to run. It's for pain control. Guy with metastatic renal cell cancer. Can I give you his name and medical record number, and maybe you can see him before you go?"

The elevator dings again, forcing me to either step out and take the consult or say I have to leave and head back to my office. *In the beginning, you want to try to work really hard to get to know your colleagues.* I remember Dr. Nguyen's advice to me about starting my first job.

"Sure, happy to," I say, stepping out of the elevator and holding it open for a nurse and a woman using a walker who fill the space we've left vacant.

1:30 P.M.

I don't have time to write my notes. I'll have to come back later this evening after home visits, I think to myself after calling Daria and leaving her a lengthy message with my recommendations for her patient.

As I gather my bag and notebook for home visits, I quickly look up the phone number for Ms. Carson, my first home palliative patient. I call her daughter and tell her I'm running late. "No problem," she says. "She's not going anywhere!"

Car, 1:45 P.M.

I have never done a home visit alone. At Stanford, I visited the homes of patients on hospice or home-based palliative care, but always with another doctor or a nurse. I always loved the concept—home visits were easier for patients and provided me with endlessly helpful information about how their health might be affected by their lives and families: Were medications stored safely? Were unruly power cords and rug edges responsible for the fall that a frail elderly patient suffered? Did the family or caregiver turn the patient gently, tend to her wounds the correct way?

These visits force me not only to observe a patient's environment closely but to also examine the patient very carefully. I can't just send them to radiology for a quick X-ray to check for fluid in the lung, or call a colleague to come by and help me determine whether red skin around a bedsore is a simple cellulitis or a more aggressive infection. Instead, I have to ask if I can turn off the television or radio to listen in silence to a heartbeat or air moving in and out of the lungs. I open a clinical examination textbook for the first time since medical school to review whether I was doing all the maneuvers I can to check for fluid in the belly; I can't just walk over to the ICU and borrow an ultrasound probe to know for sure. It is refreshing to take a patient's blood pressure as she relaxes in her living room, my eyes wandering from the cuff to the graduation photos on the wall, the copies of *People* or *Ebony* or *Men's Health* strewn about a coffee table.

In our hospital system, four teams, distinguished by the zip codes each covers, care for patients on hospice and home palliative care all over Los Angeles. I have been assigned to the South Team, joining several nurses, a social worker, and a chaplain. Working most often separately, we make home visits to patients living in specific zip codes in South Los Angeles. On Wednesday mornings during our team meetings, we discuss each patient and his or her plan of care, with input from all team members. I might report that Mr. Lewis's pain and nausea are very well controlled, but he keeps telling me he thinks he should stop taking the pain medications and suffer, because his cancer is punishment for his sins. Our chaplain, concerned, will put Mr. Lewis on his schedule. Our social worker might report that Mrs. Williams's anxiety is worse; it didn't seem that the medication I'd prescribed had worked. I, in turn, will put Mrs. Williams on my weekly schedule. Teamwork was essential.

I type Ms. Carson's address into my phone and start my car, realizing that I forgot to grab lunch. I have a bottle of water, half finished, in the cup holder. *This will have to do for now*, I tell myself.

2:00 P.M.

I drive along Venice Boulevard toward the major street closest to where Ms. Carson lives. I take in the plazas, pedestrians, signs, and storefronts that line residential roads and larger boulevards. Along Venice, there's a black-and-red billboard announcing that a popular hip-hop DJ—one I listened to throughout high school—has moved from one radio station to another. I pass at least three plazas and glance at the business signs: Mexican fast food, coin-operated laundry, a check-cashing place, a nail salon that now takes credit cards and has a new mani-pedi combo offer. Each plaza seems to have a doughnut shop.

Residential streets, smaller tributaries that branch off from Venice and La Brea, are lined with green-brown lawns and the dust and metal of ongoing construction. White paint peels off older homes and apartment complexes, some with sagging front porches or boarded-up front doors. Interspersed are newly renovated homes, navy blue or forest green, with small yards filled with succulents and Mexican sage.

Ms. Carson lives in a white house with a white gate on a quiet street. I park my car across the street and glance at my reflection in the mirror, making sure the collar of my white coat isn't turning in on itself. I carry my stethoscope, blood pressure cuff, oxygen monitor, and a first aid kit in a brown messenger bag. In an orange-colored Moleskine, I take notes on my visits so that I can write my electronic notes later. Now I review the notes about Ms. Carson that I'd gathered from her electronic chart.

Sixty years old, recent diagnosis of metastatic cancer, possibly sarcoma, had a bowel obstruction but family refused artificial nutrition, insisting that they can feed and take care of her. Decision making shared by children and husband. Currently full code. This is first visit for home palliative.

As I cross the street, I suddenly realize that nobody—except for Ms. Carson's family—knows where I am. I had been given a list of patients in the territories I covered, along with a list of those who needed visits sooner rather than later. I am in charge of my own appointments, and while I had initially thought it was great to have the freedom and flexibility to make my own schedule, I recognized now that I was not just independent, I was alone.

I'll be fine, I tell myself, remembering that Ms. Carson's daughter had sounded perfectly normal on the phone. I remember a few safety tips that one of my colleagues had given me. *Position yourself between the patient and the door. Know the way out of the house. Check to make sure you have reception on your cell phone. Park nearby.* I open the metal gate and knock on the front door.

A young woman in sweats and a headband answers, her guarded expression softening as I introduce myself. "Hi, I'm Dr. Puri from palliative care. I think we spoke by phone?" I point to my hospital badge, which I am required to show her.

"Yes, yes! Hi! I'm Gina, Alanna's daughter," she says, opening the screen door and shaking my hand.

She ushers me into a living room lined with two couches and easy chairs, and several large green houseplants. Weak sunlight filters through partially open blinds. Several black-and-white family photographs sit atop a piano covered with a white scalloped tablecloth. I inhale the sharp tang of citrus. "I was just making juice for Mom. She's in the first room to the right. I'll join you in a sec."

Ms. Carson lay in a hospital bed in a tiny room that barely fit two additional chairs. A large pink plastic basin filled with gauze, antiseptic pads, and bottles of coconut and almond oil sat on one of the chairs.

"Hi, honey, are you my new doctor?" Ms. Carson asks, turning her head to look at me. She wears a multicolored knit cap and large glasses with purple frames that she pushed up her nose. "You are so young!"

"I promise I'm not that young," I say, shaking her hand and winking. "I'm Dr. Puri. It's really lovely to meet you, Ms. Carson."

"Thank you for coming to my home. So tell me, how can I help you, dear?"

I chuckle and say, "You stole my line!"

"Oh, goodness, that's right. Sorry, I have been a schoolteacher for so many years and I just always ask people how I can help them."

I have already started to examine Ms. Carson. I observe how she is seated in bed, whether she grimaces in pain. Her hand is neither unusually cool nor warm. She is clean and well groomed, and can speak to me without losing her breath. Her skin is smooth, probably from the coconut and almond oil I could smell. A plastic container connected to a tube in her abdomen pokes out from the side of her bed. The dark contents of her intestine, a portion of which was blocked off by her cancer, empties into the container. The tube ensures that these contents, which can't move around the blockage, can be emptied and therefore spare her horrific bouts of nausea and vomiting.

"So tell me, are you married, young lady?" Ms. Carson asks, reaching for my left hand to look for a ring.

"I guess you could say I'm married to my job," I reply, smiling. This had become my way of sidestepping that specific personal question, which I'd been asked by everyone from patients to well-meaning hospice nurses.

"Why are you not married yet? You are just like my Gina. I keep telling her—"

"What do you tell me, Mama?" Gina returns with a glass of juice and a straw. My stomach growls, and I adjust myself in the chair to cover up the sound.

"You ain't married and she ain't either!" Ms. Carson exclaims as she reaches for the juice.

"Oh, please don't start with that. She'll never come back here!" Gina turns to me and mouths, *I'm sorry!*

Gina helps her mother to sit up in bed. "Mama loves her juice and her fruits," Gina says as she guides the straw to her mother's lips. "I was reading in her chart that she didn't want artificial nutrition," I say as Ms. Carson sips her juice. "Yup," Gina says. "I make juices and smoothies, and Mama has them for each meal."

Ms. Carson offers me a sip of her light green juice, which smells of citrus, apples, and parsley. My mouth waters. I decline graciously, but with great difficulty. "Do you ever feel nauseated after drinking your shakes?" I ask her.

"Not at all," Ms. Carson responds. "Every doctor asks us that," Gina says, "but what's crazy is that she feels so much better than she did on the artificial stuff from the hospital, and she even has started to have bowel movements, which they told us would never happen."

That *was* unexpected for a patient with an intestinal blockage. I am surprised at how well Ms. Carson looks with the support of mere juices and massage. Although she has an aggressive cancer, she has no pain and takes no medications. Her only concerns are fatigue and difficulty maneuvering herself out of bed. She loves my suggestion of getting a physical therapist to visit her to help her move a bit more independently, which is her main goal.

After I examine Ms. Carson, Gina and I speak in the living room. She asks me exactly what palliative care is and how often I would visit.

"Good questions," I tell her. "I'm visiting because when your mom was in the hospital, the doctor taking care of her felt that it would be good having a team visit her at home to make sure she was not suffering from any pain or other uncomfortable symptoms, and to make sure that you and your family are all well supported in taking care of her," I say. "There's a whole team that will visit. Her nurse will actually see her the most frequently, and the social worker, too, but I'll see her pretty often, too, because she's got a lot going on medically."

"But this isn't hospice, right?" she asks, cocking her head to the right. "Because I heard that hospice is only for patients who are about to die, and Mom isn't. I know she's not well but I don't want hospice here."

I don't tell her this, but I actually wondered why Ms. Carson wasn't on hospice instead of home-based palliative care. Her cancer, which has moved into her lungs and bones and liver, will probably take her life within a few months, especially since she is far too weak to undergo chemotherapy. Now I knew why.

"So it's not hospice," I begin. "But our team does some of the same things that a hospice team would do by visiting and checking in on Mom and her whole family."

"I quit my job to take care of Mom," Gina says quietly. "Dad would freak out if he knew that, so I lied to him and said I'm on family leave. My brother isn't working and he's not gonna look for a job until later. So we are basically living off my dad's retirement money and my mom's pension. But we don't need hospice. We can take care of Mom ourselves."

I know intuitively that it's not the time for me to correct Gina's beliefs about hospice. It is the time for me to listen and learn how to communicate with her. Ms. Carson is actually doing quite well, I tell her, and we can work together to maintain her current condition for as long as we can. I don't make any changes to her care other than requesting a consult from physical therapy to help with her mobility.

"Your mom did a good job with you," I observe, nodding my head. "Not everyone has the motivation or ability to take good care of their parents." I make a mental note to involve our team social worker that money is tight for the family. Maybe she can help Gina and her brother to get some sort of payment for their caretaking work.

Gina clasps her hands together underneath her chin, leaning forward in her chair. "It's really hard," she says, looking up at the ceiling, trying not to cry.

"It must be," I say softly. "It must be especially tough to be a daughter and also a caretaker." I pause, wondering aloud whether Gina had anyone in her life, maybe outside her family, who could step in to care for Ms. Carson while Gina takes a walk, or gets coffee, or goes to a movie to take a break.

"Nah," she says. "So far, we've got it covered." I tell her gently to remember the importance of self-care. She smiles and acknowledges that has always been tough for her. *We are similar in more than one way*, I think to myself.

When I return to my car, I realize that I haven't taken any notes. I open my Moleskine and begin to scribble down her vital signs, physical exam details, and the other things I'd learned about Ms. Carson:

> *Pt appears comfortable, has supportive family, children assuming all care for mother. Not open to having others care for mom. Wary about hospice. Risk of burnout and distress. Needs SW consult, maybe payment for caregiving? Pt stable with current plan, will order physical therapy at home.*

I place the Moleskine in the passenger seat and type the address of my next patient into my phone. I should be there in about fifteen minutes.

3:30 P.M.

I try unsuccessfully to ignore the hunger pains that twist my stomach. I turn into the next fast-food joint I see, a Del Taco. I scan the menu and decide on a bean burrito. I'll eat it here, not in my car, where the probability of spillage is too high. I sit in a plastic booth, wolfing down my burrito in less than five minutes. On my phone, I read mindless celebrity gossip—the latest drama on a reality show I've never watched, the cheating scandal that caused two movie stars to split. I scroll through photographs of starlets wearing five-thousand-dollar dresses and thousand-dollar shoes, their makeup so heavy it looks like they are wearing masks. The awards shows they attend and some of the studios where they film their movies are not very far from the neighborhoods I cover. But they couldn't be more distant.

4:00 P.M.

Mr. Bernard lives in a spacious two-bedroom apartment filled with sunshine. The walls are covered with photographs of kitchens and gourmet food; cookbooks fill an entire bookshelf. He tells me he was a chef at a fancy hotel before his heart failure worsened, robbing him of his breath and energy and appetite, leaving him instead constantly nauseous, dizzy, hopeless. He sits straight up in his hospital bed, almost at ninety degrees. He wears a blue T-shirt and scrub bottoms that belong to his wife, who works as a nurse. "Thank you for coming, Doctor," he tells me. "My mother died in hospice and I knew that's what I wanted for myself when the time came." His wife looks away.

Mr. Bernard tells me that his intense nausea surprises him. He pats his belly, swollen with fluid that his failing heart and kidneys cannot remove. "I don't know, maybe we should run a pregnancy test," he jokes.

I examine his belly thoroughly. "I'm going to guess it's a boy," I tell him, my expression serious.

He laughs hard. "You sure it's not a girl?"

"Well, all the old wives' tales I've heard seem to suggest that when the belly is more round than oval, it's probably a boy," I joke, suppressing a chuckle.

"If it is indeed a boy, then I'm going to need to eat a lot more than I am right now before I give birth," he says.

We talk about his nausea and his waning appetite. Sleep was his freedom from both. But he didn't want to spend all of his time sleeping in his hospital bed; he and his wife hoped to go to a colleague's restaurant opening, to spend an afternoon sitting on the lawn at the Getty. He lowers his voice and tells me one of the most degrading ways his body has changed: his legs have swollen to at least twice their normal size, and so has his scrotum. I examine him: deep imprints of my fingers remain in his legs minutes after I have pressed into his flesh. His scrotum has swollen to the size of a small grapefruit. He winces as I examine him gently for any sores or erosion of his delicate skin. "It's surreal," he tells me as I cover him with his blanket. "I don't recognize my own body, this place I've lived for sixty years."

His breathing is hard and his lips are pursed. I can tell he is trying very hard not to cry, and I tell him that it is okay to let go. Tears slide down his face and neck, leaving small moist circles on his pillow and darkening the collar of his shirt. "I was one of those hippies that did yoga and was a vegetarian, and during that time I really learned that death is going to happen for all of us, you can't live your life fearing it," he says, sniffling. "But then when it gets really close . . ." He covers his face, begins to sob.

I bow my head as sorrow shakes his body, revering this honest display of grief. "It is one thing for us to know logically that we will all die. But logic doesn't somehow take away our emotions," I say softly. We sit together for a while. His tears soak through tissues, and I give him fresh ones. His bedroom glows in the late-afternoon sunlight.

"Sometimes I wish I could just take a pill and go to sleep. The waiting, the sitting around like this . . . it's killing me," he says.

"I can only imagine," I say, thinking back over the many patients who've told me the same thing, that waiting for death to come was a bit like waiting patiently for an assassin whose unknown arrival time tortured them more than knowing he'd kill them.

We talk about the medication that may relieve his nausea, the pill that may stimulate his appetite. We discuss ways to lessen the swelling in his legs and scrotum. We talk about his mood and outlook; he isn't suicidal and doesn't think he's depressed. He wonders how anyone could get through this period in life without hoping for a quick and easy way out. We focus on getting him to the Getty, tasting the food at the restaurant opening. He is embarrassed by the size of his legs, but tells me that he'll have to bite the bullet and buy bigger pants. He tells me that he hopes his next birth will be in India. "I'm going to say a very stupid, white American thing. I love Indian food!"

"That makes two of us," I say. "And that's not stupid."

I tell him that I'll probably come back to see him in a week or so, but his nurse should visit tomorrow to make sure our plan is helping him to feel better. He reaches his arms out and I bend down to hug him. His wife thanks me and walks me to the door. Just as I leave the bedroom, Mr. Bernard calls out.

"One more question, Doctor. What the hell does an oval belly even look like?"

5:30 P.M.

I still have to write my notes on Maddy, Marco, Miss Jones, and the new patient that Dr. Lee referred to me. I race back to the hospital and rush to our basement office, grabbing a granola bar from the basket of snacks atop the refrigerator.

I log in to my computer, chewing on the granola bar, my head starting to hurt from the day and from my hunger. *I just have to bang out five notes,* I remind myself, shocked as always that over the course of such an intense day I had really seen only a handful of patients. I start with Maddy. It seems like I saw her days ago. When I click on her chart, a rectangular white box appears, informing me that I am entering the chart of a deceased patient. Did I still wish to proceed? I am surprisingly unemotional about this. I wonder if it is my exhaustion from the day, or the necessary detachment that I am cultivating. All I feel is surprise that she died so quickly.

Despite being on the ventilator and medications to artificially sustain her blood pressure, Maddy's oxygen levels and blood pressure continued to drop. Brittany met with Molly and Beatrice and tried to help them work through their differences of opinion about their mother's wishes. Brittany wrote in her note that Beatrice stormed out of the meeting when Molly insisted that her mother not be resuscitated when her heart stopped and she died. Beatrice said she was going to call the cops and have Molly arrested for murder. Maddy's blood pressure kept dropping, even while four medications to increase it dripped through her veins. She died around 3:30, after several rounds of CPR. Reading this stings me. I write her name on a Post-it, reminding myself to call her daughters tomorrow and convey my condolences.

Marco is doing about the same. He is still comatose, requiring the maximum amount of support from the ventilator. His nurses noted that his family remain at his bedside, singing hymns.

Miss Jones has enrolled in hospice and will be back in her home tomorrow. I notice that she lives in one of the zip codes that I cover, so I'll get to see her and Anna again sometime soon.

Before I return to my car, I remove my white coat and place it in the trunk. Locking away my white coat becomes my dividing line, my way of leaving my work behind as I drive home to the rest of my life.

. . . .

My mother had left me two messages that day. The first, around 12:30: *Hi, Sunita, Mom calling. I hope your day is going well. Did you take a break yet? Call me.* She'd called again when I'd been visiting Ms. Carson. *Hi, Sunita, Mom calling. Are you okay? Don't you have five minutes to call your mother?*

We've switched roles, I thought to myself. As a child, her hospital's phone number had been emblazoned in my mind. On the rare occasions that I managed to reach her between cases in the operating room, she could only talk briefly in between commitments. *Are you and Siddarth okay?* Yes, we are.

Is there an emergency? No. *Okay, then I'll see you at home in a few hours.* My conversations with my mother were sometimes just as brief when she called me in residency and fellowship. *Are you okay?* Yes, Mama, I'm just on call. *Have you eaten?* Yes, but I had to eat quickly since I had four admissions in a row. Can I call you when I get home in a few hours? When I'd asked her in my residency how she had gotten through such intense training with a husband and young children, she responded with some variation of her usual reply: "I didn't think so much. I just did it."

Mothering and doctoring were each behemoth tasks that seemed an impossible combination. Yet somehow my mother had managed to do both well. My father, brother, and I visited her call room in the evenings, bringing her dinner so that she could eat and visit with us. Piled into the same room my brother and I stayed in as young children on holidays, we spread a picnic of food from home or takeout Mexican food onto the call room bedspread, eating off our knees on greasy paper plates. My mother ate and visited with us in between responding to pages and listening to overhead alarms that might signal an emergency.

I didn't understand how much of a toll this routine had taken on her until I returned from Palo Alto. It wasn't just being a doctor and a mother. It was that, after satisfying the demands of both, she had nothing left. She hadn't ever considered that she would *need* anything else. My father supported her by caring for us when she was at work, cooking and checking homework and making sure we were picked up on time from school. But after my mother retired, she began to reflect on how thoroughly doctoring and mothering had become her sole identities.

We took a walk together one day on a beautiful coastal trail lined with succulents and chaparral, bordering a rocky shoreline. We stopped to watch the waves crash against large rocks, and we squinted in the sunlight, searching for resting seals. Over the summer, we walked here together nearly every day. My mother spoke about the yoga teacher training course she was taking and how she hoped to teach breathing exercises to chronic pain patients at her hospital. She told me about her classmates—the Indian woman who had traveled from the Midwest to take this particular course. The recent college graduate who wore his hair in a bushy ponytail and had a hoop-shaped nose ring. The woman around my mother's age who practiced aromatherapy and lived on an ashram in Northern California. "I've never met people like this before," she told me. "I wish I could have done this a long time ago."

It wasn't so much her words but the wistful tone of her voice that pierced me. She told me that taking a course for herself would have been impossible between work and taking care of my brother and me and my father. She had always felt guilty wanting to do anything that she truly loved, she told me; even the flower arrangement classes that she'd taken at the local botanical gardens were really for prayers, when she arranged beautiful combinations of flowers from our garden with store-bought flowers as an offering to God. But yoga was just for her, something she had been drawn to but never had a chance to explore. I listened carefully, more attentive than I'd been in recent years, watching foam and water engulf the rocks, linger momentarily, and then recede.

She told me what it was like to envy colleagues who took vacations with their spouses to Vietnam, France, Australia. Other colleagues dedicated time to specific hobbies that were just for them—flying planes, joining a book club, training for marathons. Some could carve out time away from their children because they had a stay-at-home spouse or a full-time nanny or nearby grandparents. "But you two were very sensitive children. You were very attached to me so I couldn't leave you with anyone," she said. I waited for her to say something about how I was probably far too sensitive to practice palliative care, that it wasn't too late for me to look for a job in primary care or hospital medicine.

But instead, she told me something I'll never forget.

I fixed my eyes on the brown-green algae floating at the top of the water's surface. "You don't have to struggle the way your father and I did in a new country with no family," she continued. "Don't make your career the only big thing in your life. If you do, the stress will kill you and it's not worth it."

I'd always assumed that my mother struggled with practicing medicine to the best of her ability because of family obligations. In fact, she told me the opposite.

"At a certain point, I realized that I could try to please everyone at work, but if I made myself sick with stress, they would easily replace me. But my family could not replace me." I could never imagine my mother, alternately the fiery anesthesiologist who would refuse to do risky cases with unreasonable surgeons and the nurturing chief who arranged for an Indian restaurant to cater lunch for her team every Friday, as replaceable. Not just because she was my mother. But because she was an exceptionally gifted physician, one who brought home awards and recognitions and cards and presents from patients.

The sea breeze turned into a momentary gust, and I grabbed my mother's arm to steady her.

"And you have a hard job, much harder than mine," she said to me. "You are very strong. I couldn't do this palliative care that you do. So you must take care of yourself, more than I did."

I was taken aback. There was nothing my mother couldn't do. This was the first time she hadn't criticized my specialty. I hadn't the faintest idea that she admired what I'd chosen for myself.

"How do you do it?" she asked, her eyes fixed on the ocean. "How do you watch people suffer so much all day, and then go back and do it again the next day?"

I watched a group of pelicans in a V-shaped formation fly along the ocean, hovering precisely above the water, close enough to identify fish but distant enough to avoid startling their prey. *Maybe like those pelicans*, I thought, watching as they glided along the blue expanse before us. *They're close, but not too close.* I wasn't prepared for her question, one I'd asked myself before and during fellowship, but stopped asking myself since becoming an attending. Did that mean I'd hardened? That what had moved me to tears just a year ago no longer did? Or was this a healthy maturation, one that allowed me to hover just above the depths without disappearing into them?

"To be honest, I'm not sure. We always talked about how death isn't the end of a person, and I think remembering that helps me. But, kind of like you, I try not to think too much about it."

She nodded, still looking at the water. "Please take care of yourself. If you get sick, the hospital will replace you. But I will never have another daughter."

I wrapped my arms around her and held her tight. The sun warmed our backs and the breeze cooled our faces. Overhead, gulls cawed. Other hikers moved around us on the trail. We embraced for a long time, until another strong breeze startled us.

. . . .

I drove away from the hospital toward my neighborhood on the eastern side of Los Angeles. I'd chosen it because, as I told my brother, I wanted to live somewhere that reminded me of the Bay Area, somewhere walkable and lively, less glossy and polished than the west side of Los Angeles where my brother lived. My neighborhood was home to quirky dance clubs and vinyl record stores, colorful older cafés and sleek eateries that specialized in just one item each: grilled cheese sandwiches, vegan doughnuts, organic vegetarian cuisine. There were two independent bookstores within several miles of my place. I both appreciated the more rugged blocks that reminded me of my trips with my parents into Los Angeles as a child and giggled at the overload of hipsters I passed on sidewalks, all of whom reminded me how uncool I am and probably always was. As I headed east on Beverly Boulevard, I called my mother back. I stopped at the grocery store as we spoke, picking up granola bars and trail mix that I could keep in my car to snack on during future busy days.

Nine

DRIVE

For several weeks, I am assigned to spend my entire day doing home visits rather than squeezing them in after mornings at the hospital; a colleague of mine will see the hospitalized patients so that I can focus on seeing my growing number of hospice patients. I drive through Baldwin Hills, Leimert Park, Jefferson Park, West Adams, Crenshaw, and Inglewood. My patients are younger than I expect: women in their early forties with breast cancer, men in their fifties with failing hearts. During my hospice rotations in Palo Alto, I'd mostly seen patients in their seventies and eighties whose failing lungs and kidneys and advanced cancers didn't surprise me. But people in the neighborhoods I cover die an average of ten years earlier than those who live in Los Angeles's wealthy coastal neighborhoods. Residents in two of the zip codes I cover live the shortest lives in the city. Those neighborhoods ranked 102nd and 103rd in life expectancy out of the 103 zip codes in Los Angeles.

Not only do many of my patients die sooner than elsewhere, they die differently as well. They die with few resources and abundant fear, even when receiving the same hospice services that their wealthier counterparts receive. Death may be humanity's great equalizer, but in my first year of work, I witness how the economic and social inequalities that shape my patients' lives also shape their deaths.

On one hot morning in March, I drive along a street parallel to the Harbor Freeway to visit my first patient that day. I pass storefronts hand-painted in red, gold, and turquoise, advertising used motor parts, *pupusas*, and books "for a Christian lifestyle." When I stop at traffic lights, I notice signs I've never seen before. One, stapled to a telephone pole, asks, "ARE YOU SCHIZOPHRENIC? EARN $7,450 IN OUR STUDY." Another promises "LIFE IN-SURANCE FOR DIABETICS." Fathers with custody issues are encouraged to call a number on a neon sign. "SELL YOUR HOUSE," another sign promises, "AND EARN FAST EASY CASH." I wonder what my patients and their neighbors make of these signs, whether they ignore them or call the listed phone numbers or try to rip the signs down.

In order for a person to be eligible for hospice care, two physicians must agree that he has six months or less to live if their underlying disease takes its natural course. Up to that point, the "natural course" of a disease has generally been slowed by dialysis or chemotherapy or an internally im-planted defibrillator. Depending on a patient's situation, these are often dis-continued when hospice care begins, when our goal shifts to comfort and solace as the body quiets.

Many of my patients feel that they have barely lived at all when I show up to help them die comfortably. I enter their lives and their homes as a stranger when familiar comforts are what many need. Our relationship will be one of brief and necessary intensity. I assure my patients that it is natural to fear the word and concept of hospice, and I listen as they tell me about an aunt who died in terrible pain even with hospice, about their fear that accepting hospice means agreeing to do nothing for their father, about their worry that hospice care actually shortens people's lives. I explain that my job as a hospice physician is to identify and treat the discomfort their disease has caused. It is also to get to know patients and their loved ones, to assess how they are coping, to ensure that they have the right resources to help with everything from planning a funeral to moving through the chokeholds of grief that will unexpectedly grip them. Some ask if I can take a family photo for them with their cell phones, and I oblige. I pray with them when they ask me to. I listen as some of them tell me about their loves, their pets, their accomplishments, their regrets. I listen also to the ones who cannot speak, who instead groan or babble, who grow quiet when I hold their hands or play them a song that their caretakers tell me they love. This is as essential to hospice doctoring as dosing medications for pain or nausea, for agitation or insomnia.

While a patient can technically be on hospice for six months, many of the patients I see die within a few days or weeks, never fully enjoying the benefits of the care we try to provide. In the United States, the median length of time patients spend on hospice is around eighteen days. Though this statistic shocked me during my fellowship, it no longer does. The term "hospice" has become so synonymous with "giving up" or "losing the battle" with a disease that it is often not presented as an option until patients are at the very end of their lives. A handful of my patients will die an hour or two after the hospice admission nurse meets them, explains hospice, and asks them to sign consent forms agreeing to hospice care. I will sign their death certificates, having barely met them and learned their names, a stranger who will attest to their departure from this world.

Yet although I am seeing a patient because I have agreed that they are approaching death, if I do my job well, what I actually encounter is the full force of their lives.

. . . .

I park and walk along a sidewalk lined with broken concrete to my first patient's home. On my way I pass a commercial building adorned with a painting of a young man with a double chin, small mustache, and short, spiky hair. Below it, in black lettering, are the words "R.I.P. ALWAYS IN OUR HEARTS." I turn the corner and walk past another home with a cross made of fresh pink flowers nestled outside its security fence. A photograph of a young man rests against it.

Loss lives everywhere here.

I knock on the door of Sergio, a newer patient I have met twice before, once on a home visit two weeks earlier and once in the hospital shortly after that. I wait on his narrow porch next to a Safeway grocery bag filled with used blue hospital gloves and empty hand sanitizer bottles. I can't see anything through the steel security screen that guards his front door, and most doors in this neighborhood; if I squint, I can just barely see the shadow of an approaching figure. Following the advice of another patient, I always wear my white coat and hospital badge on my visits, my stethoscope draped around my neck. "You should be clear," she told me, "about who you are and why you're here."

Sergio's wife, Maria, opens the door and hugs me hello. Sergio smiles widely from his bed, five feet away from the front door. His smile is out-growing his shrinking face. He cannot eat because stomach cancer has blocked off his bowels, triggering nausea and vomiting if he takes even a sip of water.

At forty-five, Sergio isn't thinking about how to die a good death. He is still grappling with why death has come for him so soon.

He tells me that he's feeling much better today than he did last week. The medications I'd prescribed took away his nausea and pain. Maria had taken him to a movie. He had the stamina to talk for nearly an hour on the phone with an aunt he hadn't seen in twenty years. He'd also been able to sleep through the night for the first time in a month. "I can dream again," he tells me with a wide smile.

I notice an open photograph album on his bed. "I want to show you who I used to be," he says. "I did not always look like this." I barely recognize the man in the photos he shows me: he was probably twice his current size, a round, joyful-looking man who lived in cotton T-shirts and a-size-too-small jeans, his wife's arms wrapped tightly around his muffin top. "My friend took these," he says as he shows me his wedding photographs. He and Maria mar-ried in the church they still attend, their reception full of home-cooked foods brought by friends and set out on folding tables like those in a high school gymnasium. Neither he nor his wife has family in the United States—each left Mexico ten years earlier and happened to meet in a dance class. "We don't have much," he told me on my first visit, "but we do have God." There is a rosary draped around the bottle of liquid morphine at his bedside.

With the help of a neighbor, Maria tries her best to get him in and out of bed, bathe him, and recognize when to give him different medications for pain and nausea. "Is this one for pain, or is it for nausea?" she double-checks with me. Her brow furrows, and there are deep lines between her eyebrows that Sergio tells me are new. I know that the hospice nurse, who visited the day before me, has instructed her to give one medication if Sergio has pain, another if he is nauseated—but Maria is afraid, as so many caregivers are. "Sometimes, I don't understand what problems I should be looking for," she tells me. "And I could never forgive myself if I missed something, if he suffered because I am not a nurse."

Her worry keeps her awake at night, watching the rhythmic rise and fall of Sergio's chest, alert to changes in its tempo, fearful that she might be asleep if it suddenly halts. She tells me that she sleeps next to Sergio as his caregiver; it's been a long time since she's felt like his wife.

It helps her when I show her the various ways the body demonstrates distress. "Does he ever breathe like this?" I ask in Spanish, heaving my own chest rapidly and wearing a look of distress. She shakes her head. I act out other symptoms aside from the obvious grimacing in pain: The rapid, shallow breathing that comes with either cancerous fluid or a blood clot clogging up the lungs. The nausea that accompanies even the tiniest sip of water. The confusion and agitation that can characterize the final hours. I start to write down which medicine to give in each instance, but remember that Maria cannot read very well, that she instead identifies medications by the color and size of each one. We instead discuss which medications can be useful in each scenario—the liquid or the pill that dissolves under Sergio's tongue. But I know she will not remember it all. I cannot expect her to. Her own breathing becomes more rapid and shallow every time we discuss these things.

I feel a heaviness in my chest when she asks me why hospice cannot pay for caregivers. "I wish I knew. I wish our system was different," I tell her, silently wondering, as I often do, why our health-care system will pay for last-ditch-effort chemotherapy for a dying patient but not for one trained caregiver to help them remain comfortable at home.

After I wrap up my visit, Maria walks me to my car. She is barely five feet tall, yet she is protective of me and walks me out every time I visit, her arm around my waist. When we reach my car, she turns and asks me if I believe in God. "I don't know why this happened to *him*. He's only forty-five. He has done nothing wrong, nothing at all. Maybe if we beg God, maybe if you also beg God, he won't need your medicines and I won't be alone." She barely finishes the last sentence, burying her face in her hands and weeping.

. . . .

I'd always assumed that dying at home was far better than dying in a hospital.

Being at home, surrounded by familiar faces and embraces, is integral to dying a good death, right? Who would want to die in a sterile hospital with arms full of IVs, the sonic chaos of overhead paging and bed alarms, and the unfamiliar voices and touch of health-care workers?

As it turned out, many of my patients did. There was Juan, a former baker in his late forties diagnosed with late-stage liver cancer. When he became so breathless that he turned ashen and sweaty, his panicked wife called an ambulance, too overwhelmed to give him the medications for shortness of breath that the hospice nurse and I had carefully taught her to administer. The thought of Juan dying in a hospital, under the watch of skilled professionals who *did* know what medicines he needed, felt like the best plan for him, she told me when I visited them in the hospital hours before he died. There was Lilah, a schoolteacher in her fifties dying of an aggressive form of breast cancer. She wanted hospice care, but not at home. She didn't want her family to go on living in the house where she would die. She wanted to be cared for by experts, not by her two scared teenagers and a handful of church friends and neighbors. After all, experts had handled every detail of her medical care during her years with cancer. Why wouldn't experts care for her in the last phase of her life?

In hospitals, my patients and their families knew that nurses wore uniforms and followed protocols instead of texting friends and stepping out for a smoke the way some family members or caregivers might. Doctors could give precise doses of strong pain medications through an IV, which was much better than a nervous son squirting liquid morphine under his father's tongue, praying that the medicine landed where it needed to. People who went to school for many years should be the ones deciding when a medication isn't working, when it's time to give another dose, when the end is near, patients and families told me. Our mothers and fathers deserve more than their grieving children doubling as rookie caretakers.

What I could not have known until my home visits began was that even when some patients accepted hospice services, the proverbial "good death at home" is often still out of their reach. Fully experiencing the benefits of home hospice requires resources that hospice actually cannot provide: Money to afford caregivers, particularly in the absence of involved family members. A nearby pharmacy that stocks opiate medications for severe pain. Insurance that covers long stretches in nursing homes for people whose families may not be able to care for them. Without these luxuries, which some may take for granted, dying at home can be even more full of chaos and suffering than dying in a hospital. The important and growing national conversation about a good death hadn't always included the experiences of some of the patients I cared for.

. . . .

I park outside Ms. Stevenson's apartment complex, but can't open the gate. I call Barbara, the friend and neighbor who had taken Ms. Stevenson in two years ago.

"Sit tight," she says. "My grandson Richard is at home and will come let you in." Moments later, a lanky teenage boy carrying a bag of Cheetos and a remote control opens the door. Jean, our team nurse caring for Ms. Stevenson, follows me into the apartment. Richard disappears into the room next to Ms. Stevenson's room, leaving the door half open. I can hear the artillery fire and bomb blasts of the video game he's playing.

Ms. Stevenson lies in her bed, her mouth pursed into a tight line and her eyebrows scrunched together in pain. Five years ago, she had developed Alzheimer's dementia but had no remaining family to help care for her; her two sisters and brother had died in their sixties. She had never married and had no children. But she knew her neighbor Barbara, first as a longtime friend and then as a savior: on two occasions, Barbara had waded into street traffic to bring a wandering Ms. Stevenson back to the sidewalk, grasping her hand tightly as they wove through the cars waiting for a green light, avoiding the gaze of their staring drivers. "I was just happy I was there when I was," Barbara told me.

After the second wandering incident, Barbara noticed that Ms. Stevenson was spending more and more time in bed, the front door to her apartment unlocked or open. She spoke less and less, mostly pointing to her backside, where she had pain from a widening bedsore. "She clearly needed to go to an old folks' home. But I couldn't bear the thought of that for her, and she didn't have the money for it," Barbara told me. "I told myself I have to take care of my friend." That afternoon, Barbara cleaned out the spare room in her apartment and took Ms. Stevenson in. Ms. Stevenson's doctor enrolled her in home-based palliative care, and we provided her with a hospital bed, wound care supplies, and the medications Barbara would need to care for her.

But even though she was bedbound and could no longer wander into the streets the way she once had, Ms. Stevenson could still hurt herself. Unobserved, she would dig her fingernails into the small bedsore on her lower back, fresh blood and occasional pus streaking her fingers. In a fit of agitation, she sprained her wrist after slamming it against the railing of her hospital bed.

Ms. Stevenson begins to moan, her cheeks streaked with fresh tears. We lift her comforter and gown to find the source of her pain, and my fear is confirmed: the feeding tube that had been surgically placed in Ms. Stevenson's abdomen had been pulled loose from the stitches that tethered it to her skin. I examine Ms. Stevenson's abdomen, looking for any signs that the dislodged tube might already be causing an infection.

"I can't believe this," Barbara says when Jean and I call to inform her of the news. "Richard was watching her, I swear." I think of the times I'd discussed with Barbara how important it was to have someone observing Ms. Stevenson—not just present in an adjacent room—because her dementia predisposed her to pulling and picking at anything from her own skin and hair to her feeding tube. I'd suggested giving her mittens and a soft ball to squeeze when she wanted to pick at something. I changed around her medications and doses hoping to minimize her agitation, pulling, and pick-ing. These had worked to a degree, but Ms. Stevenson was still safest when someone was physically with her during her waking hours.

But Barbara works full time. She had petitioned her boss for paid leave to care for Ms. Stevenson, but he told her to hire a caregiver instead. Bar-bara had already tried that. The last caregiver quit when she found an easier job in a wealthier neighborhood. The one before her stole pain medications. Another one had been excellent but broke her leg in a car accident. It was nearly impossible to find good, qualified caregivers who were willing to ac-cept the meager salary that Barbara could afford to pay.

Our social worker tried enrolling Barbara as Ms. Stevenson's paid care-giver through in-home supportive services, but Barbara couldn't make ends meet without her current salary. So she instead paid her grandson ten dol-lars an hour to watch her dear friend when he could.

"Please believe me, I'm trying my best," she begs over the phone. "I'm getting some referrals from a different home care agency so hopefully I'll have a new caregiver for her soon. I just hope I can afford it."

I'd initially been surprised that Barbara, a friend rather than a blood relative, had taken Ms. Stevenson into her home. But I've now found this arrangement to be surprisingly common: friends from work or church or childhood contribute significantly to the care of my patients. Survival meant banding together, making new families from old friends. It both pained and touched me to see Barbara struggling under the weight of her commitment to Ms. Stevenson. I know there are very few alternatives remaining.

I think then of Mary, a patient I'd seen the day before. She, too, has de-mentia that has left her vulnerable to hurting herself accidentally during fits of agitation. But every time I see her, she appears well and comfortable simply because she has three children who take shifts caring for her. All of them attended my home visits and listened carefully as I adjusted medica-tions to keep Mary's agitation and pain controlled and discussed changing the type of tube feeding she received, because her current formula seemed to be causing diarrhea.

I'd prescribed nearly identical medications and recommended similar care plans for both Ms. Stevenson and Mary. But writing prescriptions for the right medications didn't mean they would actually be filled. Describing in exquisite detail the symptom that each medication treated didn't guarantee someone would be nearby to recognize these signs of discomfort, to dispense the needed medicine. And merely emphasizing the vital importance of a caregiver's presence for both fragile patients didn't change the many reasons one family was able to oblige while another—despite valiant attempts—could not.

I think back to my fellowship training, to the first time I did home visits. My patients lived mostly in Palo Alto or the wealthy satellite cities that encircled it. Even with wealth, with paid caregivers and visits to a therapist and groceries delivered to the home, families struggled to handle the emotional and physical work of tending to a dying loved one. Without resources, this task seemed impossible.

"I'm going to call that other caregiving group right now, Dr. Puri. I'm going to keep my promise to her. She'll stay at home with me," Barbara tells me, her voice quivering. She promises to find a caregiver by tomorrow morning.

"I'm gonna be honest with you, Dr. Puri, this is a risky situation," Jean tells me when I call to discuss my visit with her. "We may just need to discharge her from our services because I don't know if Barbara can really afford the type of caregiver she needs, and the poor lady might keep hurting herself if we just keep trying and trying to keep her at home."

．．．．．．．．．．．．．

I take a lunch break. There is a Mexican fast-food joint on my way to my next appointment, and I slide into a booth with a vegetarian burrito, extra avocado. The elderly clerk behind the counter walks over and gives me a free churro, winking at me. "Just because," he says, "looks like you could use it."

I wonder how he knows this, whether my work shows in my face. I chew on the warm dough, cinnamon and sugar sticking to my fingers. A patch of sunlight warms me, nearly lulling me into a nap after I eat my burrito.

Outside the window, a rickety ice cream truck drives by, the tinkle of its song soothing me. I pull out my phone and search for the latest celebrity gossip, the unexpected breakup or cheating scandal, the reality star with the purple hair, the shoes that cost ten thousand dollars, sold probably twenty miles from where I am right now.

My phone rings just then, the number of one of the hospice nurses flashing across my screen. "Hi, Doc, this is Johnny," he begins as he always does, in a friendly, singsong tone. "I wanted to give you an update on Mr. Fryer. His pain is now much better with the increased dose of medication you gave him."

"That's awesome, Johnny. But wait—did he get to the ceremony?"

Mr. Fryer is a spry eighty-one-year-old man with bladder cancer whose bones and abdomen ached from the spread of his disease. He refused to try any medication stronger than Tylenol and ibuprofen, but would never tell me why. These medications—which he swallowed by the handful when he was desperate enough—did little more than keep him in bed or on the couch, holding himself very still in a particular position to avoid any discomfort. His wife finally pushed him to tell me more about his reasoning. "Listen, you probably know nothing about this kind of thing, but I'm going to tell you now since I just can't live like this," he said, wincing as he spoke. "A guy a few doors down, he had some accident and had oxycodone pills for pain. Someone found out and broke into his house, stole it. Pushed him down the stairs when he tried to stop them."

He was right. I hadn't considered that his pain medications, combined with his frailty, could make him an easy target for thieves. "I'm sure you've already thought of this, but what about hiding the pills?" I asked.

"That's what I've been telling him," his wife told me. "And maybe you should come into our house the back way so nobody sees that a doctor is coming home." I glanced at my white coat, unaware that my uniform might have jeopardized Mr. Fryer's safety. We agreed that I'd come in the back entrance to their home next time, leaving my coat in my car.

Mr. Fryer gave the medications a try. His wife and I emptied a bottle of allspice in her kitchen and filled it with the pain pills that I hoped would enable him to sit in a wheelchair for an hour and a half at his granddaughter's high school graduation. He took the medication gingerly, using it only when the pain was unbearable. We talked about continuing to take the ibuprofen, praying for comfort as he waited for the pain medications to work, visualizing himself completely pain free as a reminder that he could achieve that.

Johnny gives me the update: "He did, Doc! He wanted to say thank you but he's asleep now since it was a long day. But I am going to send you a photo of him from the ceremony."

I decide to look at Mr. Fryer's photograph when I need a pick-me-up. In the meantime, I imagine him sitting in his wheelchair (which always has a balloon attached to it by one grandchild or another) and smiling broadly, wearing his finest red sweater, the one he told me he loves because it perfectly conceals the port on his chest through which he received chemotherapy and the slight protrusion of the pacemaker sewn into the flesh beneath his collarbone. I imagine him focused on the graduation ceremony, taking in the cheers and balloons and flowers and inside jokes made by the valedictorian.

. . . .

The drive to Linda's takes me past streets where McDonald's, Taco Bell, Church's Chicken, and KFC line the corners of intersections, frozen in a perpetual face-off. I wave to Chaplain Matthew as I approach Linda's apartment complex, a nondescript building surrounded by brown grass, multicolored pinwheels staked in the crumpled remains of flower beds. Matthew could calm even the most squirrelly patient with his tender voice, and has looked out for me in an almost fatherly way. I find Matthew standing in a parking spot right outside, smiling broadly, wearing a crisp pink shirt and pressed pants. "I figured I'd save you the best spot!" he says.

We walk to Linda's front door, speaking softly about her situation. "I think this is going to be difficult for Linda," Matthew tells me. "She is really afraid of dying and told me she just isn't ready. Her husband is looking really worn out from taking care of her."

Linda's kidneys began to fail long before her son died of a sudden heart attack. But after his death, she'd started using cocaine and missing dialysis, leading to multiple hospitalizations, heart troubles, and her recent decision to stop dialysis. "I just want to join my son," she'd tearfully told her nephrologist, her psychiatrist, and the many other doctors and nurses who had cared for her during her numerous trips to the hospital. She was deemed depressed, but not suicidal. She did cocaine and felt better. She stopped doing it and became depressed again. Around that time, she'd enrolled in home-based palliative care and I began to visit her at home fairly often because of her ongoing nausea, weakness, and depression.

But she missed all of the appointments our team and I made for her to see a social worker, therapist, and psychiatrist. She continued to try to make it to dialysis but her fatigue—sometimes from doing cocaine and sometimes from not doing cocaine—was prohibitive. Eventually, she decided to stop dialysis and enroll in hospice so that she could be at home for what would likely be a period of a few weeks before she died. But two days later, she called Chaplain Matthew and said she'd made the wrong decision. She wasn't ready to die. She signed paperwork to end hospice services and returned to her dialysis session that very day. She came home confused, nauseated, and so weak that her husband, Charles, had to recruit three neighbors to help him pick her up and carry her back to their bedroom.

"Hello again," Charles says warmly when he answers the door. Dried bits of food cling to his shirt, and the circles under his eyes have deepened since I saw him last. The faint odor of cigarettes and singed potpourri fills the apartment. He leads us to Linda's bedroom, where she rests underneath several blankets, her glasses still on her face, a large photograph of her son mounted on the wall above the bed. She hears my hello and lifts her head. "Doctor, can I walk out to the living room and we can talk there?" I nod yes. I have never seen Linda walk.

It takes her ten minutes and Charles's full assistance to get up from her bed and hobble with a walker to a peach-colored couch just outside her bedroom. She positions herself carefully on plush bronze pillows and says to me, "I want to continue with my dialysis."

"Yes, Linda, we talked about that on the phone a few days ago," Chaplain Matthew says, leaning forward and angling his body to face her. "Can you tell Dr. Puri here what you told me about why you wanted to restart dialysis?"

"I think when I said before that I would stop it, I didn't know . . . you know . . . that I actually felt better when I was on dialysis," she says. "I think it was better for me when I was on it."

Charles cuts in. "But you didn't go to dialysis. You just skipped it when you wanted to. You know, I am tired. I am so tired. I am always here with her twenty-four hours a day, and it's a struggle to go to the clinic to get my own medicines. The only times I could leave this house were when that hospice bath aide or nurse came by. I can't afford a caregiver for even a quarter of that time and make the rent here. And her sisters don't help!" He pauses, dropping his head in his hands. Charles's frustration startles me; usually, he quietly attends to Linda's needs and brushes aside the questions I ask about his own health and well-being.

"I just think I should try it one more time, you know," Linda continues. "My sisters visited this weekend and said I was just giving up, like if I stop dialysis . . . you know . . . it's like committing suicide."

"That's a heavy statement," Matthew responds. "Do you remember how we talked about the idea that sometimes the body tires out even with all the treatments your doctors give you? And then it is perfectly all right to let go and let God. That's not a sin and that's not suicide."

"Yes, I remember, Chaplain," Linda says slowly. "But I just don't think it's my *time*. I'm not ready yet to die." I think of my conversations with Dave, who would tell me he would know when it was time to let go, that he wasn't ready to die. I wonder what it means to be ready to die, how people feel that they *know*.

Ordinarily, I'd try everything in my power to honor a patient's wishes. But when I look at Linda, I struggle to understand how dialysis is even an option for her when she is so frail and debilitated. Going to dialysis takes her seven hours from the time she leaves her front door to the time she returns home in the evening, and has to be done three times a week. She returns home more exhausted and nauseated than when she left, and goes straight to bed. Dialysis might not add many more days to her life at this point, and it certainly didn't seem to make her days better.

And if she continues dialysis, I wonder how Charles will manage without visits from the hospice team, which provide Charles with a few hours each week to see his own doctor, to buy groceries, to walk to the mall alone, and, for once, to think of anything but the weekly dialysis schedule. Frustration burns again within me, knowing that Linda's health insurance will pay for dialysis but won't reimburse Charles for a trained caregiver to help him care for her and for himself.

Linda is silent, picking at her skin. And then she asks, "What will happen if I don't do dialysis anymore?"

I think back to medical school whenever I am asked this question, recalling the moment when Dr. McCormick spoke honestly to Donna and I listened. "I will do everything in my power to make sure that you are comfortable and totally free of any pain or nausea or difficulty breathing," I tell her. "You will be here at home with Charles and we'll keep you feeling as well as possible until God calls you home."

"Okay, Doctor. Let me think about it," she tells me before closing her eyes and sighing. Charles looks down at his clasped hands. Matthew and I glance at each other and then at Linda. Her eyes have partially closed, and she has bent over to rest her head on the arm of the sofa. I wondered about the first time Charles watched Linda sleeping, long before his white hair and dark circles, before cocaine and dialysis and the death of their son, when the focus of his attention wasn't her breathing pattern or whether his neighbors were available to help him get her from their porch to the dialysis transport van. How he must have looked at her and imagined all the ways his life was about to widen and stretch and expand, how this beautiful woman sharing his name and his home would reconfigure the plans he'd always assumed he'd take on alone, making room for new ones he'd likely never imagined possible.

Before I leave, I notice an old photograph of Charles and Linda out to dinner somewhere, she in a black dress and a silver necklace and he smiling widely in a tuxedo, both barely recognizable now, in a frame engraved with the word "FOREVER."

....

When I return to my car, I take a big sip of water and exhale. I look at my phone and dread picking it up, but I know that I need to call to discuss

Linda's situation with her nephrologist, Dr. Cartwright. Preparing for conversations with colleagues sometimes takes me more time and emotional energy than conversations with patients and families. Sometimes, I have to reassure them that I don't have a hidden agenda to force patients onto hospice or to convince them that chemotherapy or surgery isn't worth it. This isn't a burden that other specialists face. And in the moments when the realities of my role weigh heavily on my mind, I remind myself that the short-term frustration will eventually give way to seeing more patients in the long term. After all, I'd signed up not just for medical practice, but also for cultural change within the field.

As I dial Dr. Cartwright's number, I rehearse my words carefully. He answers on the third ring.

"Hi, Dr. Cartwright, this is Dr. Puri from palliative care. Do you have a second to chat about a patient of yours that I just saw?"

"Yes, yes, sure, which one? I have only a few minutes because I am in clinic," he replies, and I can hear the clickety-clack of a keyboard beneath his phone. He is probably multitasking, typing in notes and orders for other patients as he talks to me about Linda. He is pressed for time, and I know that I will need to be brief.

"Thanks so much. I just saw Linda at her apartment and wanted to touch base with you about how she is doing. Have you seen her lately?" I ask, secretly hoping that he will be the one to say Linda shouldn't get dialysis anymore.

"No, she didn't show up for dialysis twice last week. But that's pretty normal for her. How is she doing?"

"She isn't doing well. She sleeps most of the day and needs two or three people to help her get up and around. We discussed the possibility of stopping dialysis and going back onto hospice."

He remains silent, and I tell myself to be confident and precise as I continue. "Based on how she is doing, I am concerned that continuing dialysis may not help her to regain function or become stronger, even though that's what she might expect. I'm worried that dialysis may instead cause her to become weaker. I'm not seeing how it's helping her right now." There is a fine line between communicating my disagreement with Dr. Cartwright and giving him the impression that I question his judgment. I hear him continuing to type for a few seconds before he speaks.

"Well, of course dialysis helps her if she shows up. I'm not sure I understand what you are saying," he says.

Don't get nervous, I tell myself. "She is very afraid of dying, which is completely understandable. But I think she will die soon regardless of whether we continue dialysis or not. And maybe now is the time to tell her that dialysis doesn't seem to be helping her, and it is okay to stop dialysis and just focus on her spending her time at home with her husband."

"Sure, but this has been going on for a long time, you see," Dr. Cartwright says. "I've seen her say she wants to stop and then she wants to start, and the cycle just repeats. It's been two years now, and she's still alive."

"This is true," I say.

I hear Dr. Cartwright tell a nurse that he's going to run about ten minutes late. "Look, if she wants to continue dialysis and not do hospice, then I cannot stop her," he says. "I'm not going to be the one to stop dialysis. She needs to tell me when she's had enough. I've told her that she really has to commit to coming to dialysis three times a week to see the benefit of it."

I want to ask Dr. Cartwright to help me understand his perspective. But the hardening edge in his voice cautions me. "Okay," I say, struggling to sound genuine. "I can continue to see her and just make sure she's feeling as well as I can get her to feel, regardless of whether she chooses to continue dialysis." I remind myself that alienating Dr. Cartwright may stop him from referring other patients in need.

"Yes, of course! I know she enjoys your visits and you do a good job with her nausea. So please keep visiting and we can talk again."

"Thanks so much for your time, Dr. Cartwright. I'll keep you posted." I hang up the phone and hit my steering wheel, accidentally honking the horn. "And fuck you!" I scream. My head throbs, and I massage my temples, leaning back into my seat for a few minutes before I start my car and begin to drive home.

My friends who aren't doctors ask me how I can deal with being around dying patients all the time. My friends who are doctors ask how I deal with the doctors whose patients are dying. As I drive away, I remind myself of the wise words that both Dr. Nguyen and my mother shared with me: *Pick your battles.*

. . . .

I try not to think as I drive home, distracting myself with a mindless mix of pop music. But eventually my mind drifts back to my conversations with Linda and Maria, Barbara and Dr. Cartwright. Had I helped my patients today? I wonder. Had I been the doctor they needed me to be? I think back to the very first time I asked myself this question, when I had been a doctor for just six months and wondered what sort of doctor Mr. Tan needed me to be for him, what it meant to be a good doctor to a vulnerable patient like him.

What does it mean to be good at this work? I wonder as my car crawls along in rush-hour traffic. Would a better doctor have persuaded Linda to stop dialysis, or Dr. Cartwright to recommend hospice to her? Would I have better served Ms. Stevenson by convincing Barbara that she'd need to find a way to pay for a nursing home to care for her? Was Barbara also my patient in a way? What did it mean to advocate for Maria and Sergio in a health-care system that couldn't provide them with the caregiver they both needed?

Maybe doing this work well means continuing to show up for Linda and Sergio, Mr. Fryer and Ms. Stevenson. Perhaps being good to them means seeing *them*, not just the circumstances of their lives, and listening as they tell me how they want to be seen. I think of Sergio sharing his photograph album with me, Linda showing me that she *can* walk, Mr. Fryer holding his red sweater up and describing how wearing it makes him feel like a normal human being, not a patient. I've often heard and read that people who are dying can teach us what is really important in life, and what it means to live fully. But though my patients are dying, part of what it means to see them is acknowledging the many ways that they are still trying to live. Some are preoccupied with paying bills, still bickering with their spouses, still buying cocaine or clipping coupons for milk and produce. Dying hasn't bestowed

upon them the meaning of life or turned them into embodiments of enlight-
enment; dying is simply a continuation of living this messy, temporary life,
humanly and imperfectly. And even as they struggle and stumble, each of
my patients offers a vivid lesson in accepting inexplicable circumstances and
choosing to live the best they can. I can see their wisdom and dignity and
strength, all of which are not things hospice can provide. Wisdom and dignity and strength have nothing to do with Linda's income or whether or not
Ms. Stevenson had a family. Yet they are perhaps the most essential compo-
nents of the very private, internal process of making peace with life as part
of the process of dying. Maybe this is the meaning of these visits, of the
visits that preceded them and all the visits that await. *Your patients are showing you that dying is still living,* I tell myself as I stop at another red light, hoping that I will remember this tomorrow when I get up to do this imperfect
work once again.

And in death, as in life, seeing and appreciating the magnitude of the
smallest things was crucial: Halting the pain if not the cancer. Placing mittens on Ms. Stevenson's hands. Finding a hospice volunteer to sit with Sergio as Maria buys groceries. Seeing the commonalities of our last days, no
matter how much money or love or family or years of life we have or don't
have. This doesn't excuse the many ways that we must improve hospice and
expand its ability to care for patients in a multitude of circumstances like
Ms. Stevenson's or Linda's. But because I know it will take years to improve
hospice services in our country, is it possible to remember the successes
alongside the endless number of formidable challenges my patients and I
face together?

The picture of Mr. Fryer comes to mind. I feel the urge to look at it immediately.

I pull into the next plaza on my right and park in front of a doughnut
shop. I open the photograph and see Mr. Fryer looking at me, a Dodgers hat
covering the patches of hair that remain. He is indeed wearing his red
sweater, and if I hadn't known him, I might have thought he was just a proud
relative of a young graduate, not a man dying of a cancer his doctor had
discovered just ten months ago, a cancer that could be treated only with

chemotherapy that destroyed his taste buds and caused uncontrollable vomiting, leaving him largely confined to his bed for weeks. His granddaughter, clad in her graduation robe and cap, had her arms around him, her wide smile identical to his. She'd tied bunches of red and white balloons, which matched her high school's colors, around his wheelchair arms. He looked just like any other proud grandfather. Such a small goal, but enormous to him. It was exactly how he'd wanted to be seen.

Ten

FIGHT

Around December of my freshman year in high school, I stopped eating. Experimenting with various diets was practically a rite of passage for teenagers in Southern California, and as I'd watched my best
friend shed ten pounds in the span of three weeks, I, too, thought I could
change my body through sheer will. If I fought hard enough to lose weight,
I would. In June, I cut out snacks. No more mini chocolate chip muffins
or string cheese. In a month, five pounds vanished. In late July, I stopped
eating lunch, substituting carrot sticks and a banana. Eight additional
pounds vanished, and I began my sophomore year in September with
classmates congratulating me on how *great* I looked. Each lunchtime, I threw
away the peanut butter sandwiches my father made every morning before
dropping me off at school. I could hook all five fingers into the new craters
behind my collarbones, and often ran my index finger along their newly apparent edges. Angular cheekbones announced themselves. My jeans' waist-
band no longer left a pink indentation on my belly after I sat down for lunch
or went to the movies. I could see the intersecting map of my blue-green
veins across my hip bones, rivers against newly prominent hills.

By early winter, I'd found a way to sit at the dinner table, chew a min-
uscule amount of my mother's cooking, and strategically spit it out clandestinely into a napkin I clutched because "I had a cold." By January, I had lost
thirty pounds.

My mother yelled and cried, in rage and in sadness, as my father grew
quiet. As she'd watched me shrink, she had initially worried that I had

cancer, and took me to my pediatrician almost every two weeks. My pediatrician ran a battery of tests and reassured us both that I didn't have cancer or an overly active thyroid. I wasn't using cocaine or speed. She suggested instead that maybe I had "a mental issue" that was leading me to believe I shouldn't eat. My mother was aghast. She had never heard of anyone who willfully stopped eating. She reminded me that she and my father never knew where their meals were coming from as children, that I was selfish and stupid for shunning food. At that point, on the advice of my pediatrician, my mother took me to a nutritionist (an appointment, she'd told me, that only diabetics and overweight people should need) and then, despite her shame, to a therapist. As far as I could tell, my father tried to maintain a semblance of normalcy. He spoke to me as if he noticed nothing wrong, asking me about my grades, handing me a bagged lunch with a sandwich and a banana and pretzels every morning, indulging my request to drop me off a few blocks from school in the morning so that I could "walk the rest of the way and get a little exercise." Instead of walking, I ran those blocks, my purple backpack stuffed with the heaviest of my textbooks, so that I would burn more calories. My father would tell me later that he'd never been so afraid to speak to someone. Saying the wrong thing to me, he worried, might worsen my seemingly steadfast commitment to destroying myself. So he pretended that nothing was wrong, until one morning he couldn't.

"I can see the vein on your forehead," he said stoically as he drove toward my high school. I had been in the middle of another of my rituals, trying to chew a piece of sugarless gum ten thousand times. I stopped chewing. When we paused at a red light, he told me to look in the mirror. A squiggle had appeared overnight at the corner of my right temple, just below my hairline. "I saw that on my mother before she died." The light turned green, and I quietly watched familiar scenery speed by: blocks of apartment buildings surrounded by tall trees, a plaza with a gas station, a bigger plaza with a Burger King and banks, a Taco Bell and a TJ Maxx. My father drove me right up to the curb in front of the high school's gymnasium and stopped the car. I waited for an outburst, the one I'd expected months ago. *What is wrong with you? How can you be so stupid? Don't you know the value of food? Don't you know what starving yourself will do?*

"I feel sad when I look at you," he said. He asked me if I remembered what we had talked about when I was younger: That the body is temporary and it will always change, no matter how much we try to stop it. The soul, the spirit within the body, makes us who we are. Who we are has nothing to do with how our bodies look. Did I remember these things? he asked. I think I nodded. If you remember, then please feed your body, he said. It's not who you are, but you need it to be who you are.

Throughout that day, I ran my finger across the vein on my forehead, thinking about my father's words. By the age of ten, I had learned and could say aloud what my parents had taught my brother and me about the temporary nature of human life and the eternal nature of the soul. They'd told us that even our friendships with others were probably temporary. Change was the only constant. Living well would necessitate remembering what truly endured—the soul—and what didn't—the body. But hearing and intellectually understanding these ideas—many of which I had no real way of understanding as a young child—didn't translate into embodying them.

It would take me months to regain some of the weight I'd lost, but years to really begin to understand the many sad and complicated reasons I'd wanted to vanish, taking my body with me. Throughout those years, my father would remind me of what he had said that morning: That who I am is fundamentally distinct from my body. That my body was temporary and subject to both constant change and, eventually, its own physical limits. That I could not will my body into doing or being something it couldn't.

I would need to return often to this duality between my self and my body during stretches of sadness when I felt that everything in my life would be simpler if only I didn't weigh whatever I did. In the middle of one such stretch during residency, my father sent me a copy of the Bhagavad Gita, telling me that this particular translation was the best he had read. As I read each verse of the epic poem recounting a conversation between man and God, my eyes caught a phrase that I have returned to since: *The soul wears the body like a cloth and discards it at the time of death.*

Understanding this duality not only would help me personally, but would also shape how I spoke to my patients years later.

....

Several months into my first job, I received an unexpected voicemail from Dr. Coffey, one of the senior ICU physicians. "Unfortunately, I need your help with Joe Brown," he said when I returned his call. I opened Joe's chart and learned that, over the past five years, Joe's heart had slowly been failing, struggling to circulate blood to the rest of his body. His lungs became waterlogged with fluid to the point where even walking from his bed to his bathroom in the morning exhausted him. His legs swelled and he couldn't make it through his workdays at the post office. He took his diuretics and his diabetes medications regularly. But one day, while at work, he suddenly slumped over onto the counter and couldn't move or talk. When his daughter, Teresa, heard he had been rushed to the hospital, she assumed he'd had another worsening of his heart failure. But this time, Joe had suffered a stroke. A large tide of blood flooded his delicate brain tissue, drowning some parts and depriving others of necessary oxygen. At the hospital, a ventilator filled his lungs with oxygen, and a tiny yellow tube that snaked through his left nostril and into his stomach provided him with artificial nutrition and most of his medications. But even when all sedating medications—which he needed to stay comfortable on the ventilator— were discontinued, Joe didn't open his eyes or react when Dr. Fan, the neurologist, pinched his arm or rubbed his knuckles across Joe's breastbone. Joe's pupils, wide and dark, became only slightly and sluggishly smaller when confronted with a fluorescent flashlight. He barely coughed when his nurse tickled his throat with a suctioning device. Multiple parts of his brain weren't working, at least not right now, and possibly not ever again.

If Teresa wanted to give his brain more time to rest in the exceedingly tiny chance it might recover, Dr. Fan said, then Joe would need a tracheostomy—to keep him on the ventilator more comfortably—and a feeding tube surgically inserted into his belly instead of keeping one in his nose. These measures would give him oxygen and nutrition. But whether his brain would recover, whether he would ever wake up and become who he once was, remained at best a remote possibility. "He will need to live in a nursing home probably for the rest of his life," Dr. Fan told Teresa. "A nurse will need to clean him and turn him. He probably won't be independent again. Do you think that's something your father would be okay with? It's something you need to think about before we put a tracheostomy and a feeding tube into him."

"I don't know how to talk to this family anymore," Dr. Coffey told me, describing the meetings he and Dr. Fan had held with Teresa and her brother, Ray. I listened cautiously as he spoke, still surprised that he'd requested my help. Months ago, he'd told me that if he had to consult palliative care, it meant that he'd failed his patients. If *he* was asking for help, I thought as I listened to him, the situation must be *really* tough.

Dr. Coffey and Dr. Fan had held three prior meetings with Teresa and Ray, explaining that Mr. Brown's stroke was among the most devastating they'd seen. If Joe was to survive, they'd told his children, it would be solely with the support of machines. He'd never go back to the post office. He might never recognize or speak to them again. But instead of talking about her father's predicament, Teresa talked around it. The stroke would never have happened, she insisted, if *his doctors had just done their job.* She noticed her father twitching, which she interpreted as him trying to move even though Dr. Coffey and Dr. Fan both told her gently that those movements were involuntary and signified the extent of his brain damage. Still, she *knew* her father recognized her. She insisted that he would make a full recovery no matter what Dr. Coffey or Dr. Fan said. She wanted everything possible done for him.

"I'll be honest. I'm tempted to just do whatever Teresa says just to shut her up, but first of all, we are already doing everything possible, and second of all, I know that doing whatever she says to do is not the right thing to do for Joe. Dr. Fan has explained to her so many times that he's not going to wake up, that all his supposed movements are just involuntary twitches that actually mean he's doing terribly. But she doesn't listen to anyone. She thinks he's trying to fight and a miracle is going to happen," Dr. Coffey said. "Maybe she just needs to hear it from a new person, to get the perspective of a total stranger."

....

Around the time I met Joe Brown, I realized that I doubled as an accidental linguist, helping patients and families to excavate the many layers of meaning they assign to a word or phrase. In the first few minutes of our conversation, Teresa would describe Joe as a fighter. Countless patients described themselves this way to me. When I first met her, Linda had described herself as a "warrior" against her failing kidneys. Back in fellowship, Dave told me he felt more like a "soldier" in his "battle against emphysema" than he ever felt he'd been in Vietnam. Recently, I'd seen an elderly patient with end-stage lung cancer hospitalized with severe pneumonia. Her granddaughters superimposed an image of her face—thinned by cancer, crusted over with a slowly healing zoster rash—onto Hulk Hogan's body, and hung photocopies on every wall in her room. "Don't be fooled by her looks. My grandma is every bit as tough as the Hulk and there's no way she's losing to this wimpy old cancer!" her granddaughter said when I first met her. Her grandmother moaned, trying again to remove the oxygen mask over her nose and mouth. "See? She's so strong, she thinks she can fight this without even the oxygen!"

I understood this impulse to fight. When faced with anything life threatening, our instinct to preserve our lives is so strong that it's practically a biological response to fight an enemy in every way possible. Our bodies want to keep living, which is why they have so many built-in mechanisms to stay alive even when faced with life-threatening illnesses or injuries. When, for example, heart failure worsens, the kidneys work harder to preserve blood pressure. If we suffer blood loss in a car accident, the heart pumps harder and faster, and our rate of breathing increases to meet the body's needs for blood and oxygen. But what do we fight for when, despite the best possible effort made by the body and mind and medicine, the disease grows stronger?

In residency and the early months of fellowship, I had the impression that self-described fighters would be difficult patients. Fighters were the ones who didn't actually understand how sick they were. They demanded unrealistic treatments and berated doctors who wouldn't provide them.

They vocalized their courage and strength more loudly as their bodies weakened, as though the militaristic ferocity of their words alone could halt or reverse the territorial gains of their invisible enemy, be it cancer or heart disease or liver failure. When fighters died, their obituaries underscored their battles. Celebrities who died of cancer "lost their long battles" or "succumbed despite fighting."

But what did these fighting words actually *mean* to the people who used them? Their use had become so pervasive that they were now de rigueur descriptors for anyone confronting mortality. Fighters wanted "everything" done to treat their disease. Fighters hoped for "miracles." They refused to entertain any discussion of "giving up." Some physicians I knew interpreted the descriptor "fighter" as an indication that they should provide all treatments possible, regardless of their harm. Who were they, as physicians, to challenge or unpack the word "miracle"? I had seen many a conversation stalled with the use of these phrases, and began to wonder if the way to advance a challenging discussion was to explore these word choices, to force clarity about what fighting for a miracle might mean in a very specific set of unfortunate circumstances. After all, didn't the word "fight" imply a conflict? Did the fighter grasp the complexity and nuance of the battle? What did the fighter know about his or her enemy? How, specifically, did they understand the consequences of the fight, and what they were fighting for? How did they define "giving up"? What was worth fighting for? With what consequences for the battleground, which was inevitably one's body and life? Could there be miracles aside from curing a disease, especially if that wasn't possible?

The body has its own language, and Western medicine has become its adept interpreter. Using a blood pressure cuff, we can identify high blood pressure as the cause of chest pain. Through blood and urine samples, we can tell whether a person's confusion is due to failing organs or an infection or taking too much of a certain medicine. But do we know how to listen when the body tries to tell us that it is dying despite our best efforts to forestall death? If we are giving patients the weapons to fight these so-called battles, isn't it our responsibility to help them understand what may and

may not be possible to fight for, with what ammunition, and with what consequences? Doesn't that merit as much discussion as the ways in which a
patient may want to fight?

As I thought about Mr. Brown's predicament, I felt myself reaching for
the language my father gave me years before about the body: that it was our
home but not our identity, that it was scientifically known but infinitely
mysterious, that we could try to make it bend to our will but nature would
always prevail. I'd fought to understand this duality when my own life and
well-being hung in the balance, but it had taken years for me to move from
intellectually understanding this concept to inhabiting it with more ease.
The soul wears the body like a cloth and discards it at the time of death. I wondered
if I could use these words to help Mr. Brown.

. . . .

Teresa Brown wanted me to know that she was a dutiful daughter. She sat
in the visitor's chair next to her father's bed, empty coffee cups and a banana
peel on the counter behind her. She opened two spiral notebooks, one filled
with his medications, vital signs, daily weight, and notes taken during her
father's visits to his cardiologist over the past two years. The other was
filled with feverish scribbles documenting the name of every nurse who
took care of him, the time each nursing shift started and finished, details of
what the nurse did for him, and verbatim accounts of her discussions with
Dr. Coffey and Dr. Fan, some of them highlighted, clearly reviewed over
and over again.

Over the last three days, she told me, she'd sat next to her sixty-year-old
father, observing how the nurses turned him from side to side, taking notes
on every medication given to him, quickly pointing out errors or misunderstandings.

*No, that's not his dose of metoprolol. Didn't you read his home medication
list?*

*This is the third time I've had to tell the nurses not to come in here in the middle
of the night. Don't they understand he needs to get some sleep?*

I want to talk to the doctor directly about why this ultrasound was rescheduled.

It's the second time they told us there was an emergency and they have to delay the test.

"He is my father, and I don't mess around," she said, peering at me, eyebrows raised, over the top of her cat-eye-shaped glasses. When someone we love is fighting a formidable battle, we want to try to give them every chance of success. For Teresa, that meant never leaving her father's side and struggling to control the aspects of his care that might help him pull through. Powerless in the face of so many unknowns—why her father had suffered a sudden stroke, whether he would recover, and what recovery would actually look like—she focused on the ways she could advocate for her father. I knew that she meant well. I could see myself acting from a similar place of fear, protectiveness, and love if my own father had been hospitalized. But as she spoke, I sensed a familiar, growing unease in my belly, a sensation akin to a hand pressing inward, squishing my innards, shortening my breath. I'd come to recognize this sensation as my body's visceral reaction to patients or families who could quickly become adversarial. Not all scared daughters took notes on every aspect of nursing care or wrote down verbatim conversations with physicians. I tried to maintain both compassion for her and caution about the situation.

I'd struggled with this balance before with other patients and families, like the sister of a patient who yelled at me in the middle of a family meeting, "WHY ARE YOU ALWAYS SO NEGATIVE?" as her entire family and three of my colleagues looked on, stunned. Or the elderly man who asked me if I was the Grim Reaper. Or a patient's wife who once said, "I can't call you 'Doctor' the way I call other people here a doctor. Because you're the opposite. You're like a human killer." The insults cut deep, even though I knew logically that patients and their families under tremendous duress spoke and acted in ways they might not mean. But even when my mind told me I could find a way to make an alliance with most people, my body tried its best to warn me that, sometimes, I simply couldn't.

Teresa spoke again: "I'm sorry, what is your specialty again?"

She had been so intent on relaying various aspects of her father's care that I realized I hadn't had a chance to introduce myself in the fifteen minutes I'd been in the room. I resisted the urge to describe myself as a member of the "supportive care team," a popular euphemism for the palliative care service. I decided instead to be straightforward with her. There was no point delaying the tension I was certain would follow.

"I am from the palliative care service," I said, looking her in the eyes, keeping my voice even and gentle. "I work closely with many patients like your father who are in the ICU, and try to help in two ways. First, I help make sure that the patient's symptoms like pain or nausea or difficulty breathing are all treated so they are comfortable. Second, I help families and the medical team with discussions about how to help match the medical treatment plan with the patient's goals and values."

Her expression changed from welcoming to surprised. "Well, you know, I'd say Dad is pretty comfortable right now. He's just resting. I can tell you that his goal is to get better and go home. Simple. Does that answer your questions?"

"Yes, that's most people's goal, so I hear what you're saying," I began. "Has Dr. Coffey given you any updates about how your dad is doing?"

"Yes, he has," she said. "I've written it all down here. Dad needs the respirator and the feeding tube, and we're going to just take it day by day and see how he does."

While her summary was technically correct, it didn't acknowledge the fact that her father was likely *not* to make a meaningful recovery despite everything Dr. Coffey was doing for him. I wondered about his *personhood*, and what Joe would want if, at best, he might be a mere shadow of his former self.

I pushed back against the invisible hand as I took a deep breath. "I think what might be helpful is a meeting with your father's doctors and both you and your brother. We can discuss exactly where we are in taking care of your father, and make sure that all of your questions are answered. How does that sound?"

Teresa responded with exasperation. "You folks always want to talk and meet and waste my time," she said. "Do we really have to do this? Haven't I already answered your questions?" I could feel my patience wearing thin, but reminded myself that if I were her, I, too, might be suffering from conversation fatigue, especially if most conversations were about my father's failing health. But since we couldn't talk with Joe about his care, we had to talk to Teresa. After all, she was his advocate.

"I know there seems to be endless talking, Teresa, but it's because your dad's situation is pretty complex, and we want to make sure that what we're doing for him is what he'd want for himself."

"I'll tell you exactly what we are going to tell you—do everything you can to save his life." Teresa stared at me with her eyebrows raised and her arms folded across her chest. "But fine, if there's no getting out of this, then let's just meet tomorrow at noon." Even though I understood that an intense jumble of emotions led Teresa to speak this way, I could feel my exasperation begin to outweigh my empathy for her. Just before leaving Joe's room, I watched as she bent over him, moistening his brow with a cool towel, whispering that she loved him and would never leave his side. She pressed her forehead to his for a moment before removing her glasses and dabbing her eyes with a tissue. I set aside my frustration with Teresa and tried to look upon her as a loving and scared daughter, alone in a hospital room, unprepared to lose her father. Joan Didion's words came to mind: "A single person is missing for you, and the whole world is empty."

....

What People Might Mean When They Say
They Want "Everything" Done:

I want you to do all possible medical tests and procedures to cure my mother, all the things I see the doctors do on television, because those patients recover.

If I don't ask you to do everything, then I'm giving up on my father.

I'll sue you if you don't do everything you can.

I can't be the one to tell the doctors to stop. I need to feel like I gave my father every chance to fight, even though I can't answer you when you ask me what my father would want to fight for at this point. I don't want to be the one to say "let's just make him comfortable."

I feel guilty that I haven't seen my aunt in ten years. But now that I'm here, I want her to get everything you can give her for her heart disease. Leave no stone unturned, no test undone, that sort of thing.

I am so frightened that I'm going to lose my wife. What if she is the one-in-a-million person who will survive? How can you know for sure she's going to die unless you try everything possible to keep her alive?

If we don't do everything we can to treat his cancer, isn't it just like allowing him to die?

Please, return her to me whole. Give me back the person I know and love.

You're not God. So who are you to say that you know for sure that he won't survive a liver transplant? Do everything for him.

I am overwhelmed, scared, worried, angry, confused, resentful, numb, unable to sleep, and deeply sad, and frankly it's just easier for me to tell you to do everything than to have to take it in and digest the truth.

Doctors told my father that he wasn't going to survive his cancer but he told them he wanted everything done and he's still here, three years later. I don't trust what doctors say anymore. I want everything to be done for my mom.

. . . .

During my fellowship, I might have spent hours with Teresa, convinced that if I heard and fully understood her opinions about her father's care, I could gently refocus her attention on the gravity of her father's neurologic devastation. I knew logically that her sharp words and adversarial attitude had nothing to do with me personally. But even just bearing witness on a daily basis to the strong emotions that accompanied death and loss dulled my own emotional response to the suffering that surrounded me.

And yet, to take care of Mr. Brown, I'd have to find a way to talk to

Teresa and her brother. A year ago, I might have asked how I could muster the fortitude to put up with Teresa's behavior, her insistence on conflict rather than collaboration. Where I had once strived to be understanding with people like Teresa, I now grew impatient. I glanced at clocks during contentious family meetings. I cringed inwardly and tried to change the subject when a patient complained in great detail about how every physician they met had failed them. I'd force myself to listen to their monologues, waiting for a pause so that I could divert the discussion back to the topic at hand. I'd convinced myself that in order to do my job well, I had to forge an alliance with the Teresas I'd met. But now I began to ask myself a different question: What was my responsibility to patients if their families could not hear what I was saying no matter how many different ways I tried? Could I use compassion to soften their anger, and what might that look like? Would it be more compassionate to indulge avoidance of a tough discussion, or to force it?

Despite meeting Teresa just once, my frustration with her swelled like a tide that threatened to engulf me. In retrospect, I can see that when I heard her voice, I also heard the chorus of difficult patients and families I'd encountered over the past two years, the ones whose anger I remembered more than their vulnerability. Teresa, her brother, and her father appeared in my mind as though I looked at their reflection in a fun-house mirror: Teresa, angry and controlling and unrelenting, was outsized, both tall and wide, inescapable. Mr. Brown, who was really the central character in this unfortunate drama, was short and squat, squished to the side by Teresa's largeness. What was reflected back to me in this distorted image, the product of my frustration and impatience, was my own distorted sense of victimhood. Mr. Brown's suffering, which I told myself was my focus, was not a part of this picture.

. . . .

I had intended my move to Los Angeles to be permanent, a placement of roots firmly in the ground. But at first, permanence—or the hope for it—was an unexpected challenge. After all, transience had characterized the past ten years of my life. I cycled through everything from teams, patients, hospitals, clinics, apartments, pager numbers, and furniture. If stability was the intended payoff of all the transience, why did it feel like such a difficult adjustment?

Just around the time I met Teresa and her father, I had started to feel just as comfortable outside the hospital as I did within its walls. Making friends in Los Angeles became easier. I worked closely with the hospital medicine physicians, many of whom consulted me regularly. They were a lively group with great senses of humor, appreciative of my work and sympathetic to the challenges it brought my way. They began to invite me to happy hours at local bars, Christmas parties at their homes, and departmental picnics. A number of them were around my age and had recently finished their own training; they could relate to the jarring adjustment of becoming an attending, and the curious discomfort of having newly free time to fill after training had ended. Over drinks and dinners, we talked about the more challenging parts of our jobs and the fun things to do in LA that made coming back to work easier.

I gradually settled into a routine in my neighborhood. I found several welcoming coffee shops where I read and wrote, and a handful of restaurants that I explored with new friends from work. I hiked in Griffith Park with my brother, who had begun his residency training at UCLA. And I met a man whom I would come to love deeply. In the early days of our courtship, he would bring me Tupperware full of coffee cake he'd baked himself, and send me texts in the afternoons letting me know he was thinking of me. As was the case in residency, hours would pass before I'd reply. But he took no offense, telling me he didn't send the notes with the expectation of an immediate reply. He just wanted me to know he was thinking of me, that was all. I found myself looking forward to the texts, scrolling through our conversations from start to finish when I took breaks from writing my patient notes, warming to the idea of someone I missed who missed me equally.

This life, the beginning of what I'd hoped would be the permanence I'd craved, had for so long been a shimmering mirage at the end of the long road of training. As it came into sharper focus, I could feel some of my long-held anxieties about whether I was a good enough doctor begin to soften. Perhaps the best way to be a good doctor, I was learning, was for me to revel in everything outside of medicine, everything I'd wanted but never really believed I could have. The task now was to protect it from the long shadows that work—particularly thorny situations like the one at hand with Teresa—could cast.

....

I struggled to find a place to meet with Teresa and Ray. They trailed behind me as I stopped first at the waiting room (full of visitors, two with young babies who wailed), then at a peach-walled conference room (occupied by two nurses on break, one of whom responded with only an annoyed stare when I asked if I could use the room for a family meeting), and finally the tiny ICU conference room (where several colleagues were discussing a difficult case). I considered taking them to the cafeteria, which was usually empty around this time, but recognized my growing desperation and stopped. It was as though places to have family conferences were deliberately engineered out of hospital architecture. There were plenty of spaces for every possible procedure, but not for a conversation. Just then, I felt a buzz in my pocket and saw a text message from Dr. Coffey: *Meet in the nursing conference room.*

The nurses had agreed to let us use the large conference room where they often had staff meetings. Surrounded by blue-gray walls, it housed a large tan table and chairs with plush seats and firm, supportive backs. Teresa and Ray filed in, followed by Dr. Coffey and me.

"So the reason we are all here today is because we need to talk about your father's medical condition," Dr. Coffey began right after we all sat down, his impatience already apparent. He spoke directly, evenly, his hands clasped together on the table before him. "I think we all know each other by this point, so let's skip introductions and get started." I glanced at the clock: 1:30 p.m.

"As you know, your father had pretty advanced heart failure for several years now, along with diabetes, and his kidneys weren't working that well, probably because of both those issues."

Teresa cut in. "I'm going to stop you right there, sir. Because I don't think that his diseases just got worse on their own. They got worse because my dad was totally neglected by his doctors." She tapped her pen on the table to emphasize the end of her sentence, glaring first at Dr. Coffey and then at me. "Now what I'm interested in is telling you all the ways that mishaps by his other doctors led us to this situation, and then you can tell me what your plan is to correct it." She opened up one of her notebooks.

"Um, Teresa, we've talked about this before and I don't think it's ultimately helpful to your father if we go over things that happened months and years ago, because he's in a very different situation now and I—"

"Yes, he is," Teresa interrupted, raising her voice slightly, "and I want to see how you are going to correct all the things that weren't done properly before. There is no way I'm going to let my father die because of all the screwups by the doctors here."

A type of filibustering followed for the next hour. Teresa talked about every detail of her father's care except his current situation, which she talked around. There were the times the nurse in cardiology clinic had told him medications were ready for pickup from the pharmacy when they weren't. There was the time his kidney doctor didn't return Teresa's phone call to confirm the next follow-up appointment day and time. Once, his primary care doctor suggested that he start a medication he was already taking. Teresa wondered aloud why doctors like us were paid so much when we couldn't call patients back or remember the details of their treatment plans.

"People sometimes feel like they need to go over every detail of everything that has gone wrong because they are hurt and angry and can't cope with the situation," Dr. Nguyen told me when I asked her how she sat through a similarly lengthy monologue during a family meeting once. "You just need to listen and try to remember that you're there to help them try to think about what their relative would say is best for them." I tried to pay attention as Teresa spoke, reminding myself that she was simply overwhelmed, that the combination of frustration, fear, anger, and grief she was expressing was understandable. Yet by making it nearly impossible for us to have an honest discussion with her, she was making it harder for us to care properly for her father—the person who mattered the most.

Ray, who had been silent, spoke when Teresa paused after speaking for nearly twenty minutes. "I can't believe all the ways my dad was treated not even like a human for so long. I didn't even know all this stuff Teresa is telling you. Now that I know it, I'm asking myself, well, what can we do to correct this situation? Why isn't that what you all are asking yourselves?"

Ray's tone became harsher and louder as he accused us of trying to euthanize his father and save the hospital system money. I wondered whether his words were an expression of his grief or whether he truly felt that this was the most effective way to advocate for his father to receive the best possible care. I wondered what Teresa and Ray were really asking for, and what they hoped we could do for them, for their father.

This gridlock stalled Mr. Brown's care. I looked on as Dr. Coffey tried to explain at least three different ways that Mr. Brown's maladies had always been incurable but well addressed by his doctors; that unreturned phone calls and an hours-long delay in receiving a prescription for routine medications, while understandably aggravating, were not the reasons for his massive stroke; that he thought Teresa and Ray should simply consider the possibility of allowing their father a peaceful death, since his chances of survival were extremely small. But Dr. Coffey couldn't make it through his sentences without fiery interruptions. He could never get to the part where he'd say he'd support their decision either way, but wanted to be sure they knew all the details of their options so they could discern which one their father would choose if he could.

And the brighter Teresa and Ray's anger burned, the less interested Dr. Coffey became in returning to the conversation's original purpose. Eventually he grew silent, glancing at the clock on the wall. Silence, he would tell me later, was his only real option. Challenging Teresa would have weakened his ability to have any further conversations with her, should the need arise. His face, once concerned, had relaxed into apathy. These were exactly the types of situations that made many physicians wary of difficult conversations with patients and families. After all, it was far easier to do whatever a difficult patient or family requested than to help them understand that their request might be impossible or dangerous or the cause of tremendous suffering. It wasn't right, but it was human.

My idealistic side wondered whether there was a way I could cut through Teresa and Ray's resentment of their father's physicians and appeal to their love for *him*? The tired part of me wondered whether it was really my responsibility to understand and work with their anger.

"I know that this has been a really tough ordeal for you both, tougher than any of us can imagine," I said softly. Teresa snorted. Ray looked down at his lap. "We aren't trying to gloss over the way your father's care might have been handled in the past, but we do think it's important to try to talk about how he's doing *now*."

Teresa started laughing and Ray shook his head. "Have you been listening at all?" Teresa replied. "Or do you need some hearing aids? We understand how he's doing. We know that this wouldn't have happened if you people hadn't fucked up. What we are respectfully asking you, on behalf of my father, is to do everything you can to fix him!"

My anger—not my empathy—got the best of me.

"You've said that many times, that we should do everything we can for your father. What we are trying to explain is that there are different ways we can care for your father, different ways that we can do everything for him, depending on what he would consider most important at this time," I said, narrowing my eyes. "You've already heard this, but I want to be one hundred percent sure that we both have the same information about his condition. He's had a major stroke, and we are worried that he may never wake up, talk, or be in any way independent again because he's shown no signs of improvement in a timeframe when many other patients would have started to open their eyes or move. In addition to this stroke, he's suffered from heart failure and diabetes, and these conditions might make it even harder for him to survive his stroke."

"Wait, wait, wait," Teresa interrupted. "Why are we going back to this? The heart failure, the diabetes—that has nothing to do with this stroke. Those are problems that you people caused."

"Sister, shut up and let her talk," Ray said. "I really want to hear what this one has to say about Dad's so-called options. Even though we keep saying the only option is for him to keep fighting."

I paused, considering whether I should continue. But remaining silent angered me more than the prospect of further confrontation frightened me. No matter what Teresa and Ray's response might be, I felt responsible for telling them about the same options that any patient in Mr. Brown's position would be given.

"Actually, before we get into options, I want to learn more about something you've both said. You describe your dad as a fighter who would want everything done for him. Can you tell me what that means to you? These are words that mean different things to different people."

Ray laughed and Teresa shook her head. "You went through so much school and you're asking me what I mean when I say Dad is a fighter?"

"Yes," I said. "I want to hear what you understand the fight to be, and what you're envisioning the outcome will look like if he wins this fight."

"Fighting means overcoming," Teresa said. "It means keeping going no matter what the circumstance. He is fighting for his life. I see it every time he kind of shakes in the bed."

"He is fighting a very tough battle," I said. "Winning the battle would mean that he wakes up and goes back to his normal life, correct?"

"Yes," Teresa said. "And I know that is going to happen."

"You've mentioned that he would want everything done for him so that he can win this battle, and I think it's important that you know everything possible is already being done right now. But the breathing machine and feeding tube can do only so much. For him to go back to his normal life, his brain needs to start waking up. It has been so badly damaged that he may never wake up. So we need to talk about what we should do if doing everything for him doesn't seem to be helping his brain fight and get better." I raced through my sentences, hoping they'd let me finish.

"So what are you saying?" Teresa asked, exasperated.

"You've given me a sense of who your father is as a person, as someone who would fight tooth and nail to get better. But we are seeing that, no matter what we do to support him, his *body* may not be able to fight the way *he* would want to. And while we can have hope that his body may recover, we also need to talk about what we should do if it continues to get sicker, which seems to be the more likely outcome." Teresa and Ray remained quiet, which made me nervous. I kept talking.

"We all want to see your father get better. But we all need to be on the same page about what 'better' really means. In his situation, there's a chance that, at best, he would need to live in a nursing home on a breathing machine for the rest of his life. He might be okay with that. But if you think he wouldn't want that for himself, we can talk about another option, which is to focus on keeping him comfortable and free of pain without the support of machines, and allow him to pass away."

The invisible hand returned, and I pushed against it to breathe. That was the first time I'd been able to say the words I'd been holding in—that there was another way to care for Joe if our default plan, continuing all current support, wouldn't be what he'd want if he heard what his life would likely be like. In the brief silence that followed, I braced myself for the fallout.

"Are you saying it would be better if we just unplugged him and let him go? Not give him every chance to fight? I don't know why I need to keep repeating myself," Teresa said, looking incredulously at her brother. "Here's what you are all going to do. You're going to fix the mistakes you made. You are going to do everything for my father. You asked me last time what my goal was? We expect him to be given every medical treatment known to man and he better be able to go home."

Just as I drew in a breath to respond, to use different words to re-explain the complexity of her father's condition and the exceedingly low chance that he would recover even if we "did everything," she pointed at me and began to speak. "And I am not interested in hearing you ask any more questions about what he wants if this or that happens. I don't know how else to get through to you. Ray and I want everything done. *E-ver-y-thing*."

I wished I could understand what they saw when they looked at Joe. Did they see the father they loved? Did they really believe that his twitches were his attempts to move? Did they think that his eyes, glassy and vacant, saw and recognized them?

I had been looking at Teresa, but glanced at Ray just then. He appeared to be holding his phone upward, as though he were making a video. I blinked, stunned by what I saw. "Are you recording this conversation?" I said in a voice I didn't recognize, a panicked mixture of shock and dismay. "I'm going to have to ask you to stop. We don't allow that."

"Why not?" Ray said, looking at me only through his phone screen, his expression an angry sneer. "You're probably afraid because if I post this online and the world can hear what you are all saying to us, then you'll think twice about treating anyone's family this way. You people are crazy if you think we're going to let you talk us into this, whatever, comfort bullshit because YOU'RE THE ONES WHO SCREWED UP!" He began to yell. I looked at Dr. Coffey, guessing that he would be okay with me wrapping up the meeting at this point.

But before either of us could respond, Teresa and Ray began speaking to each other in Spanish, a language they didn't realize I spoke and understood. Teresa told Ray that their father was in the hands of stupid doctors. Ray responded by wondering whether we were ashamed of ourselves for how we'd cared for his father. They exchanged a few thoughts about how they might use the small stretch of video footage Ray had captured. When I heard Teresa mention hiring a lawyer, I spoke.

"Yo hablo español y puedo comprender todo lo que ustedes están diciendo," I said quietly. *I speak Spanish and I can understand everything you are saying.* They stared at me, briefly quiet, until Ray told me he was glad that I heard they thought we were terrible doctors who deserved to be sued.

"You know, I think we're done here," Dr. Coffey said decisively. "I don't think that this is a productive conversation, even though Dr. Puri and I are trying our best to help your father. If we can't talk about this, then I think I may need to call someone from our hospital's ethics board to speak with you further."

"How many conversations are you going to make us have?" Ray said. "Haven't we been crystal clear with you?"

"I don't think there is any point in continuing this discussion," Dr. Coffey said again, signaling to me that we should leave the room. As we walked back to the ICU, he told me he suspected that Teresa and Ray might not actually be representing what Joe himself might want in this situation, instead ordering us to do what they want. "That isn't the role of a surrogate decision maker, as you know," he said. "It's always to tell us what the patient himself would want." Theoretically, this was true. But reality was complex; a grieving child could easily convince herself that her father would agree to an intervention that she might want for him. In the face of death, love and fear made porous the very boundaries we hoped families would respect. "I know that wasn't a fun meeting. But thanks for being there with me. I would have given up and walked out long before if you weren't there," he said.

. . . .

It was raining when I drove home that evening, the roads slick and the traffic formidable. I admired the water on my windshield, the way it caught the red of brake lights and the bright stream of headlights coursing by on my left. I half listened to the mindless mix of pop on the radio and the rhythmic swipes of my windshield wipers. I was exhausted, partly from the meeting with Teresa and Ray and partly from the sheer logistics of spending half of my days in the hospital and the other half doing home visits. Numbers mattered in new ways: The strength and effectiveness of our service was measured by how many patients we saw. But the more patients we saw, the less time I could devote to each person. My conversations with patients and families became more compact and, occasionally, incomplete. I felt forced to rush through discussions that required focus and care. This was a different exhaustion from what I'd experienced in residency and fellowship; those years had been an endurance test from which I emerged fatigued, but not depleted, the way I'd felt recently.

I thought back to a conversation I'd had a few weeks ago with a colleague, the director of a palliative medicine program at the University of Southern California. She and I had met the year before at a conference and had kept in touch in the months after I moved back to Los Angeles. *I may have a job opening up in a few months*, she'd called to tell me. *I think it could be a great fit for you. Lots of teaching opportunities with medical students and residents, and very interesting patients. I'll keep you posted about what happens.* I hadn't been looking to leave my job, but her call made me remember what I missed about being at a university: Being in the company of other learners, teaching others and being taught, taking in noontime lectures by experts in lung cancer or coronary artery disease or geriatrics. I missed working with residents and medical students. Back then, I'd had not only the opportunity to teach them how to care for a patient but also the chance to debrief with them about the tough situations we encountered.

But though I'd considered staying on as an attending at a university, I was drawn strongly to the idea of working at the same medical group that had employed my mother. Even when my days were tedious, I took unexpected comfort and pride in having followed my mother here. I was secretly over-joyed when a patient mentioned that she'd called my mother's office instead of mine, or when I received emails intended for my mother. But eight months in, I wasn't sure that this connection was reason enough to stay.

. . . .

When I returned to work on Monday morning, I learned that Joe had died.

At eight o'clock on Friday night, a few hours after the end of the family meeting, his blood pressure began to fall: 120, 100, 80, 75, 50.

During the weeks he had been in the hospital, nothing had changed in his condition, until, over the span of thirty minutes, everything had. Dr. Coffey had returned from the family meeting to find Mr. Brown sweating from a new fever, his percentage of blood oxygen lower than normal. An X-ray of his chest revealed a new pneumonia that hadn't been on the morning chest X-ray hours ago. His blood pressure dropped as his infection bloomed. When Dr. Coffey told Teresa that her father's kidneys were also starting to fail, Teresa asked the nurse to call the kidney doctors so that Teresa could speak to them directly and make sure that Dr. Coffey was telling her the truth.

4, 10, 25, 30. The dose of one of the medications to sustain his blood pressure increased rapidly over those thirty minutes. His blood pressure continued to fall even at the maximum dose. A second blood pressure med-ication was added. 5, 10, 20, 30. The dose rose as his blood pressure fell, a rising arpeggio and a falling one, each with a certain macabre grace, ending in silence.

Around 10:30 p.m., Mr. Brown's heart slowed and then stopped.

Dr. Coffey led the effort to resuscitate him, ordering one of the nurses to begin chest compressions, to try to force life back into Mr. Brown's dying body. The nurse pushed into his chest two inches deep, one hundred times a minute, for two minutes at a time.

Teresa and Ray were pushed outside his room, forced back by the crowd of doctors, nurses, and respiratory therapists and pharmacists who hovered around his bed, each charged with the task of doing everything. The crash cart, a cream-colored vessel containing all of the medications and tools needed during a Code Blue, took its place at the rear of the room. There was no space for the two people Joe had probably wanted at his side.

Everything. The 30 and 30 and the 100 compressions per minute, each deep into his chest.

"10 rounds of CPR were performed," Dr. Coffey wrote. "No return of spontaneous circulation." No heartbeat despite the compressions, the 30 and 30.

I wondered what I could have done differently in talking with Teresa and Ray. I felt ashamed for my frustration with them. A dull ache grew in my chest as I thought about what Joe went through as he died.

Our father wants everything to be done to keep him alive. You people couldn't do your jobs in the clinic, so now he's here and you better do your damn best to keep him alive because that's what he wants.

I hadn't expected that he would get sicker so quickly. And I certainly didn't anticipate that he would die hours after our conversation. I scrolled through Mr. Brown's chart and found Teresa's number listed as his emergency contact. Minutes passed as I stared at her number, wondering if I should call to see how she was doing, to tell her how sorry I was to hear of her father's death. I started to punch in her number on my office phone, but stopped a few numbers in. What did I plan to say to her? Given our last interaction, wouldn't my call only upset her? Was I calling for her or for myself? I hung up the phone.

Maybe I was just jumping to conclusions and assuming that Teresa would have only harsh, unkind things to say, I thought. If I regularly called other patients' families to offer my condolences, I should call her. I picked up the phone again and began to dial her number. I hung up after two rings.

Eleven

THE GRIP OF LIFE

I wore freshly pressed gray pants and a pink top to Ms. Carson's funeral service. "Please don't wear black," Gina told me when she'd called to invite me. "Mom specifically told me that she wanted lots of color, none of the usual funeral dreariness."

"I feel like your mom would want me to bring a date," I joked with Gina, who laughed.

"She never stopped talking about that," Gina said. "She was hell-bent on meeting the boyfriend you told her about." I hadn't had to tell Ms. Carson much. She somehow knew that I'd started seeing someone. "You're in love, aren't you?" she exclaimed one day as I knelt down to determine the exact amount of dark fluid that drained from her abdomen into the plastic container at her bedside.

"Mom, stop!" Gina exclaimed, rolling her eyes.

"So let's talk about your belly," I said to Ms. Carson, winking. "Gina told me you were in a lot of pain over the last week." As I pressed my hands around her abdomen, she let out a long, loud fart.

"Good Lord, I am so sorry, Doctor!" Ms. Carson exclaimed, turning bright pink. Gina bit her lip, shaking silently as she held in her laughter.

"Don't apologize! I'm just glad you're passing gas. Means that your intestines are moving around. Do you feel a little bit better?" I asked, shocked that a woman with a near-complete blockage of her bowel had managed to fart.

"How can you stand it, doing this sort of work when you are so young and have your whole life ahead of you?" she asked, sidestepping my question. "Why are you here with this farting old lady?" Back in fellowship, I realized I'd committed to an interesting symmetry, building my own life as I cared for people confronting their mortality. I'd made the choice to practice this field of medicine, but I'd also been drawn toward it, maybe ever since the time my father taught me that impermanence defined every life and being, from myself to my parents to the clouds in the sky above us all.

"I think it's just what I was meant for, just like you were meant for teaching," I said, smiling. "I can't really explain it."

I sat toward the back of the church in a pew lined with copies of the program, which was filled with photographs from every stage of Ms. Carson's life. A photograph from her wedding, when she'd clutched a bouquet of white flowers tightly and stood next to her beaming husband. Gina in a red and black robe, flanked by her parents and brother at her college graduation. Ms. Carson as a new mother, gazing at her sleeping newborn swaddled in a blanket. I read her biography and realized how much about her I hadn't known: that half of her family was from South America, that she'd been both a teacher and a swimming coach.

The service began, and I took in the remarks by Ms. Carson's family, her colleagues at the school where she'd taught, a former student. I wiped my eyes with my bare hands until a kind usher brought me soft tissues. I cried not because I was sad, but rather because I was moved by the words spoken, the tone in which they were delivered. If death is the dropping of a stone into a still lake, perhaps the ripples toward the shore are the imprints we leave behind, the change that we effected simply because we existed. We may disappear into the water, but our significance doesn't drown.

"Say 'death' and the whole room freezes," writes the poet Jane Hirshfield.

even the couches stop moving,
even the lamps.
Like a squirrel suddenly aware it is being looked at.

Say the word continuously,
and things begin to go forward.
Your life takes on
the jerky texture of an old film strip.

I'd used the word "death" more in the past two years than most people probably did in a lifetime. I'd watched my patients look death in the face almost every day, until it had become as ordinary as the photographs that filled Ms. Carson's funeral program, just as natural as the sunrise and sunset, words Gina used in her speech to describe her mother's birth and death. Death still moved me, still struck me as profoundly sacred, a force I regarded with great respect. It could still frighten and overwhelm me, though it did so less frequently. Because I'd also seen that death wasn't mighty enough to strip away the meaning and lasting impact of a human life. Death was even an unexpected reminder of human equality, demonstrating that no matter how different we might be, we were unified in the brevity and fragility of our lives. Death didn't have the power to undo a life and its legacy. But perhaps the fact of death amplified life's significance.

"The grip of life," Hirshfield reminded me in the closing lines of her poem, "is as strong as the grip of death."

. . . .

A few weeks later, my colleague from USC called to tell me that she'd been able to secure funding for a second position on the palliative care team, and she wondered if I could come in for an interview the following week. The day after I interviewed, I received a call from the division chief of internal medicine offering me the job. For weeks, I wrestled with what it would mean to leave the same hospital system where my mother worked for thirty years, to leave a job after just one year. But when I imagined what awaited me—being a part of a young and growing palliative care team, teaching and mentoring medical students and residents and fellows, maybe even having some time to write—my exhaustion gave way to excitement.

Days later, I said yes.

. . . .

During my last week of work, I opened up our electronic palliative care list to find a new patient with a Punjabi name. Even though I had trained in cities with good-sized Indian populations, I could count on one hand the number of times I'd cared for someone from the same region as my parents.

Her name was Amrita Singh. She had suffered a sudden and large hemorrhage in her brain, so large that pooled blood had pushed her brain against her skull. She was just fine until one day she complained of a splitting headache and lost consciousness. Her daughter, Anu, called 911 immediately, and grew fearful and silent when the neurologist reviewed her mother's head CT, telling Anu that her mother might die that night. But Amrita survived that night, and the next, though she hadn't yet woken up and couldn't seem to breathe without the support of the ventilator. The ICU team had requested my help talking with Anu about the possibility of a tracheostomy and feeding tube if Amrita survived the next few days.

With her dark hair and smooth skin, wide smile and slightly hooked nose, Anu looked like she could be my cousin. "When I saw that CT scan, I just couldn't stop crying," Anu told me as she sat next to her mother's ICU bed, stroking her hair. "I mean, what do you do with a picture like that?" She began to cry again, and I reached for tissues. The neurologist had asked her tough questions. "Have you considered what your mother's wishes might be in this situation?" he'd asked. Anu was still wrapping her mind around the enormous implications of the CT scan she'd seen. Thankfully, she worked as a lawyer, and had helped her mother fill out an advanced directive the year before.

"She is a firecracker," Anu said as she described her mother. They had just attended a U2 show together. Amrita had bought Anu her first U2 concert tickets when she was seventeen. "She loves U2," Anu said, smiling, "and she was right there with other fans screaming, 'I love you, Bono!'" Anu had been planning their outing to the concert for a long time, and finally had convinced her mother to take a break from caring for her father. "I'm so glad we made it to that concert, but I just don't know . . . I mean, how did she go from being healthy and totally loving life to how she is now?" A deep sadness stirred within me. Anu was just around my age, and her mother was just a few years older than mine.

As we sat together, I studied Anu's mother, whom I called "Auntie." She wasn't a blood relative, but I couldn't imagine referring to her as "Amrita" or "Mrs. Singh," the way I generally refer to other patients. It was second nature for me to call older Indian men and women "Uncle" and "Auntie," and I did just that the handful of times they had been my patients. Auntie's beauty reminded me of my mother's. She had thick dark hair streaked with gray, and skin the color of almonds. Her eyes were always closed, but I imagined them to be just like Anu's: large, warm chocolate brown, framed with long lashes that required no mascara. Although she was on a breathing machine, her face was relaxed, peaceful.

I listened to her heart and lungs and pressed gently on her belly. Everything sounded and felt fine. Everything but her brain and mind. I did a complete neurological exam, ending by asking her gently, "Auntie, can you squeeze my hand if you hear me?" and I thought I felt her attempt, quivering fingers trying to close around mine. "Can you squeeze my hand if you are in pain?" I waited to feel the squeeze I'd hoped for. I leaned in close and whispered, "I am so sorry you are going through this, Auntie. I want you to know that you are safe and that Anu is right here with you. You are loved, and you are not alone." It was something I would come to say often to patients who couldn't speak either because of their condition or because of the machines they depended on to survive.

I ordered her pain medications and spoke with her nurse to ensure that she'd check Auntie's pain level as often as she could. Anu and I then sat down in a conference room in the ICU to talk more. "Mom was always the healthy one," she told me. "My dad has Alzheimer's, and taking care of him is her whole world even though he doesn't recognize her. And now, even if I told him that she's sick, he wouldn't understand. He will never know that this happened to her."

Anu looked at her lap, twisting together and pulling apart the tissues she had.

"I think it would devastate her if she were alive but couldn't take care of him," she said. "She would have such a hard time depending on someone to take care of her, or to do anything for that matter."

"I hear that so often from people in our parents' generation," I offered.

"Totally! I think there's something about them having survived Partition time and knowing they need to be independent to survive and take care of each other in a new country. I can't imagine how she would stand being in a nursing home if she even survives this." We sat in silence for a few minutes, and Anu told me that she'd have to leave for a little while to take care of some work at her legal practice, but that she'd be back later tonight. Her brother, a surgeon, would be flying in the next day and she hoped that we could all meet.

"He might be more realistic about her situation than I am," Anu told me. "I know she wouldn't want to be dependent on machines . . . but I feel like we need to give her a chance to try to get better."

"I can understand that," I told her, "and even when we might have a general idea of what our parents might want, it is one thing to know it and it's another to honor it when there is a lot of uncertainty about whether she might recover."

"I just wish she could talk to me," Anu whispered, looking down at the table and resting her head in her hands. "I wish she could tell me what to do."

. . . .

I drove home that night thinking about my own parents. I knew that they had drawn up wills and advanced health-care directives around the time I'd graduated from college, when they were both in their fifties. I didn't admire their foresight. I instead refused to discuss their plans with them, becoming angry when my father tried to reason with me. "I don't want to talk about that stuff," I said, interrupting him as he explained that it was important for my brother and me to know their plans and to understand the intricacies of the document. "No," I had said. "Nothing is going to happen to you." My brother, then a college freshman, had a much easier time listening to my father. I'd learn years later that my brother knew all about the content of my parents' wills and the very specific instructions they contained for handling every aspect of their lives. He hated talking about these matters, he told me, but it was a necessary part of life.

Now in their sixties, my parents were quite healthy. Both exercised regularly, ate a vegetarian diet, and took their medications every day. Ever since his cardiac procedure back in 2004, my father hadn't had chest pain, though I asked about it regularly. My mother's arthritis flared at times, but she turned to Ayurvedic therapies to help her feel better—castor oil massaged into her knee, turmeric powder added to the glass of almond milk she drank every night before bed. But Auntie's situation reminded me that everything could be just fine, until suddenly it wasn't. I thought again of Joan Didion's words: "Life changes in the instant. The ordinary instant."

. . . .

Auntie was neither better nor worse when her son, Ajay, arrived for our meeting. Auntie's brother joined us, too. Just before our meeting, I stood outside Auntie's room and watched her brother cradle her head and speak to her in Hindi, telling her to be strong, to fight through, to come back to the people who love her.

Ajay listened quietly as I gave him updates on his mother's condition. He'd reviewed her CT scans with the ICU attending, and knew that not much had changed since she first arrived at the hospital. "Have her ventilator settings changed much?" he asked. "She's actually on pretty low settings," I said, "but since she's not waking up, it would be risky to try to extubate her. This is why the neurologist thinks that if we are going to keep trying to support her artificially, we should probably do a tracheostomy."

Anu remained quiet for most of the meeting, as she'd already heard my explanations. "We must give her a chance," Auntie's brother said, turning to me. "You know, miraculous things happen. One must never give up hope," he continued, tears starting to fall from his eyes. "Yes, Uncle," Ajay began, "but we also have to be realistic. If she isn't going to get better, then why make her suffer like this on machines?"

"No, no, I cannot accept that. We cannot just stop the machine that is keeping her alive," he said firmly, shaking his head. "We cannot take my sister's life," he said, looking at me, his hands pressed together as though in prayer. I would have ordinarily reminded him of the purpose of the breathing machine, which was to support her as her body tried to recover, though I doubted that it would given the magnitude of her hemorrhage. But he spoke to me as though I were his niece or granddaughter, begging me for mercy in a way he probably wouldn't have if I were of any other background. So much about the Singhs felt familiar and familial: Anu's hand gestures, the mixture of English and Hindi that Uncle spoke, the unspoken shared history. I was tempted to bend the rules, to err on the side of comforting them rather than discussing the reality of Auntie's situation. *They need you to be a doctor, not a purveyor of false hope*, a strong voice reminded me. *Don't let your empathy get the best of you just because they remind you of your own family.*

I responded in my gentlest voice to Uncle's fear of losing her just as suddenly as she'd gotten sick. "Uncle, nobody is going to take Auntie's life. I know this is very scary. Nobody could have predicted this would happen to her. No wonder it is so frightening."

"But the breathing machine won't fix the stroke," Ajay pointed out to his uncle before I could. "She may never be able to come off it."

"Anu and I spoke a bit about this, but I was wondering what you thought as well," I said to him. "Did your mother ever talk about what she would want in a situation like this?" Uncle wiped his tears as we spoke.

"No, not really," Ajay told me. "She was always really healthy and everyone was really mostly concerned about my dad. But I seriously doubt she'd be okay living with a trach in a nursing home."

"Sorry, but what are the odds that a miracle could happen and she could get better?" Anu asked suddenly. "I need to know that."

"It's natural to want to know that," I reassured her. "But I think we need to be really clear about what getting better would mean for her. Sometimes, getting better means that she needs less support from the breathing machine. But that's different from her waking up and being herself again. That sort of getting better might be very difficult to achieve," I said. When I looked at Auntie's CT scan myself, I couldn't believe that she hadn't died the night of her hemorrhage. Maybe that had been the miracle, the fact that she was still alive, able to sense the love around her, giving Anu and Ajay and Uncle a chance to say their good-byes.

. . . .

Two days later, Anu told me it was time for her mother to be at peace.

The ICU team had done another CT scan of Auntie's brain and things looked worse. So did her physical exam. "I know I can't be selfish even though I want to," she said, her eyes red. "We all agreed that we just need her not to suffer like this anymore. She's lived a good life, such a beautiful life."

Anu proceeded to tell me the things she would never forget about her mother. She told me that her father was supposed to have had an arranged marriage, but that he had met her mother and fallen in love with her, marrying her shortly thereafter. Anu had found some of the love letters they had exchanged while her father was pursuing a master's degree in the United States while her mother was still in India with their two children. Love marriages were exceedingly rare in India in the 1960s, when Anu's parents married; they required bravery, risk, and enough certainty about one's intended to push back against the heavy weight of societal and parental expectations. "I keep telling her that Dad is going to be okay, that we're going to take good care of him," Anu told me. "I don't want her to hang on thinking that nobody will be there for him."

"Telling her that is so important, Anu," I said. "I am sure she worries for him, and she needs your reassurance that he will be cared for well. Are there other things that might be important for her, things I can help you in any way with?"

Anu paused and spoke hesitantly. "Actually, yes. I know this is a really random question, but my mom loves my dog. I know you might think I'm crazy, but I just don't think she can go without a visit from Buster."

I chuckled, shaking my head. "You are not crazy at all, Anu," I reassured her. "Pets are family. I'm sure Buster also would want to have a chance to say good-bye. I think it should be okay, but I'll double-check with the ICU nurses and staff."

"Thank you for everything," she said, sniffling. "There's just no way I could have made this decision without talking to you."

Although for many years I had chased the praise and approval of others, I now found it hard to respond to comments like Anu's. I'd shrug them off and instead praise the patient or family for their own forbearance and courage. This time, I experimented with saying the simplest thing: thank you.

"Thank you, Anu," I said, finding it easier than expected. "You are so strong that you could have definitely done this without me, but the privilege is truly mine to help out."

"She would have loved you," Anu said, and suddenly I began to cry without warning, hot tears spilling onto my cheeks. I covered my face in shame and told Anu that I was sorry, that I usually didn't cry in front of patients and families. She gave me a hug and told me it was okay, that I was just as human as she. We cried together there in Auntie's ICU room, arms wrapped around each other like sisters.

. . . .

It happened to be my last day of work at the hospital, and I rushed around to sign paperwork, say my good-byes, and turn in my white coats and pager. I stashed thank-you cards and gifts in my office and rushed around to say good-bye to the patients I'd seen in the hospital. I'd said my good-byes to my hospice patients, giving their families my new contact information and encouraging them to keep in touch. As the day wound down, I wrote my notes and logged out of my computer for the last time, taking one last glance at the adjacent photos of my mother and me when I searched for our last name in the online physician directory. I sat at my desk in silence for what seemed like a long time, bewildered that it had been a year since my arrival. It had passed so slowly, and then so quickly. Time, at once as expansive and compact as an accordion, always beguiling.

. . . .

That weekend, I went home to see my parents, thinking of Auntie as I drove. It was relatively early on Saturday morning and the traffic on the Harbor Freeway was minimal. I took an exit near my mother's hospital, driving past the cluster of buildings that had been my second home. I drove along Anaheim Street as I'd done dozens of times on my way home in the past. On my left was a large factory with spirals of smoke twirling upward; on my right was a series of empty lots with patches of brown grass and green weeds. I drove up Hawthorne Boulevard alongside groves of pine trees and eucalyptus, past my old high school. Without thinking, I turned onto a street that led to my elementary school, parking my car in the exact spot where my mother would pick me up, a spot that had undoubtedly hosted millions of pickups and drop-offs since then. I continued, driving six blocks away to the street where we'd rented a home with a lush, verdant backyard and a kids' room off the kitchen where I'd read *The Berenstain Bears* aloud as my mother cooked. I thought of our year in this home, our first in Los Angeles, when my father first took my brother and me trick-or-treating, when my mother took up gardening and taught me how to plant begonias and marigolds underneath a wilting banana tree. It had been nearly thirty years ago, but the clarity of my memories—the smell of the dirt around the flowers, the gentle grip of my father's hand around mine on Halloween—suggested otherwise.

How many moments make up a life, I thought then, realizing how lucky I was to have had my parents with me for these thirty-five years. I thought of the ways they had nurtured and protected my brother and me as children, how they had thought about and prepared for every aspect of our lives. I thought of Auntie's vulnerability as she lay in a hospital bed, how she appeared almost childlike in her rest, her future hanging in the balance between her family's grief and medicine's educated guesses. And I knew then that no matter how much I dreaded it, I had to talk with my parents about what they would want when—not if—their bodies failed them. That would perhaps be one of the greatest gifts I could give them—dignity and presence at a time of their own great vulnerability. I looked again at our former home, renovated into modernity with a gleaming oak door, a driveway free of deeply fissured concrete, and neatly linear flower beds in place of tangled knots of green-brown bushes and ivy. I remembered my father's familiar refrain: *Change is the only constant in life.*

. . . .

When I reached home, my mother was in the garden, drinking tea. She sat on a small terra-cotta-colored wall that bordered our small green lawn. A peach tree, a guava tree, and bunches of tomatoes and cucumbers crowded the other side of the wall. My mother often sat on the wall between the greenery, meditating, raising her face to the sun, playing with our cats, Snow and Winter, who mewed and napped next to her. I watched her from the kitchen window as she played with them, remembering her hesitance to pet the first kitten I'd brought home in 1986, fearing it would bite or claw her.

I opened the sliding screen door and she smiled widely, her face glowing as though she hadn't seen me in years. I inhaled the mixture of sandalwood and coconut oil in her hair as I hugged her. "I didn't think you would be home till later," she said, "and I haven't made lunch yet!"

"Don't worry, Mama, I'm not even hungry," I replied, suddenly nervous as I thought about how to open a discussion with her.

"So? How was your last week at the hospital?" she asked, squinting in the sunlight. Although she'd told me that she supported my decision to take the university job, I knew she was disappointed. We'd both relished being a mother-daughter pair in a large health system, our second home over the years.

I knew myself well enough to know that if I didn't talk about it now, when I was inspired to, I might never do it. What followed came mostly from my heart rather than my head. "My week was okay," I said. "Something happened that made me think a lot of you."

I told her about Auntie, about how Anu's description of Auntie made me think of her, of how both of them had defied Indian societal expectations of women to build alternative lives courageously. I told her that Auntie was a firecracker and she was, too. I told her that I couldn't live with myself if something suddenly happened to her and I didn't know what she would want me to do for her. I struggled to remember the questions I asked my patients and their families every day. Language, my reliable workplace ally, vanished as I looked at my own mother's face.

"I don't want to think about life without you. But I know I need to be prepared for it," I said, leaning on her shoulder as she put her arms around me.

My mother stroked my hair, just as she had when I was a child afraid of the dark. I forced myself back into my doctor role, leaving my daughter role briefly. "What would you want me to do for you, Mama, if you got so sick that you couldn't talk to me? What would be important to you at that time?" I was glad that we could speak about this in English; these weren't questions or concepts that I could easily translate into Hindi. When I'd tried in the past, I spoke haltingly, my sentences confusing and awkward. There was simply no good way to translate "goals of care" or what one "might hope for when time is short."

"I don't want anything aggressive," my mother said immediately, waving her hands. "I just want you to let me go." Her response was so quick and terse that I realized she'd thought about this for years. Her words stung, and I reacted just as I'd seen many children react to their parents' similarly expressed wishes in family meetings. *But what about me? Don't you want to try to stay alive for me?*

"But what does that mean exactly?" I pressed, trying to remain in doctor mode. "If you had something reversible, something like a pneumonia, and needed to be intubated for a few days, wouldn't that be okay with you?" I was back in daughter mode. I couldn't imagine my mother forgoing a few days on a ventilator for pneumonia, especially when she'd intubated so many patients in far worse situations. "You've intubated and taken care of so many people who were on the vent for no good reason," I thought aloud. "How could you possibly say no to someone else taking care of you that way for a few days? Wouldn't it be worth it to you to have more time with Siddarth and me and Daddy?"

I could sense my mother softening her stance. "Yes, okay, I think if it was something reversible, then yes. You can tell them okay if they need to intubate me for a few days. But no tracheostomy, no nursing home, none of that. I wouldn't want all these things we do to patients." This didn't surprise me. Most physicians I knew noticed the irony inherent in our offering patients intubations, CPR, tracheostomies, dialysis, and so on, when many of us wouldn't choose such interventions for ourselves in their circumstances. We often joked about wanting DNR tattoos and generous doses of pain medications at the end.

But there was more than just this to my mother's reasoning. Stories about her life structured her thoughts about her death. She described how her life had always bulged with dizzying amounts of activity—medicine, child care, volunteer work, engaging with our spiritual community. She couldn't stand the thought of drawn-out debility, forced by disease into a state of dependence. If her organs were failing, or she had an incurable diagnosis, her main concern was living well. She didn't want therapies that would just prolong her dying process. "And I would never want you and Siddarth to have to take care of me," she admitted.

"But why?" I asked, hurt and angry. "How could we not? You deserve the same love and care that you gave us. We would both do whatever it took to make sure you and Daddy were okay. Don't you have that faith in us?"

"Yes, but we don't want to be dependent on you both," she explained. "You have to understand that your father and I are completely self-sufficient. Nobody gave us a thing when we moved to this country. You see that, *na*? It would be very hard for us to start depending on others at that point." I knew this was true. While they readily responded to the needs of others in crisis, they asked for help only with small matters, like feeding the cats and collecting their mail when they were away.

"I know that you are both very independent," I said, validating her words in the most doctorly way possible. When I was doctorly, I enunciated words clearly and slowed the pace of my sentences. Keeping a professional distance actually helped me to have this very personal conversation with her. This meant trying to look at my own mother as though she were a stranger. "But Siddarth and I would both *want* to take care of you if you needed that. Can you accept that from us?" She said she would, but that she couldn't live well without her independence. If she could not take herself to the toilet or sit in the garden with the cats or move without severe pain, she would take these signs as God calling her. "Then I would want only comfort. I wouldn't want anything more than my family and God's prayers at that point," she said. I tried to push aside my anguish at this thought, reminding myself to be doctorly and not daughterly, to listen carefully to what my mother was saying. She wasn't saying anything remarkably different from what many of my patients told me; most valued their independence and quality of life with their loved ones, and wouldn't want medicine to sustain their bodies at the expense of the quality of their days.

But then she said something that most people don't tell me, words that captured the essence of who she and my father are. "Sunita, your father and I are not afraid of dying. We will miss you, but we will never leave you," she said. "I know that my Lord is waiting for me, and that gives me so much comfort. I know in my heart that you and Siddarth will not have to make many hard decisions because He will make them for me and your father."

I let her words sink into my mind like handprints on wet concrete, hardening into permanence. Everything she now said echoed everything she had always said. The same faith that propelled her from poverty to medical school, from the challenges of immigration to the stability of her current life, would of course be her main guiding light as she aged. She wanted to die as she had lived.

"It is very important when I am at that point to pray," she continued as I looked past her at the hummingbirds floating between the leaves of the peach tree, a crow perched atop its highest branch. "You must pray continually and keep Swami's photo on my chest, over my heart. Just stay next to me," she said. "I will be ready when my Lord takes me back."

A breeze rustled the grass and stirred the cats from their nap. A bee zipped around us toward a patch of lavender. I looked at my mother's face for what seemed like a very long time. I noticed the patches of gray hair that glistened in the sun, the dark brown circles underneath her eyes, the mole atop her upper lip surrounded by faint peach fuzz, her hazel eyes, the ones my brother inherited. She'd passed on to me the shape of her torso and her wide smile; my first strands of gray hair showed up just above my ears, exactly as hers had. She and I even both suffered from a patch of eczema on the same part of our left legs.

She was half of the DNA in my cells. She'd literally live on in me, in every cell of my body, long after she left me physically. But my inheritance from her was more than just physical. She'd also passed along her dreams. I followed her into medicine not only to heal others as she did, but also because, in some way, I wanted her cherished role in the world to live on through my own work. It brought me immeasurable comfort to have heard her thoughts directly from her. My task at some point—a point I couldn't fathom—would be to follow her careful instructions. It would be to use what I knew of her to allow her peace, knowing that my love for her would make her immortal.

"You will know what to do for me. You and I have a direct connection," she said, leaning in and pressing her forehead against mine. I thought of the day when sitting next to her on this ledge would be another memory in my mind's kaleidoscope. "Don't you know that I'll always be with you?" she said, her face close to mine.

. . . .

My father had watched our conversation from the kitchen window as he prepared lunch. He eyed us with an amused expression as we walked hand in hand, Snow trailing behind us mewing for treats. "So, what were you discussing?" he said, chuckling as he noticed my serious expression.

"Come on, don't tease her," my mother said as she approached the fridge. She had always rescued me from my father's jokes. "Are you making the salad or should I start it?"

"Are you having doubts about the new job?" he asked, eyebrows raised, a joking half smile on his face.

My mother snatched away the radishes and lettuce he was washing. "You need to sit down and talk to her. This is important," she said, winking at me as she forced him to take a seat.

"Okay, Krindy," he said, using my childhood nickname as he always did. "Your mother is being dramatic again," he said, laughing as he glanced over his shoulder at her. "What is it that you want to know?"

Leave the emotion out of it, I reminded myself. *Doctorly, not daughterly.* "I know that I haven't wanted to talk about this in the past," I began, "but I really do want to know your thoughts on what you would want from your medical care if you couldn't tell me yourself." I had carefully rehearsed this sentence on the drive down from my home, particularly in preparation for my discussion with him. Thirty-five years of knowing him had taught me that he responded best to logic. Because he had the mind of a rational engineer, I gave him the context behind my question. I told him about Auntie, about the questions that her situation had made me ask, and about why caring for her had compelled me to talk to him.

"Well, here is how I see it," he began. "The body is like a machine. Sometimes you can easily fix a problem, and other times you can't. If there is something to try to fix a problem I have, like when I got the stent ten years ago, then do that. If there is something not fixable, then don't let me suffer." He spoke with the same even tone of voice he'd used when he taught me algebra in middle school. The image of him hunched over a legal notepad with me, teaching me the Pythagorean theorem, came to me. It was a warm summer day and he'd insisted that we do math problems together instead of going to the YMCA to swim. "If you solve the problems, we can go swimming," he offered as a compromise. "You have your whole life to swim, but now is the time for your father to teach you math."

"Okay," I said, "but sometimes it isn't that simple. Remember Rajiv? The doctors fixed certain broken things in his body, but the way he ended up . . . would you want that kind of life?"

"No, absolutely not," he said firmly. "If I become so dependent on others that I can't go where I like, do what I like, then I think that's it."

"What about being on machines temporarily if you needed that?"

"Well, you are a doctor! I would trust your judgment. If you think that a machine or the CPR or whatever it's called would help me, then you can tell them to do it. But if I will just be in bed, weak and with a nurse doing everything for me, then just let me go."

"So you don't want to be like Lieutenant Dan, then?" I said, smiling, knowing that the mention of his favorite character from *Forrest Gump* would cheer him.

"Well, Lieutenant Dan wasn't just lying in bed doing nothing," my dad pointed out seriously. "He just had this idea that he should have died on the battlefield like his ancestors. But who are we to think we can plan exactly how we are going to die? Some people have this very silly idea about all this stuff," he said, laughing, then suddenly serious.

"Do you remember another movie we watched, *Gandhi*? Do you remember what I always pointed out to you, the most important moment of the movie?" he asked, and I immediately knew which scene he was referring to. We must have watched the film when I was around ten years old, and the scene I remember most vividly was when Gandhi was shot, when the last words that he murmured were *Hai Ram*, one of the many invocations of God in Hindi. I was sprawled on my stomach on our thick brown carpet, and I remember my father telling me then that the most important thing at the time of death was to say God's name.

My memory was accurate. "Remember in the Gita that at the time of death you must always remember God. But to train your mind to remember God at the very end, you must remember Him all the time," my father said. "You know, I don't even think there will be a need for you or Siddarth to do anything for your mother or me," he continued. "I really do think, and I feel this in my heart, that He will just come and pick me up one day. He will say, 'Okay, time to come with me.' None of these machines or anything will be needed. I will just go quietly."

I couldn't imagine which was worse: making a decision for my father to make use of life-sustaining technology or waking one morning to find him gone, at peace but without a chance at remaining with us.

"Okay," I said, doctorly again, trying to be objective as I summarized what I'd heard. "It seems to me that you would be okay with some interventions if Siddarth and I and Mama thought that you had a reversible condition," I began. "But if you were going to end up dependent on machines or mostly bedridden, that wouldn't be what you would want."

"Yes, Krindy," he said, smiling. "That is all correct. Make sure also that you and Siddarth are there with me, praying. This is what I would want the most."

I wondered if my brother and I would be able to remember my parents' words when we needed to, or whether our fear and disbelief might lead us to act like Teresa and Ray, whether our shock might prompt us to hang on like Anu. As I sat in the thick of this discussion with my parents, I could identify with each of their reactions and with the reasons why they probably hadn't had this sort of discussion with their parents. I could barely get through it even though I had these talks for a living. I recognized that not all people would have such discussions, that it would naturally be tougher for those who weren't close to their loved ones or who had strained relationships or who had to negotiate multiple family members' input about these matters. But though it had been challenging now, I couldn't imagine broaching these topics in the midst of a true emergency. Still, even though I had heard and understood my parents' words, I knew that I would need to rely upon a wellspring of strength to honor to their wishes when the time came.

"One thing I can say for certain is this," my father continued. "I don't think I'm going anywhere anytime soon. I'll be around to bother you when I'm old and walking with a cane and yelling at you!" He started laughing, which I'd also expected. Standing up from the chair, he shuffled over to my mother, leaning on an imaginary cane. "Hey, don't laugh about this!" she said, shooing him away.

"Hey, don't laugh about this!" My father imitated her as he swiped a handful of chopped bell peppers and broccoli and munched loudly.

Our usual routine resumed. I pulled out the bag of cat treats stored beneath the sink and tossed a few out to Snow, who gobbled them quickly and mewed for more. My mother plunked a handful of garlic and ginger on the counter. "Please cut them up." My father went to the adjacent living room and began to watch Indian news in Hindi just as he always did after completing his part of lunch preparation. I chopped the garlic and ginger as methodically as I had when I was in eighth grade, handing them to my mother. Outside, the crow returned and leaped around our yard, cawing. The breeze rustled the trees and disappeared, leaving behind crystalline tones of a wind chime.

. . . .

I drove back to my home the next day, pensive. In my kitchen that evening, I picked at a burrito I'd grabbed from a food truck down the street. I drove home starving, but lost my appetite after a few bites. Outside my window, Sunset Boulevard was a river of light, a constant stream of headlights and bike lamps, colorful blinking restaurant signs and fluorescent streetlights. In a shadowed parking lot, dark figures moved quickly toward cars.

Something weighed on me, though I couldn't articulate it precisely. It wasn't about my conversations with my parents, which had brought me a deep peace. I wandered around my place, sitting on my couch and moving to a chair, picking up a book and setting it down to watch TV instead. I turned the TV off and considered going to bed early. Maybe a good night's sleep would fix my restless mind.

And then a question surfaced. What if what happened to Auntie suddenly happened to me? Her situation had at first reminded me of my parents' mortality, but what of my own? Perhaps this crossed my mind because Auntie and I shared a common heritage, and she had suffered a sudden catastrophic event, which could happen to anyone regardless of their age. Maybe the fact that I had faced another transition point, my last week at my first attending job, contributed subconsciously to my mind's sudden insistence that I consider the meaning of endings. Whatever the reason, I began once again to consider my own answers to the questions I had asked my parents.

I knew that I was mortal, that at some point my body would shut down. But though my rational mind knew this, sometimes it felt like mortality didn't apply to me. I was a doctor. I was there to tend to *other people's* mortality. I thought back to all the years I'd clung to the idea of delayed gratification, the times when I'd put my life on hold until I'd completed an educational milestone. If I persisted in my studies, I'd told myself countless times, I'd someday have all the time in the world to enjoy life. I panicked now as I considered what my life would mean if it ended tomorrow in an accident.

What had I learned about death in doing this work? I'd seen that no amount of considering or preparing for it made it easy. Talking about it to prepare frightened loved ones, saying or writing good-byes (if one was lucky and lucid enough to do so), and trying to make peace with a higher power might soothe us and help us. We feared it and sought to control every aspect of it, even considering physician-assisted suicide to give us a sense of agency over an unconquerable aspect of human existence. But if death was not only a medical fact but also a spiritual and sacred passage, then it would always have a certain mystery that was perhaps worth accepting rather than attempting to control. Because we can't control it. We can't always anticipate or prepare for it. What we define as a "good death" may not be in the cards for us. But maybe we can use the inevitability of death to live differently. Maybe we need the promise of death to guard against taking life for granted.

I thought back to the many times I feared death as an outcome for my patients, convinced that it was my job to forestall it, to control and manipulate nature. Giving death this much power distorted my view on life—my own, and that of my loved ones and patients. Fighting and fearing death obscured finding meaning in living moments.

What if I regarded my own death with reverence instead of fear? I wondered. Or, even more radically, what if I had some sort of *gratitude* for the transience of my life? Would it change what I worried and cared about? Wasn't it necessary to think about this when I was in the midst of building a life? Or rather, *living* my life? And the more I thought about mortality and what it had come to mean to others and what I thought it meant to me, I realized that life was simultaneously so vast and so small.

It was daybreak after a good sleep and exhaustion as the stars emerged. It was the first crisp bite of an apple, the taste of butter on toast. It was the way a tree's shadow moved along the wall of a room as the afternoon passed. It was the smell of a baby's skin, the feeling of a heart fluttering with anticipation or nerves. It was the steady rhythm of a lover's breathing during sleep. It was both solitude in a wide green field and the crowding together of bodies in a church. It was equally common and singular, a shared tumult and a shared peace. It was the many things I'd ignored or half appreciated as I chased the bigger things. It was infinity in a seashell.

I thought and thought that night, making mint tea and taking a few sips, watching the steam rise from the cup and then disappear. It felt strangely calming to focus on the cooling of heat, to appreciate the fact of temporary warmth. Maybe this, too, was the lesson of mortality: appreciating what we have now, in the midst of life, knowing that it is all a temporary gift.

I didn't want the sum total of my life to be only a collection of my worldly achievements, boxes of degrees, and lists of patients I'd treated. I thought of what I had pushed off or considered unimportant, the things I promised myself I'd do when I "had the time." I'd call the friend I had been meaning to call for the past year since I moved to LA. I'd take my mother to the beach in Santa Barbara. I'd take a pottery class. I'd write regularly to my uncles in Mumbai. I'd learn to cook Thai food. I'd adopt a puppy. I'd deal with my fear of bugs and go camping. These all seemed like such cheesy wishes as I thought about them. But these were the things I didn't want to leave my life without doing. Which meant they weren't small things.

That night was the beginning of a conversation I continue to have with myself, especially in the moments when the wrong parts of my life feel big and cast shadows over the smaller things. Those are the times I return to my copy of the Gita, having stumbled across a passage that perfectly captured how the fact of death has taught me to live differently:

> No matter how strongly you ascribe to the universal delusion that you can avoid pain and only have pleasure in this life (which is utterly impossible), sooner or later you must confront the fact of your inevitable aging and eventual death. . . . Therefore, because death stirs people to seek answers to important spiritual questions it becomes the greatest servant of humanity, rather than its most feared enemy.

And there it was—the life lesson, and the death lesson. Vast and small, interlinked. Infinity in a seashell.

Twelve

TRANSITION

My new workplace is a shiny white and gray building that towers over a fountain with frothy jets of water that bubble continuously. Green shrubs and tiny flowers hug its perimeter. Above the fountain, white pillars hold up a red and white banner: KECK MEDICAL CENTER OF USC. Sparrows dart between a crisscross of beams underneath the banner and the dark crevices above the hospital's main entrance. A short walk away is the Norris Cancer Center, flanked by a cluster of trees that burn gold and scarlet in California's autumn. Outside Norris, residents and fellows bustle through a quad filled with trees, rectangles of grass, rose bushes, a library, and a bookstore. They glance at patient lists as they juggle cups of coffee and stethoscopes. Students alternately lunch together and hunch over books and computers on a cluster of tables outside the cafeteria. I wander into the student store and scan its offerings: short white coats and scrubs, Red Bull and protein bars, iPads and study aids. I shake my head in disbelief, realizing eleven years have passed since I walked into the student store in medical school for the first time.

Because USC is an academic teaching hospital and a regional referral center, patients travel from across the United States—and, occasionally, the world—for treatment here. Some come for liver transplants or to enroll in a clinical trial for metastatic lung cancer. They are among the sickest and most complex patients I've ever encountered, suffering from the rarest sarcoma, recovering from risky surgical replacement of a heart valve. And many are quite young; there are weeks when the oldest patient I see is fifty years old. There are other weeks when the majority of my patients are in their twenties and thirties. Their hopes for a fix or a cure are palpable. They believe we can offer them miracles. In this milieu, some of my colleagues remarked that calling a palliative care consultation could feel like giving up on a patient, crushing their long-held hopes. I could only see those patients referred to me by my colleagues, who in turn supervised the teams of residents and fellows rounding on patients each day. Though I'd returned to a university hoping to teach medical students and doctors in training, I realized quickly that the most important—and unexpected— audience was my peers. I would have to find a way to teach palliative care and its value to surgeons, oncologists, cardiologists, and an array of other physicians who might have had minimal exposure to the field in their training and practice.

I joined a palliative care team that at first consisted of me, a social worker named John, and a coordinator named George. Formed just two years before my arrival, our team was young and busy. Together, John and I saw around seven hundred patients in my first year, walking together between Keck and Norris, reflecting on the many sorrows we witnessed, laughing at the surprising moments of levity we also took in.

John, George, and I quickly became friends. Light poured into our office window, through which we enjoyed a view of a grove of trees and a small park across the street from the hospital. John brought in doughnuts for special occasions, always careful to include the ones that George and I liked best. On days when we saw especially challenging patients—those with difficult-to-control symptoms, others struggling with fear, anger, acceptance—we would go out to lunch at a local Mediterranean place and debrief. We laughed at celebrity gossip and bemoaned local and national politics. In an homage to a rap song that John loved, we adopted a panda as our team mascot. Despite the transience that remained a part of my work— the comings and goings of patients, residents, and attendings—our team, a comforting constant, anchored me.

Just over a year after I joined, fellows in oncology and intensive care medicine joined our team for two-week stretches, learning how to lead discussions with patients and families about their goals and reviewing the best ways to treat bothersome symptoms. Around my two-year anniversary, our team began to host and teach fourth-year medical students as well. One of them, Adrian, Gonzales, emailed me shortly after participating in a family meeting for a patient he cared for who was dying of heart failure. "You and your team were consulted on a patient of ours," he wrote in his email. The patient came to mind as I read his note. He'd been in his sixties, a stargazer who was looking forward to the solar eclipse just a few days away. But his heart started to fail for reasons we never determined, and he'd been in the ICU for more than a month, repeatedly requiring the support of a ventilator and continuous dialysis. In the meeting, we had to discuss the ways that our best treatments simply weren't working; his family agreed that he would want only peace and comfort under the circumstances. I talked them through how we would undo the breathing tube and dialysis, how we'd give him medicines to prevent pain and difficulty breathing, how he'd likely be with us for only minutes after the breathing tube was removed. He died two days later, his family surrounding him in his ICU room.

"It was a very difficult and emotional experience for me that has really stuck with me the last week but it was a very valuable experience," Adrian wrote in his email. "I had not, up to that point in my medical career, had to have a conversation with a family like that." Adrian wanted to observe more of those conversations, in hopes of learning how to have one himself. He began his rotation a few weeks later, seven and a half years after I'd watched Dr. McCormick speak to Donna in a way that split my heart wide open.

. . . .

Jared Douglas was one of a small handful of patients I'd seen in oncology clinic. He struggled with pain from a particularly aggressive form of kidney cancer, one that had spread to the bones of his legs and arms and to his spine. On his most recent CT scan, tiny holes dotted the ordinarily smooth surfaces of his bones, rendering them prone to fractures. "He's been managing on a few Norco tablets each day, but his wife tells me he's still in a lot of pain so I wanted him to see you," Dr. O'Brien, his oncologist, told me over the phone. "You should probably also know that he's on his fourth line of treatment," he added, "and I'm not sure how much progress we are going to make."

"Have you discussed that with him?" I asked.

"I've tried, but his wife is really reluctant to talk about that word, 'hospice,' and they both seem to want to keep fighting," he said. "But if you can talk about that with them, I think they would appreciate hearing it from you."

When I first met Jared and his wife, Sylvia, he was sitting upright at the edge of the clinic exam table, swinging his legs rhythmically as though he were an excited young boy. He had a mane of brown hair, green eyes, and deep wrinkles around his eyes and mouth. His voice had a melodic cadence to it, and he appeared remarkably peaceful despite his circumstances. "Taking these medications makes me nervous, Doctor," he told me. "But I know that I have to try."

I asked him what his pain prevented him from doing. He told me he could still dress and bathe himself, but had to use a walker to get around, and lacked the energy to go on outings with Sylvia. "It's been a real shock to need a walker," he told me. "Not being able to walk around on my own has been a real blow." We talked about whether he'd be willing to try a small dose of strong pain medication to see if that might lessen his use of the walker.

"Can I stop the medicine if it's making me feel weird?" he asked. Of course, I told him. And if the combination of medications and physical therapy I suggested didn't help him sufficiently, then we would change them around. "Controlling your pain is a really important way to help you enjoy life," I told him gently. "The objective is not to keep you sleeping in a bed, but to find the right combination of medications to keep you doing the things you love."

I asked what his oncologist had discussed with him about his cancer and its treatment. Sylvia grimaced at the question. "Well, I've gotten several types of chemotherapy and radiation, and right now we're trying a pill that I hope will work."

This was the type of moment in conversations when I had to decide whether and how to probe a patient's answer. Especially over the last year,

I'd become more sure of the structure and language of my conversations with patients, and could tend a bit more to the emotion underlying their words and body language. Mr. Douglas's tone of voice was even, and his body language appeared open rather than defensive and closed off. I decided to proceed.

"What has your oncologist told you to expect if the pill works?" I asked.

"Well, to be honest, he hasn't been too clear. All I know is that since I've been taking the pill he says my blood tests look better, but I haven't been feeling better," he told me. Sylvia cut in. "We're hoping that the pill will work," she said firmly, looking at him. I could sense that this wasn't a topic Jared and Sylvia had openly discussed, and I was wary of forcing a conversation that neither person might be prepared for. I considered wrapping up the brief discussion by encouraging them to talk together about Jared's expectations of treatment and his hopes if treatment didn't work for him. But Jared spoke instead.

"But for me, I'll tell you that quality of life is the most important thing," he continued. "If I'm so sick that I'm sitting in bed all day and can't do anything for myself, then I wouldn't want that kind of life." Sylvia looked away. He looked over at her. "I know it's hard, honey, but that is my honest opinion."

Because he'd brought up quality of life, I asked Jared to tell me what that meant to him. He'd clearly thought it through. He wanted to spend his time as active and independent as he could be, and did not want to end up bed bound. He wanted to spend his time at home with his wife and dogs; he dreaded the hospital and wanted to minimize his time there. If his heart stopped, he wouldn't want to undergo resuscitation. Not only did it sound violent to him, he knew that it wouldn't ultimately fix his cancer and he simply wanted a peaceful exit from this world. He didn't want to be placed on a ventilator at the end of his life, and also wouldn't want artificial nutrition through his veins or through a tube in his stomach. He'd be okay with antibiotics and gentle fluids to treat an infection if he had one, but that was it. "No machines," he told me. "I want as long as I've got to live, but only if it's a good life."

I could tell that he meant every word.

I hadn't expected such a detailed conversation. And because of the dense combination of sadness and surprise in the room, I didn't bring up hospice. Jared knew that his disease had no cure, and he had a clear set of expectations from his chemotherapy: improved mobility and energy and independence. The clarity of his goals could guide all the decisions that lay ahead—up to and including the question of hospice. Jared's responses had been so quick and thoughtful, so free of hesitation, it was as though he'd had the same conversation with himself and had been waiting to have it with someone else.

"Please call if the pain medications aren't working or if you need to talk about anything we discussed," I reassured them as they left. "And thanks for talking with me so openly. I know it couldn't have been easy."

"It was a pleasure, Doctor," Jared said, extending his hand. "And we will definitely be in touch." Sylvia forced a smile.

We wrapped up around lunchtime, and I headed first to the cafeteria and then to my office. It was late August, and the mood on campus was one of renewed energy and excitement at the start of a new school year. I squinted at the azure sky and felt the ninety-degree sun and thick, humid air press mercilessly upon me. I thought about my conversation with Jared and Sylvia, grateful that we'd had a chance to meet before a crisis, especially since it seemed that Jared hadn't shared his wishes openly with Sylvia before our discussion. As difficult as it had been for Sylvia to hear Jared's thoughts on his last days, I hoped she'd find some measure of relief in hearing his wishes directly from him. Had Jared ended up in the hospital, unconscious and unable to communicate, I could envision Sylvia floundering to make sense of the crisis and also to serve as Jared's decision maker in the absence of a conversation like the one we'd had. It still wouldn't be easy for her to follow Jared's instructions, but I hoped the memory of his own words would guide her to choose for him what he'd have chosen for himself.

And my gut told me that a crisis would come soon for Jared. I couldn't always explain these flashes of intuition, and they weren't always right. But there was something about the sharpness of his cheekbones and temples, the replacement of muscle with loose skin on his arms, a sense of his accelerating fatigue that nagged at me. And maybe it was also the fact that he'd declared his wishes decisively and quickly, free of hesitation. His clarity made me wonder if he knew he was dying and had made peace with his realization. On both a physical and spiritual level, Jared left me with the impression that his time was short.

. . . .

Six weeks later, shortly after Adrian began his rotation with me, Jared came to the hospital in the throes of a pain crisis. Dr. O'Brien had called me earlier that morning to let me know that Jared's pain control had improved substantially for several weeks, but suddenly worsened. He'd increased the doses of Jared's pain medication nearly tenfold over the past week, to no effect. "I'd really appreciate it if you could see him," Dr. O'Brien said. I promised I would.

I found Jared in his hospital room, sitting in a wheelchair. Sylvia perched on the edge of his hospital bed. He appeared to have aged ten years. His tan skin appeared leathery and dusky, its wrinkles and creases deeper, filled with shadows. He slumped forward in his wheelchair like a wilting flower, too weak to hold his body upright. His feet and legs had swollen, though his face and torso had thinned. Skin peeled off his ankles. Even on massive doses of pain medication, he could barely tolerate lying still in one particular position in bed. He was mostly bed bound. Moving independently was out of the question. Going to the bathroom required Sylvia's full assistance. "I've been losing power in my legs," he told me, placing his hands on his thighs for emphasis. "And my feet have become too heavy to lift," he said, pointing downward. Despite his tenuous circumstance, his voice was calm and even, and his face radiated the same tranquility and peace I'd observed six weeks ago.

"I need to use all of my strength to move him from his bed to a wheelchair and then to the bathroom," Sylvia told me, visibly exhausted. "I don't even know if I'm moving him around correctly. I'm just kind of making it up as I go and I think I'm hurting him." Sylvia's eyes were puffy and shadowed with fatigue.

Adrian sat next to me this time as I spoke with Jared and Sylvia. Jared told me that for a few weeks his pain had been well controlled on the medications we had started, but once the pain worsened, it amplified exponentially. "I'm desperate for relief," he told me, and I took his hand.

I told him that I wanted to get his pain under control with intravenous medications instead of pills for now. I also asked if he'd spoken to Dr. O'Brien recently about his cancer treatment.

"Well, his lab tests are getting better," Sylvia said, opening her notebook to tell me his most recent result. "So my impression is that it is working."

I wondered for a moment how much I should say about the fact that his cancer treatment was so obviously not working. It hadn't helped him to feel better or gain back independence, which is what he'd hoped for. And those were the goals of treatment he'd identified six weeks ago. I had to find a way to bring those clear-minded goals back into the conversation.

"Sometimes, when a cancer is very advanced, lab results alone don't always tell us whether the treatment is helping someone," I began gently. "I think it would be important to talk with Dr. O'Brien about whether he thinks the treatment is helping you. I remember you telling me that you were hoping the pill would help you to feel better and be more independent. And from what you're telling me, it seems like you're actually feeling worse." Jared nodded.

"Well, I can tell you I definitely don't feel any better. I just want to get my pain under control," he said. "I can't live like this."

"I hear you," I told him. "And I am worried that your pain has gotten so much worse, and that you appear to have become much weaker since I last saw you a few weeks ago. I want you both to know that we can switch our focus just to controlling your pain and giving you the best quality of life possible. Dr. O'Brien and I discussed our thought that hospice might be a very good way to do this for you."

As I'd expected, Sylvia recoiled. "No, I don't think we're there yet," she said.

I had two options: stop or continue. Delaying this discussion wouldn't prepare Sylvia for it. She would never be ready, and I would never expect her to be. And the longer I waited, the higher the chance that Jared would suffer a complication that might prevent him from getting home. I chose to continue.

"I know that hospice can seem like a scary word or concept," I said. "Tell me what you know about it."

"It's basically when you give up and say there's nothing more we can do. That's when they call hospice in," she said. Jared looked on, not saying much.

I explained that hospice was a type of care that Jared could receive at home, and its main focus would be on controlling his pain and any other discomfort he might have. The entire hospice team would also support Jared and Sylvia emotionally and spiritually, and make every effort to help Jared do or enjoy what meant the most to him in the time he had left. Sylvia wondered whether Jared could continue his cancer treatment on hospice, and I told her that generally that isn't possible, that cancer therapy at this stage didn't always improve quality of life and could instead worsen certain symptoms. "It is also important for you to know that in order to be eligible for hospice, two doctors have to say that you probably have six months or less to live," I said. I dreaded saying this to Sylvia. She could see that Jared had suffered worsening pain and become more debilitated, but she didn't know that these might be signs of dying rather than a setback that chemotherapy could resolve. She looked stunned. Jared nodded.

"I know this is a lot of tough information," I said, "and my intention in telling you about this option is just to make sure you know it is an option, and one that Dr. O'Brien and I have discussed."

"Well, we will talk about it together," Jared said after a brief silence.

"Certainly. And in the meantime, I'm going to make sure that we have all the right pain medicines ordered for you," I said as I shook his hand. "I'll be back in the morning."

. . . .

As Adrian and I walked to see our next patient, I wondered aloud whether I'd spoken about hospice too soon.

"She seemed so scared when you mentioned hospice, but he didn't at all," Adrian observed. "She really wants him to get more chemo. But if he wants hospice, what do you do?"

I had become so used to these complex situations that Adrian's question startled me. I'd asked something similar of Dr. McCormick years ago, when I still believed that our duty as doctors was to respect patient autonomy regardless of family members' potential disagreements. "That's a good question, and these situations aren't really ones we teach you much about in medical school," I began. "What you learn in medical school is that we should honor whatever a patient wants. But it's more complex than simply thinking about patient autonomy because patients sometimes agree to do what their families want, not necessarily what they would choose for themselves." Adrian nodded, and I continued. "This is why I try to come back to a patient's goals and their own definition of suffering. I try to help a family hear what the patient has to say about their own life and what they want for themselves. In Jared's situation, I think Sylvia will come around and see his perspective, but it is incredibly painful for her to acknowledge what Jared seems to know already. And I totally get that."

"Okay. So for Mr. Douglas, his goal is good pain control, and the best way to do that would be hospice?" Adrian responded, his inflection a cross between a statement and question.

"When I first met Jared, he told me that his goal was to have his pain controlled to the point where he could walk without a walker. And even at that time, he wasn't sure if chemo was helping him to meet that goal. In the six weeks since I've seen him, he's only gotten weaker and less mobile despite being on chemo. I think hospice would be the best plan for him to be in his own home, suffering as little as possible," I said. "And I think that's the part Sylvia is having a hard time understanding—hospice isn't giving up. It's acknowledging that cancer treatment may not be the right choice anymore. When someone's got a limited amount of time left, and their goal is comfort and quality of life, hospice can be a great way to help them."

We walked past groups of students and hospital volunteers in training as we made our way past the fountain and palm trees outside the hospital lobby. "I think Sylvia needs some time to wrap her mind around what's happening," I continued. "Usually, most family members are pretty shocked when hospice comes up, but they become supportive when they understand that it's the best way to address their loved ones' suffering at this stage. I try really hard to remind everyone of the patient's goal, and that usually helps."

"It was really good to see that," Adrian said when we returned to our office. "Thank you, Dr. Puri."

"Why don't you see him in the morning, Adrian? You can check in on his pain and see if he's more comfortable. Then we can go see him together later in the morning," I suggested, and Adrian agreed.

. . . .

An MRI showed that Jared's cancer had spread to the middle of his spine and put pressure on his spinal cord. This explained the loss of power he'd described, and it also explained why, just over the past day, he could no longer urinate and needed a catheter to collect his waste. The oncology team wanted to start radiation therapy to decrease the amount of pressure on his spinal cord and hopefully relieve some degree of his weakness and urinary retention. Interestingly, this area was not where Jared experienced pain, and he was hesitant to accept radiation treatment. He'd had radiation before and thought it only made him tired and weaker. The oncology fellow asked if I might be able to help persuade him to try radiation. "I know he doesn't have much time left, but we could just give him four or five treatments. That might at least prevent him from the worst-case scenario, becoming paralyzed," she said.

Jared's main goal at this point was to remain pain free, I told her. I'd be happy to discuss the option of radiation with him, but I knew Jared well enough to know I couldn't persuade him to do anything he didn't want to do.

On our way to see Jared, Adrian and I talked about my discussion with the oncology fellow. Adrian reported that Jared felt much better on the pain medications we'd started yesterday, and he was able to sleep through the night for the first time in weeks. He still had trouble moving his legs, though they were less swollen because we'd given him a diuretic. "So what are your thoughts on radiation for him?" I asked Adrian.

"I don't know," he confessed. "He says he only wants to focus on pain control, and the area where he has pain isn't the area they want to radiate. But if he has cord compression, then how can we not give him radiation?"

"Great question," I said as we stood outside Jared's room. "And let's go back to his goals. He wants to be pain free and as independent as he can be. It's not clear to me that the radiation will really accomplish either goal, but it would stave off paralysis, which I think he wouldn't want to experience. But the trade-off would be staying in the hospital longer than he might want to."

"Can he go home and come back for radiation?" Adrian wondered.

"He could," I said, "but making that trip every day might tire him out to the point where he couldn't actually enjoy his time at home."

. . . .

When we entered the room, Jared lay in his hospital bed and Sylvia sat in a chair next to him. "Hi, Docs," he said brightly when we entered the room. His pain was quite minimal, Jared said with a grin, but he was really torn about radiation. He wasn't sure how it would help him at this point; a prior round of radiation had only worsened his fatigue and pain, and at that point he'd been much stronger than he currently was.

"That's an important observation," I told him, "and there is a chance that radiation will make you more tired. It may also worsen your pain for a little while. But it may also help prevent your legs from becoming paralyzed and can possibly improve your ability to urinate. What do you think?"

When I considered his predicament, I thought of his dignity. Dignity, like suffering, was a word I'd never thought much about in medical school. The first time a patient had used that word with me, he'd referred to the many indignities of being a patient, from having a catheter in his penis to wearing a backless gown to showering with supervision. I had always considered these aspects of a patient's experience to be a series of temporary but necessary nuisances on the path to recovery from an illness. But especially these days, I'd observed how often patients felt their very self-respect compromised in the course of their illness and its treatment. "Is this worth it?" a middle-aged man with heart failure asked me once. "I feel like I'm a child again, with the nurse measuring how much I pee and people waking me up at night to check my temperature and only being able to eat what they tell me I can," he said. "This is all supposed to make me feel better, and I appreciate that. But if this keeps happening, and I need to be controlled in these ways, maybe I'd be okay with less time on earth." Compromising dignity had to result in a serious payoff. And for patients who had very little time to live, clinging to dignity was sometimes the way they could reclaim their power and humanity. Dignity was the last thing they could protect. Sacrificing it was too high a price for many.

I went out on a limb, hoping it wouldn't backfire. "To me, the possibility of paralysis and being unable to urinate seem like issues of dignity."

"Dignity," Jared repeated. "I think I've lost so much of that by this point. But yeah, I agree. There would be nothing much worse than being paralyzed and not being able to pee. I could try it. But I don't want my pain to get worse." I assured him that we could give him extra doses of pain medication before radiation to keep him comfortable, and that if he felt radiation made him feel worse rather than better, we didn't have to continue the treatments. He and Sylvia agreed. I let the oncology team know of their decision.

"No discussion of hospice today?" Adrian asked as we walked down the hallway to the stairs.

"Nope. If he had said he wanted to go home no matter what, I would have broached the subject again. But he's here for at least four more days now, so we have time to address it. We don't have to bring it up each time we see them," I said.

Adrian reflected on the other patients he'd seen in his training who'd needed to have a conversation about goals. He wondered if it was realistic for all physicians to have these discussions. They seemed to require special skills. "When we did have conversations, they were more about whether or not the patient wanted a surgery or whatever other procedure, but not about what the patient understood the goal of the surgery to be."

"I can understand why that is, even though I don't agree with the reasons," I said. "I personally believe all doctors are capable of having basic conversations about goals of care, but it's a matter of helping them understand why these talks are so important. That's never discussed with us really in medical school, and we're more wired to do things rather than talk about them."

Other patients we saw that day had different goals. A gentleman with heart failure told us that he wanted to die comfortably at home, but adamantly refused hospice care at home. If he were at home in Armenia, he explained, he would go to the hospital to be treated, so why wouldn't he do the same here?

Adrian wondered why anyone would really want to come to the hospital when they could get hospice care at home. My own hospice patients had taught me that the theory of a peaceful death at home wasn't realistic for everyone. Taking care of someone at home can be a very foreign concept to people who strongly believe a hospital is the only place to be treated, I explained to Adrian. Suggesting care at home can feel like abandonment to them.

A particularly cantankerous gentleman with advanced esophageal cancer grew frustrated when his oncologist and I tried to ask him about his goals. He had told his nurses he was tired of suffering, but also refused the medications prescribed to treat his discomfort. "I just want to make sure you really want chemotherapy," his oncologist said, "because it's important that you take all of the medicines we give you. It is okay if you don't want it, and we'd just focus on keeping you comfortable. But I do want to hear your thoughts either way." He grew angry then, insisting it was obvious he wanted treatment because he was in the hospital. "Years ago, doctors just gave me the treatment, they didn't stand around asking me whether I wanted it!" he yelled. He rolled his eyes at us and mocked me when I asked if it was okay for me to ask about his symptoms. His wife tried to cajole him to cooperate with us—"They are trying to help you and you are not making it easy for them!"—but he mocked her, too. At a certain point, I spoke firmly, telling him that we needed him to take his medications exactly as prescribed in order for him to feel well enough to get chemotherapy. That was the plan. He seemed to respond to my frank paternalism.

Adrian and I had to laugh after this discussion. "I don't know how you kept your cool," he said. "I would have been really offended!"

"In all seriousness, I think he's probably very scared and is acting out a bit because of that," I said after my giggles subsided. "But also, his reaction is a good reminder to me that some older patients really do think the doctor should just tell them what to do. Just as he was saying, forty, fifty years ago, we didn't really pay as much attention to patient choice as we do now," I said. "If he was expecting us to tell him what to do, then I can see why he got annoyed. The disagreement was really a big cultural difference, just the way that our other patient said he'd always go back to the hospital if he felt unwell."

It was late afternoon, and the shadows cast by the hospital buildings grew longer and darker. As Adrian and I walked back to my office, we passed Dr. Thompson, an oncologist, who stopped to talk with me. He told me that one of his patients, a young man in his early thirties with widely metastatic cancer, had just been admitted to the hospital with severe pain. "I need your help with managing his pain," he said, "but do not talk about anything else with him." He wagged a finger at me and continued. "You always ask me about my plan for the cancer treatment, but that is not your concern. And do not talk about hospice or any of that. I only need you to manage his pain. Okay?"

I blinked, pressing my lips together to avoid blurting out a retort I'd regret, especially since Adrian looked on. I thought of the time I'd seen another of Dr. Thompson's patients, one whom I'd found crouched on the floor, suffering from waves of nausea. Through tears of concern, his parents asked me what hospice could offer their son if he chose to stop chemotherapy for the cancer that had invaded his brain, lungs, and liver. When he heard about our discussion, Dr. Thompson publicly chided me at the nursing station of the oncology ward, asking who I thought I was to offer hospice to *his* patient. It wouldn't have helped the situation to explain that I'd simply answered the appropriate questions of parents who saw that their son was slowly dying, had been for months, and he wanted to spend his last days at home in his own bed. He would die three days later, after Dr. Thompson told me that hospice was an absurd idea, that he wasn't about to throw in the towel on this young man.

He used the same tone with me now that he had then, his wagging finger emphasizing every word.

I was tempted to decline the consult. I considered telling him he had no right to speak to me this way, and to assume that I'd inappropriately discuss hospice with his patient. But in the space between his request and my response, I thought of the advice that John had given me when I'd described my earlier interaction with Dr. Thompson, and how it made me want to refuse to see any of his patients. Though he had listened sympathetically, John reminded me that a patient's pain relief mattered more than Dr. Thompson's bad behavior. "You're right," I'd told John. I had to do for my colleagues what I did for my patients: meet them wherever they were in their understanding of palliative care.

"Okay," I said to Dr. Thompson, "I'll see him after lunch. But just so you know, I ask about the overall treatment plan just like any other consultant would." I pretended I was speaking to Adrian, which helped me to keep my voice neutral.

Dr. Thompson nodded and went on his way. Adrian and I walked together silently, though I could sense his discomfort with what he'd just witnessed. Embarrassed, I said, "I'm sorry you had to see that."

"It was weird," Adrian replied. "It seems like he doesn't really understand what you do during a consult."

"Yeah, it's an ongoing challenge. I have to reassure some of my more skeptical colleagues that I'm not going to put everyone on hospice or persuade them to stop treatment," I said as we approached the elevators at Keck. "It's sort of an occupational hazard," I added, and we both laughed.

....

After writing our patient notes that afternoon, I checked in with Adrian to see how he was handling the emotional heft of the rotation. "I'll be honest, it's been tough," he told me. "When I'm driving home, I think about the people we see and I wonder, what if it was me? What if it was someone I love?" He talked about his days with his girlfriend, a nurse at a nearby hospital. "It makes me feel grateful for the life I have because you never know what's coming or could happen to you or someone you love."

"This work certainly forces you to keep that perspective," I told him as

we wrapped up that day. "I think it's really healthy to reflect on those questions. Death is an experience we will share with our patients."

. . . .

Several days later, after Jared completed his radiation treatment, he and
Sylvia were ready to talk about hospice. Dr. O'Brien had visited them the
night before and told them that any further chemotherapy would only harm
him and possibly even hasten his death. He'd called me before and after his
meeting with them, and I thanked him for stopping by. "They really trust
you, and I think it was important for both of them, but especially Sylvia, to
hear that information from you, someone they have known for years," I
told him.

Jared told us that his pain had worsened. "I had trouble sleeping again
overnight," he said. He wasn't sure if radiation had made a difference. "I'm
still weak in the legs, just less swollen," he told me. He was looking forward
to going home.

"Dr. O'Brien came by last night," he said, looking at Sylvia. "And he told
us that the cancer treatment isn't working. He said continuing to take it
might actually shorten my life because I'm so weak." From the disbelief on
Sylvia's face, I could tell she was still processing the news. "So I think it's
time for us to hear more about hospice."

I described what hospice offered and told Jared that he could get hospice
care at home or in a nursing home. He looked at Sylvia. "Well, I don't want
her to overstretch herself. I require a lot of care these days. I was thinking
maybe a nursing home."

Sylvia didn't blink but responded, "Absolutely not. You're coming home."
She looked at him intently from her chair near the window. The morning sun
threw alternating patches of light and shadow on her patterned blouse.

"Honey, I think we should think this through. I don't want you to go on
living in a place where I'd die. I don't think that's fair to you."

Sylvia spoke firmly. "I want you at home. You need to be in your own
home, with me and the dogs and . . . everything. I am not putting you in a
nursing home. You will be with me until the end."

Four days ago, I didn't know whether Sylvia's resistance and fear would soften into acceptance. I held my breath as I watched them speak to each other as though they were alone. Everything was out in the open: his worry for her after he died, her commitment to caring for him no matter what.

Because many of my patients were so sick, I knew that I'd eventually lose each of them. But they and their families don't always know this. Many can't hear it when I try to tell them. Yet somehow, through hours' worth of conversations, a shift would take place. And the credit belonged entirely to the patients and families I spoke with. I could tell them the hardest of truths, but they ultimately had to decide whether they could accept and endure the most heart-shattering information, or the greatest loss. I'd watch as a mother's rigid belief in a miracle might loosen, contemplating for the first time a possibility other than a cure for her daughter. I'd see a husband whisper to his dying wife, "It's okay to go. We will be okay," and watch her take her last breath minutes later. I looked on now as Sylvia told Jared that he belonged in his home, so that he could die his death where he had lived his life. This was the work of the spirit.

Sylvia turned to me and asked what type of support she could expect from hospice. We discussed logistics for a little while, until Jared said that he was tired and wanted to rest. "Not a problem," I said, holding his hand with both of mine. "Thank you, Jared." Sylvia stood up from her chair and hugged me. Outside their room, I put my hand across my heart and took a deep breath in and out, reminding myself never to take for granted the invitation to witness and shape conversations like theirs.

. . . .

Just before Jared left the hospital on Friday morning, he told me he felt like a million bucks. Our conversation drifted from his symptoms and a question about hospice to his love for his dogs. I mentioned to him that I had considered adopting a therapy dog as part of our palliative care service. Jared and Sylvia lit up as I described my idea, and both heartily endorsed it. "That would be so calming and healing for everyone, really," Sylvia said. "I can imagine that in a heated or tough meeting, people would probably be more civil and calm than usual because nobody would want to upset the dog." We laughed together.

A serious expression crossed Jared's face. "If you ever need anything from me to support that idea, you just let me know," he said. "If you need me to write a letter from a patient's perspective, or go to a meeting with you to advocate for your idea, you just call me." Sylvia nodded. I was astounded by his generosity. I was convinced that if I asked for his help, he would follow through on his promise, even though he knew his days were numbered and his energy was limited.

"We're just planning to stay positive and hope that we still have a good amount of time together," Jared said, looking at Sylvia. "I can't wait to go home with this beautiful woman."

Jared looked at me. His brown hair, mussed from days of being in the hospital, looked longer and thicker than I'd remembered. His eyes, glassy with tears, nonetheless radiated a wistful joy. "Thank you, Doc. For . . . well, for everything. You are . . . well, you know." I took both of his hands in mine, as I'd done before. "You are a gem, Jared. Thank you for letting me be a part of your team. Please, please call if there is anything I can do for you."

Adrian shook Jared's hand and thanked him for his generosity. Not all patients would want a medical student visiting with them at this tender time. Adrian had visited with Jared every morning, asking him about his discomfort and his emotional state. One of Jared's lasting gifts was talking with Adrian, inviting him into the physical and emotional experience of his illness and his life.

. . . .

Jared died at home two days later in the company of Sylvia and their dogs. He'd died on Sunday afternoon, Dr. O'Brien informed me over email, shortly after lunch, when he'd managed a few bites of grilled cheese and asked to take a nap. He didn't wake up. I thought of my last conversation with Jared, of the shine in his eyes, and was grateful that his death was as akin as possible to simply falling asleep. I scribbled a note on a Post-it reminding myself to call Sylvia. And I emailed Adrian, who had just completed his rotation.

"Thank you for letting me know that," Adrian replied. "I only had the privilege of knowing him for a short time but as odd as it may seem, I feel like I learned a little about life, a little about death and pain, and a lot about the comfort and dignity we have the opportunity to offer our patients when their days on this earth are numbered. I'm truly grateful for having met him."

As a teacher, I felt a deep sense of pride as I read Adrian's words. All I'd ever hoped to achieve was a slight shift in a student's thinking, to suggest that perhaps there was another way to doctor, a way we didn't necessarily learn in medical school but perhaps knew intuitively, as human beings. I closed my patient charts and thought of Jared. I hoped that he wasn't in pain as he died. I hoped he'd run his hands through his dogs' fur. I wished that he'd had more time with Sylvia than he did.

And then I reminded myself of what I often tell my students: sometimes, people go when they are ready.

Thirteen

SPEAK

From a seat near the podium of a lecture hall on the medical school campus, I watch as medical students, residents, and attendings in the department of surgery take their seats in the brightly lit auditorium. It is a Friday morning in October, and I am about to give a Grand Rounds presentation on palliative medicine. A long-standing tradition across different specialties in medicine, Grand Rounds lectures are an opportunity to learn about important updates in medical research or clinical care.

In the ten minutes before my talk begins, I study the audience. A transplant surgeon sits to the right of the podium, drinking coffee and catching up with a colleague. He and I had debated his suggestion that I rename my team the "supportive care service," since he felt that the vague and confusing term "palliative care"—and its association with hospice—frightened patients and their families. Several rows behind him sits a trauma surgeon with whom I work closely in the intensive care unit. He recognizes the benefits of palliative care for his patients and consults our team frequently, though he finds it harder to talk to the family of a dying patient than to perform a high-risk surgery. In the very last row sits a cardiothoracic surgeon who once described to me what it felt like to touch a human heart—an exhilarating mix of excitement, fear, and rapture—and the guilt he endured when he had to tell a patient's family that their loved one's heart was too broken to fix. He led the toughest conversations beautifully, but still asked how he could do better. I took a deep breath and tried to calm my nerves. I reminded myself that although the people before me practiced the all-consuming, awe-inspiring art of surgery, they were also simply human beings, hardwired to fix problems and devastated when they couldn't.

We physicians are all fixers. We want to help our patients live long, healthy lives, and we value the role we can play in achieving that. We even derive a sense of our own identity from helping our patients to outlive their ancestors, to outsmart death. But although modern medicine has helped us make enormous strides in preventing previously lethal infectious diseases, improving the safety of surgery, and advancing techniques to diagnose and treat everything from cancer to heart disease, we cannot fix everything. In fact, we can only slow down rather than cure most debilitating chronic diseases, maladies including heart failure and emphysema and multiple sclerosis, all of which slowly progress, claiming our lives. This realization shouldn't dissuade us from discovering new therapies and pioneering new technologies to extend and improve our patients' lives. I wondered if, at this moment in the history of Western medicine, an important revolution could consist of both pushing the limits of nature while simultaneously accepting our patients' mortality, nature's ultimate limit. Can we do both as physicians? Can we strive to minimize the suffering inflicted by disease while also embracing more fully the truth that mortality is not a condition medicine should seek to cure?

What if we learned how to identify and talk about suffering and dignity while still in medical school, right alongside our efforts to learn how the heart and kidneys work, and how we diagnose and treat the body's myriad afflictions? What if we learned how to discuss with patients both medicine's offerings as well as its limits? What would the future of medicine look like if every medical student learned that scientific discovery and remembrance of our ephemeral existence go hand in hand? Would perhaps the greatest advance of all be a future in which the separate specialty of palliative medicine is indeed unnecessary?

As the audience continued to file in, I searched for my mother. Though her hospital had been my second home in childhood, this was only her second visit to USC, and the first time she would see me give a lecture on palliative medicine. It seemed fitting that she sit in an audience filled with surgeons, the group of physicians with whom she'd shared years of triumphs and arguments. There she was, at the end of a row in the middle of the auditorium, next to John and a senior surgical resident I considered a friend. As I watched her nibble on a muffin and sip a cup of tea, I thought of her surgical colleagues, the ones who'd first met me when my main interests were Grandma's brownies and *Scooby-Doo*, the ones who'd suggested I pursue any career but medicine, the ones who'd bicker with my mother in the operating room but tell me how lucky I was to be her child. Though she'd worked alongside surgeons for nearly thirty years, this was the first time that she, an anesthesiologist, had been able to attend a surgical grand rounds. Her presence was both comforting and anxiety provoking. I still longed for her approval.

It was time to begin. The director of the surgical residency program introduced me, and as he spoke from the podium, I reminded myself to keep my goal small: if I could communicate what palliative care is and isn't, and explain that our field complemented rather than contradicted the care of surgical patients, I'd have done plenty. *Just a small shift in thinking*, I reminded myself. *That's success.*

I cleared my throat, looked at my mother, and began.

"How many of you have been confused about what palliative care is?" I asked, raising my own hand, surprised that my mother remained still, her hands folded in her lap.

About two thirds of the audience joined me. "I have to confess that even though I thought I knew what palliative care was when I applied for my fellowship, I don't think that I fully understood the meaning and impact of the field until I became an attending, seeing patients on my own and learning from the many mistakes I made during my training."

Though I'd spent weeks writing a fact-filled presentation organized around a patient case, I struggled to get through my slides. What followed was mostly a conversation rather than a lecture, which was secretly what I'd been hoping for. An introduction to communication strategies in palliative care simply didn't lend itself to a PowerPoint presentation the way a review of lung cancer therapy might. The hour whizzed by as we discussed the right time to call a palliative care consult, common communication pitfalls, and the struggle to make enough time for difficult discussions with patients and families. Though I'd worried that the audience would remain mostly silent, detached, they instead asked thoughtful questions, answered the questions I posed, and confessed how they grappled with their own worries about disappointing families and guiding complex decision making when a patient was critically ill or dying. One surgeon worried about scaring patients if he opened a discussion about goals too early, but also feared the consequences of waiting too long to have a tough conversation. Another told me he struggled to frame discussions about goals without causing a family to lose hope. In response to this comment, one of his colleagues said he emphasized to patients that he'd never abandon them even if, despite his best efforts, he could not promise them a cure. As they spoke to one another and to me, it became obvious that the questions they voiced weighed heavily on their minds, perhaps just as heavily as the difficult choices they'd made in the operating room. But though they had forums in which they together discussed and commented on operative errors, I wondered whether and how they debriefed challenging family meetings or thorny ethical questions that emerged in the care of the very sick patients we shared.

Since they were forthcoming about their own difficulties, I shared the many ways I fumbled in my own training and practice. This hadn't been part of my plan, but I wanted them to know that communication, like the tying of various surgical knots, was a skill they could all learn, no matter how daunting it seemed. But it does take practice. I mentioned that a cheat sheet didn't help me organize a successful discussion with Mr. Tan and his family, that I took and studied my notes on countless family meetings, that I'd had to practice what to say to Alice in front of a mirror each night until the words came easily to me, that there would always be family members like Teresa and Ray who tested the limits of my compassion. I shared my regret that most of us learn how to communicate with our patients about mortality and loss only through trial and error rather than with structured teaching and close supervision. Despite our very human impulse to run away from frightening discussions, ultimately communication is the basis of everything sacred in the doctor-patient relationship: trust, vulnerability, honesty, compassion. We could all learn to do it clearly and well.

As the audience clapped, I stole a glance at my mother, who met my eyes and raised her hands higher to show me how hard she was clapping. She stopped momentarily to give me two thumbs up, her smile wide and bright and proud.

....

My mother was waiting for me when I returned home from work that evening. The scent of onion and garlic welcomed me, as did the sizzle of cumin in coconut oil. My house smelled like home.

"Why are you so late?" she asked me, annoyed. Bits of ginger and cauliflower stuck to the edges of her red spatula. "You said you would be here an hour and a half ago." My recently adopted kittens, Comet and Chiclet, crowded my mother's feet. She looked down and spoke to them in Punjabi. "Hey! You want Grandma to give you treats?" They looked up at her, wide eyes fixated on the spatula to see if a nibble would fall.

"I know, I'm sorry," I said, giving her a hug. "We got a lot of consults later in the day." A yellow *daal* bubbled on the stove next to *saag paneer* that my mother made out of frozen spinach and fresh paneer that she and my father made themselves. She threw a crumble of the paneer on the ground, and Comet beat Chiclet to it.

"Do you and your boyfriend ever cook?" she asked, smiling slightly. "There is nothing in your fridge." I felt ashamed. In the three years since finishing my training, I still hadn't abandoned certain habits of student life: getting cheap Thai takeout or tacos, cooking enough *daal* and rice for one week but tiring of it by day three.

She'd recently started to wonder aloud whether she'd taught me any life skills. Why didn't I cook as she always did? She worked full time and cooked fresh meals for her family even after a long day. I only had a job—what was my excuse for not having prepared a meal for her or organizing the papers that piled up on the dining room table? When was the last time I'd weeded my garden? Why was I not married and settled, with a family of my own? She wondered if I wasn't married yet because she hadn't taught me how to run a household. I knew she wasn't trying to be hurtful, but her words stung.

I knew I could never be like my mother, though I'd spent long stretches of my life trying to emulate her. I couldn't fathom how she balanced everything she did. Unlike her, I'd never known poverty or the uncertainty of my next meal's source. While I could imagine moving to a new country, I couldn't fathom doing so with a new husband I barely knew, or raising children an ocean away from my parents. The concept of cooking for hungry children after work, of giving them the parts of myself that were left over from a job that took almost everything, exhausted me. But my mother had done these things without questioning them. *I didn't think so much about it. I just did it.*

"I wish I could be like you," I told her. "But I can't. I've tried."

The cauliflower she pushed around with the red spatula browned and softened as we spoke.

I began to set the table and my mother scooped the *daal* and *saag* and *gobi* into serving bowls. "You know what would make me very happy?" she told me as she brought them to the table. "Maybe one day you can invite me here and just cook me a meal. That would make me very proud. I hope I've taught you something more than just how to work hard."

She asked of me what I had always craved from her: nourishment, though mostly emotional, and presence. I couldn't have foreseen that one day we would switch roles, and my mother would be the one waiting for me to return from work, wishing for me to do the simplest things: cook some lentils, make her some chai, sit with her with no distractions as we ate, all thoughts of work far away. "I promise I will," I told her as we began to eat.

After dinner, I put away the dishes and gave my mother a clean towel and nightgown, telling her that she should sleep in my bedroom and I would take the guest bed. She lay down to read a book of prayer that she read every night. I lay down next to her to read before finding my way to the guest bedroom to sleep. I opened up *Meatless Days*, a memoir written by an English professor who co-taught one of the few literature classes I'd taken in college. Though I'd bought her memoir back in college, I hadn't read it yet. Just a few weeks before, I'd found it on the bookshelves in my parents' garage. I read and reread the opening chapter, but found myself restless and distracted, unable to concentrate.

I rested the book on my chest, noticing a gray strand of a cobweb draped along its spine. I stared at the striking cover photograph, one I'd loved the minute I'd first seen it, nearly fifteen years ago. A young child clutches her beautiful mother's hand, almost as though she is trying to pull her mother along with her though her mother appears to be trying to let go. The child's back is turned toward the camera, and I can't see the expression on her face. I wonder whether she pulls her mother insistently or playfully, with frustration or sweetness. I glanced over at my own mother, remembering the many times I'd felt like the child in the photograph, pulling my mother toward me until I figured out it would be easier for me to follow her instead.

My mother had fallen asleep while reading, her glasses still perched on her nose. I watched the rise and fall of her chest and listened to her slight snoring. Her gray hairs, gathered mostly at her temples, glistened like tinsel in the light. New lines ran across her forehead and along the corners of her eyes.

It had been many years since I last curled my small body against hers after school, studying her face and waiting for her to wake up, hungry for her full attention. As I watched my mother sleep now, I was nearly thirty-seven years old, but I still looked at her with the eyes of the same longing ten-year-old, the one who was acutely aware of how quickly the time she spent with her mother would pass, how she would never have as much time as she wanted with her mother.

Time folded on itself.

I reached over gently to remove her glasses, easing them upward to avoid brushing against her peaceful face, interrupting the sleep she hadn't enjoyed during those endless nights of call when her patients needed her, and the following afternoons when my brother and I needed her.

She didn't rouse. Afraid that I might wake her if I tried to leave for the guest bedroom, I instead lay next to her, watching the rise and fall of her chest until I, too, fell asleep.

Acknowledgments

Though I have always believed in the power of language, I'm not sure that words can fully capture my deepest and most sincere thanks to the people in my life without whom I could not have written this book.

Many thanks to my extraordinary literary agent, Amanda Urban, whose wisdom and expertise have been a blessing at every turn. The smart, insightful, and kind Melanie Tortoroli first saw the potential in this book, and championed it before I had even written it. Without Melanie, this book would not be in your hands, and my debt to her is indescribable. It's been an honor to work with my editor, Laura Tisdel, and I cannot thank her enough for her brilliance, deep understanding of what I was trying to convey, and her good humor and patience with me throughout this process. I am grateful to the entire staff at Viking and ICM—especially Amy Sun, Andrea Schulz, and Maris Dyer—for shepherding this book from an idea in my head to something tangible and real.

I couldn't have written this book without time away from the hospital. I am grateful for the writing residencies I was given at the MacDowell Colony, the Ucross Foundation, and the Mesa Refuge. Without the spiritual and material support those gorgeous places provided, I would have written a lesser book.

The exceptionally gifted Katy Butler is not only my mentor, but also a dear and cherished friend. Katy took me under her wing, gave me invaluable advice and guidance, and emboldened me to say clearly what I have to say. Her generosity is a huge part of this book's journey, and it is my luck that our paths crossed in this life. I am grateful beyond words to the inspiring Meghan Daum. Her belief in me helped me through the moments when I thought I could never finish this project. Thank you, Meghan, for the incredible standard you set for all writers, your wicked sense of humor, and your wisdom in all areas of writing and life. My deepest thanks to Samantha Dunn and Bernard Cooper, both inspiring teachers, who provided much-needed encouragement and thoughtful comments on the early drafts of this book.

Thank you, Rod Flagler, for being a demanding and kind English teacher during my sophomore year of high school. I wish you were here to read this; your influence is on every page. Felice Hunter has read everything I've written (including my horrendous teenage poetry) since I was a freshman in high school. Thank you, Mrs. Hunter, for being a trusted reader, one of my dearest friends, and my adopted Jewish mother.

My deepest thanks to the physician-educators who made me a doctor. Dr. Robert Nachtigall is one of the best people I know. Thank you, Bob, for your mentorship, guidance, and support. I couldn't have made it without you. Dr. Gurpreet Dhaliwal's steadfast belief in me for the last decade buoyed me through my training. He manages to combine brilliance with humility, and will always be a model physician to me. Thanks also to Dr. Thuy Pham, Dr. Gary Hsin, Dr. Gary Lee, Dr. BJ Miller, Dr. Eric Widera, Reverend Denah Joseph, Dr. VJ Periyakoil, Dr. Chris Barnett, and Dr. Rita Redberg, all of whom it was an honor to work with and learn from. Special thanks to Vivian Robinson and Amy Forsythe for their kindness and support. I am also very grateful for the support and the community of the Paul and Daisy Soros Fellowship during my medical training.

I am deeply grateful to my friends, who have been with me on many, many journeys. Alex Fay, fellow lover of both books and medicine, has been my closest confidante since medical school. I treasure the many laughs we've shared, and your close reading of this book. My deepest thanks also to Patricio Riquelme (girlfriend!), Harsimran Sachdeva Singh, Marissa Mika, Aarti Rao, Sara Catania, Yashu Yeragunta, Byron Decuire, Ronald Kall, Anna Martinez, Kareem Sassi, Jill Piacente, Brian Kaufman, Elle

Johnson, Sophia Bicos, Nicky Jatana, Amy Van Dyke, and Fred Macri. Your friendship is a gift, and I love you all very much.

The community I grew up with is near and dear to my heart. Thank you to Manoj and Rajni Joshi; Rika and Shivani Jain; Pradeep, Neeta, Diviya, and Sonali Loomba; Niranjan and Hema Reddy; and Valerie and Jim Real for your kindness and support over many, many years.

Thank you, Dr. Pamelyn Close, for the opportunity to work at USC and for your guidance in everything from palliative care to the tending of elephants. It is a gift and a privilege to work alongside Dr. Carin van Zyl, Dr. Aaron Storms, and Dr. Emily Beers, treasured colleagues whom I admire deeply and who provided so much support and friendship as I wrote. Many thanks to Dr. Michael Karp, chief of General Internal Medicine, who gave me the opportunity to build a palliative care program at Keck and Norris, and supported me throughout the writing of this book. John Pappas, LCSW, is the embodiment of compassion, integrity, and dedication to his patients and our team. His friendship means the world to me. Thank you to Char Elorta for her good humor, her reassurance that I don't have *that much* gray hair, and our memorable trips to the Farmers Market.

USC is a wonderful academic and clinical home, and I consider myself very lucky to work with colleagues who have made work a joy and a worthy challenge: Dr. Ronald Hall, Dr. Stephanie Hall, Dr. Sebina Bulic, Dr. Damon Clark, Dr. Yuri Genyk, Dr. Andreas Kaiser, Dr. Armin Kiankhooy, Dr. Joongho Shin, Dr. David Quinn, Professor Alex Capron, the late Dr. David A. Goldstein, Dr. Jennifer Marks, Dalia Copti, RN, and Jacob Spruill, RN.

I have been fortunate to participate in the education of medical students, residents, and fellows, and I'd like to acknowledge the following trainees for having become the sorts of physicians that all patients deserve: Dr. Allison Kennedy, Dr. Derek Antoku, Dr. Daniel Klein, Dr. Brittany Abt, Dr. Matt Martinez, Dr. Kelly Fan, Dr. Lucas Cruz, Dr. Jennifer Loeb, Dr. James Shen, Dr. Ming Li, and Dr. Hillel Bocian. You've all helped me to grow as a teacher and as a doctor. Thank you.

Thanks on behalf of my mother and me to the physicians who worked alongside her and inspired me first: the late Dr. Robert Nejdl, Dr. John

Kondon, Dr. Gary Belzberg, Dr. Eric Robins, Dr. Brian Sturz, and Donna Konarski, RN.

Without my *naniji*, my maternal grandmother, so much of my life wouldn't have been possible. Thank you for believing in my mother's wild dream of becoming a physician, and for believing—ahead of your time—in the importance of women's education and independence. I wish you were alive to read this book, but I hope that you will live on through the stories in these pages. I am so grateful to my uncle, Raju *mama*, for sharing stories about my mother and grandparents, and for graciously hosting me whenever I visited Mumbai. Thank you for reading this book closely and pointing out factual errors or errors of my own memory. My mother's cousin, Dr. Hans Raj Manchanda, guided my mother every step of the way when she was in medical school and has always been kind and generous to her and my family. I love you very much, *papaji*. I've spent many a fun time in San Francisco with my cousin Ashwin and am grateful for his friendship over the years.

I am very grateful to dear Tony for his support, witty humor, and friendship throughout the writing of this book.

My deep thanks to my brother, Siddarth, for his friendship, kindness, intelligence, and inspiring embrace of life. You are my best friend, and you make me a better person.

My mother and father don't understand why their lives have inspired me, or why I included their stories in this book. They are humble people, and I am immensely thankful that they gave me permission to write about experiences in their lives that they'd rather forget. I am so grateful to my father for being the source of endless wisdom, much of which he learned as he persevered through great hardship. Thank you for your example, for being tough on me when you needed to be, and for loving me no matter what.

My mother is the person I've always strived to be, though I'll always fall short. I am here because of her love and her encouragement for me to be exactly who I am. Thank you for the gift of your friendship and endless support. I can never repay you for mothering me as you have.

ACKNOWLEDGMENTS

And to my patients and their families, past and present: You remind me every day what a privilege it is to do this work. Thank you for allowing me into your lives, to be there with you in times of great pain and great joy. You shape my practice and my thinking, and challenge me to open my heart ever more widely to the beauty and fragility of this human life. It is an honor to be your doctor.